BALANCE

First published in 2018 by Westland Publications Private Limited
61, 2nd Floor, Silverline Building, Alapakkam Main Road, Maduravoyal, Chennai 600095

Westland and the Westland logo are the trademarks of Westland Publications Private Limited, or its affiliates.

ISBN: 9789387894518

10 9 8 7 6 5 4 3 2 1

Typeset by Garamond Premier Pro by Jojy Philip, New Delhi
Printed at Thomson Press (India) Ltd.

BALANCE

Responsible Business for the Digital Age

Namrata Rana
Utkarsh Majmudar

Contents

Introduction

Balance … is everywhere. It exists at many levels. As a skill, as an art form and as a perspective. Action needs to be balanced too.

In football, balance is a skill. Running at breakneck speed, changing direction, moving the ball around and yet keeping track of the opposition needs tremendous agility and perfect balance that comes with years of practice. In birds, balance is taken for granted. Birds can hang upside down on telephone wires, fly flawlessly in all kinds of climate and do perfect in-air acrobatics. Natural systems also maintain a balance. All species and natural systems depend on each other, and when the balance in one is disturbed, the others act as a counter balance. Almost everywhere, balance is the vital difference between chaos and order, between winning and losing and the difference between living and becoming prey.

Today, balance needs to be created.

The current world systems are askew. Extreme poverty exists face to face with extreme wealth, Mars missions coexist with children dying due to a lack of basic medical aid and excessive consumption exists along with extreme deprivation. Waste, water, energy, biodiversity, inequality and data are just words. Words that describe discrete elements that need to be fixed. Though it's moot whether they can at all be fixed, unless we fix ourselves first. At the heart of the problem is us. You and me and our friends and our families and our children and what we have come to believe defines us. This then translates into how we work, how we govern, how we live and how we communicate. Designing a better world will not just be about new processes but a better way of thinking and communicating. Balancing the impact of our actions on people, the environment and everything around us.

Today's world is already facing immense challenges and responsibility and balance can't just be a few additional words that are tossed into the discussion or a couple of new elements that need oversight. Responsibility and balance have to be about people. Awareness of actions, their unintended consequences and maybe, a better language of business communication.

From the wanton destruction of forests, concretisation of civilisation, reckless emissions into the atmosphere and dumping of egregious waste in the seas has emerged a consciousness about the earth. Helped by this consciousness and the tremendous technological developments of the past decade, strategies have emerged that can help mitigate our misuse of the planet. We are slowly but surely moving from a linear mode of production to a circular one. Words like reuse and recycle are starting to dominate our conversations. But still, there is a case for more.

Increasingly, companies are dedicating teams to work on social responsibility and sustainability issues. They map the material risks that their companies face, interface with stakeholders, develop strategies to mitigate or eliminate them. The finance function that until recently merely counted the pennies that the company made has started to look at ways to measure the impact of the company's sustainable and social actions. The production department tasked with improving the efficiency of operations now also concerns itself with using sustainable materials. The marketing team not only promotes the products but also promotes the well-being of people. The human resources function now actively scouts for filling sustainability departments. Sustainability departments are now emerging from the shadows of the corporate communications teams. The CEO's thinking is moving from shareholder value maximisation towards maximising value for all stakeholders.

Parallely, industries are evolving their own coping mechanisms for the changing world. Power companies are gradually increasing the share of renewables in their portfolio. Cement manufacturers are increasingly worried about water depletion and atmospheric pollution. Metal and mining companies are increasingly coming under public pressure to eliminate hazardous impacts on ground, water and air. FMCG companies are acting to reduce plastic and other non-biodegradable packaging and moving to biodegradable ones. Electronics manufacturers are deploying methods for the collection of e-waste to enable reuse and recycle. Banks are moving towards responsible banking where they refuse to entertain loans to companies that are not environmentally or socially conscious. Chemical companies are becoming careful about their waste. Investment management firms are cutting out companies with dubious social credentials.

While many of these actions have been prompted by writers and activists, some have been on account of governmental activities too, both through cooperation at the international level as well as action in their own countries. Al Gore, the former Vice President of the USA has done tremendous work to raise awareness about climate change in public discourse. Dame Ellen McArthur promoted sustainability through the circular economy model. Karl-Henrik Robèrt set out the system conditions for the sustainability of human activities in his path-breaking work in *The Natural Step*. John Elkington coined the word Triple Bottom Line (TBL or 3BL)—people, profit and planet—that led to the development of thinking around measuring social and sustainable actions of companies. Writers like Roger Martin, Naomi Klein and Peter Senge have also contributed towards discussions on this subject. At an international level, governments have long tried to build a consensus around sustainable actions. The Rio de Janeiro Earth Summit in 1992 laid the groundwork for climate cooperation among companies. The Kyoto protocol in 1997 extended the achievements of the Earth Summit and started formal mechanisms for climate control. The 2015 Paris Agreement (COP21) that led to a formal agreement among countries to reduce the increase in world temperatures was a landmark event. Nations in their own right have also contributed. Several European countries have taken actions to reduce or eliminate waste, impose stiff pollution norms and move to greener options. India and China are actively promoting renewable energy. Agreements on Millennium Development Goals and the Sustainable Development Goals have further progressed international action.

Yet, something is amiss. None of the environmental or responsibility challenges seem even close to being solved. On the other hand, the arrival of data as a new area of responsibility has created a fresh set of challenges.

The future will witness a rate of change at a velocity never seen before. Acceleration due to technological change may bring the world closer, but it could also lead to a faster pace of wanton destruction.

Technology today permeates our lives. The smartphones that we already use to connect with friends and the world through social media applications, the e-commerce sites we use to order goods and services, the drones that will soon deliver products to our homes, the 3-D printed products that are coming our way very soon, the smart homes that we will live in are all linked by technology. Terms like artificial intelligence, machine learning, deep learning, big data, and analytics are fast becoming an integral part of people's vocabulary. In several ways, technology has made lives more manageable and has helped people connect with their families and the world at large.

However, there have also been many issues that have brought home the dangers of technology and at the same time, turned the spotlight on corporate responsibility. Data privacy is one such key issue. Rapid developments in data analytics, artificial intelligence and robotics have already begun. Aggregation of data is already resulting in changing customer and voter behaviour. The Facebook-Cambridge Analytica episode and the fight against Aadhaar have brought this issue to the forefront. Another issue is how companies use artificial intelligence to manipulate our lives. The deployment of algorithms in many technologies is replete with consequences, many of which the world has still not completely come to grips with.

People, planet, data, each of these areas is undergoing a significant change. All of this needs to be managed. In order to do so, we need to look at tools and technologies but even more we need to change at a fundamental level. The problem of plastic waste is not one of companies alone. It is also that of consumers who consumed without a thought. The problem of data misuse is not one of social media companies alone, it is equally ours since we shared data without thought.

India and its businesses are not immune to these changes. Steps have been taken to initiate change on these lines in India as well. Since 2013, India has seen the birth of a new ecosystem for social responsibility with the passage of the Companies Act 2013 which mandates that companies spend 2 per cent of their profits towards CSR projects. But, responsibility can't emerge through compliance alone. We need to therefore enable it through action, words and conscious thought. Models, frameworks and technologies are tools to assist us. Equally, we need individuals to think in terms of circular systems, financiers to think about real options, CEO's to think about business models and policy makers to think about better design.

More than at any time in the past, we need the language of balance if we need to create a better future!

CHAPTER 1

Responsibility Goes Mainstream

The current scenario

Global wealth stood at $280 trillion by mid-2017.[1] Much of this can be attributed to the capitalist mode of economic growth—a framework which mobilises resources, human and natural, and transforms them into tradeable goods and services. Conversations about national economic growth often centre on the need to increase a nation's GDP, which is inherently a measure of goods and services produced by its economy and how they are consumed. An increase in global wealth is on account of increasing GDP in countries throughout the planet, and this points to an increase both in the production and consumption of goods and services.

We are now living in perhaps the most innovative time in history when everything is changing at breakneck speed. Some of the most pressing problems that humanity has ever faced now have solutions. Better education, better health, better communication, advances in science and technology have transformed our lives like never before. Life expectancy has risen considerably, and people do not die of simple diseases like in the past. Sanitation conditions have improved as have education levels. Greater opportunities are now available to more people. As increasing numbers of women join the workforce, gender parity has received a boost. We live better, eat better and work better than ever before, and this is only the beginning.

However, as technological advances take place at a rapid pace and life changes like never before in recorded history, the twenty-first century world that seems so full of promise is also equally in peril!

The current model of economic growth as measured by growth in GDP has had serious consequences for the environment. Pollution, water security, deforestation, ocean acidification and increase in natural disasters are just some of the critical issues that have been the consequences of overproduction and consumption. The substantial increase in global wealth has also meant a significant rise in consumerism as we have moved from mere market-based economies to societies that seem to be based entirely on how much we own and how much we consume.

Growth has also been unequal. While the wealthiest people, the biggest companies and corporate leaders have unparalleled wealth, the poorest still struggle for food. The wealthiest eight men in the world own as much wealth as the poorest half of humanity consisting of 3.6 billion people.[2] The biggest and most prosperous global companies are richer than the next 180 countries combined. The fruits of economic prosperity, globalisation, industrialisation and ongoing growth were meant to be shared across all strata of society, but that hasn't turned out to be the case. Just 16 per cent of humanity is responsible for 78 per cent of the total consumption of the world.

Industrialisation has brought with it prosperity and improvement in the quality of life. However, it has failed to fully take into consideration the interconnected nature of our world. Our consumption patterns have contributed significantly to this exhaustion of natural resources, through the systematic generation of 'waste'. Take for instance, metal cans that are used and thrown away. Bauxite would have been extracted to produce the aluminium that went into making the cans. Once a can is thrown away, the bauxite used in it is effectively lost forever. This is merely one instance of 'waste'. Many other such instances abound.

Almost all our existing processes are linear in nature. They take in resources and change their form by concentrating, altering and synthesising them into products, many of which cannot be reused or recycled at the end of their intended use. Part of the reason for the inability to reuse or recycle is because it is often cheaper and easier to replace an article than to get it repaired. This pattern is furthered by product designers who design products (electronics, for instance) with a inbuilt obsolescence period. These products eventually either end up in a landfill as industrial waste, since the raw materials cannot be recovered, incinerated or released into a water body leading to air or water contamination. While some of these products do get recycled with similar products resulting in a down-cycling of precious metals and other resources, this proportion is on the lower side.

Figure 1.1: The linear and circular economy

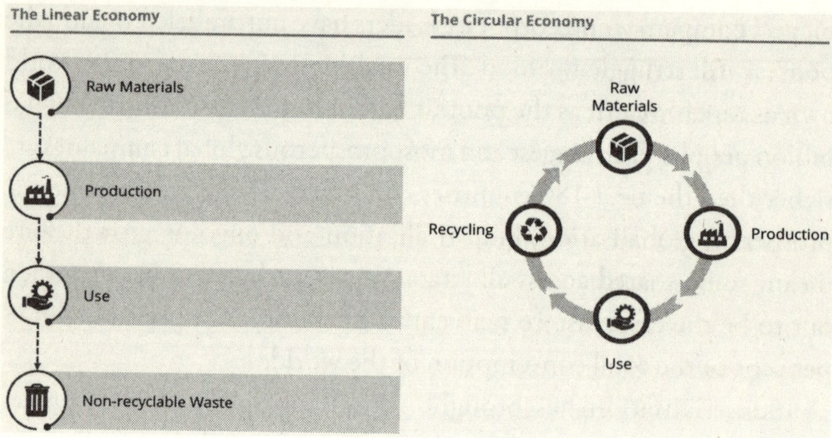

Our cars, food, clothes, and almost everything else that we consume are made from resources from around the globe. Take the case of a car, whose components are made in countries as diverse as Japan, China, Taiwan, Korea and Mexico. Each component, in turn, is composed of materials sourced from various locations. These components are then shipped to factories in the USA, Japan, Germany, India and Australia for assembly. Once assembled, they are transported to the various countries where the cars are sold. Once the car reaches the end of its life-cycle, all those components sourced from different parts of the world eventually reach a landfill. This addition of metals, minerals, plastics and electronic components to the soil via the landfill degrades the environment and adds to pollutants. In a nutshell, this is perhaps the biggest problem with the industrialised model of growth—our inability to design manufacturing systems that are harmonious with nature. This has meant that concentrations of pollutants in the world have also increased dramatically. For example, mercury, which is used in making CFL bulbs, refrigerators, LCD screens, thermometers and more, once discarded, finds its way to landfills, even though it is highly toxic to the soil and to human health. There is nothing to prevent it from entering the soil and water systems, causing significant damage to both plants and human beings. The same is the case with petroleum products. The polluted skyline of most global cities is a testimony to the pollution caused by carbon emissions from cars, trucks, bikes and planes. Clogged drains and bloated landfills have heaps of plastic, which is not biodegradable. The list is endless.

The prevailing discourse around the environment currently is one that foretells a grim future—rising seas, food shortages, water wars, scarcity of almost all materials and minerals and many species of flora and fauna becoming extinct. Unrestrained extraction of natural resources enormously impacts the ecosystems that they are a part of. Whether it is overfishing that has depleted the fish in the oceans, making waters alkaline and bringing some species of marine flora and fauna near extinction; the transportation of products to centralised manufacturing hubs that result in harmful carbon emissions; or the vast quantities of waste generated from raw materials, one thing is becoming clear, and that is that this kind of growth, at this pace, is perhaps not sustainable. However, this notwithstanding, companies operate in a feigned reality of sorts where they, despite being aware of potential risks, adopt a policy that assumes growth, positive outcomes and a future where they have a role to play.

The world needs sustainable growth and so does India

The two unintended consequences of the current model of growth—increase in income inequality and increased consumption—have led to the current crisis of sustainability, where we are consuming more natural resources than the earth can regenerate. Sustainable development was defined as 'development that meets the needs of the present without compromising the ability of future generations to meet their own needs'.[3] Given the preponderance of consumption and its deleterious consequences, it has also been rephrased recently as 'consumption that meets the needs of the present without compromising the ability of future generations to meet their own needs.'[4]

The global push towards sustainability is happening because of several macro forces around food, population, water and climate change that are altering our world. World population is over seven billion and is expected to reach eight billion by 2030. Asia will see the greatest increase in population, leading to the rapid growth of a number of mid-size cities on the continent. If current population and consumption trends continue, humanity will need the equivalent of two Earths to support it by 2030.[5] These consumption trends are of significant concern, particularly with regard to food. The amount of land per head available for food production is falling, and the proportion of agricultural land that is being degraded or diverted to other uses is increasing. Also, as population and per capita incomes increase, the demand for food is becoming more intensive.

Water, mainly freshwater, is also becoming a scarce resource and efforts are being made to conserve it, reuse it and recycle it. However, because water is difficult to transport, its scarcity tends to be a serious local or regional phenomenon. Globally, countries are facing a water crisis because of two key reasons—depleting groundwater aquifers due to over-extraction to support expanding cities, industries and food production and seepage of untreated water into water bodies which is making them unfit for use, causing various waterborne diseases. Some scientists predict that India, China and the Middle East will actually run out of water by 2030 due to over-extraction. Both governments and corporations are developing and deploying various technologies to address this crisis. These range from the active adoption of water management and conservation techniques to the recycling of waste water and desalination of sea water. India has even started a project interlinking all its major rivers to help it manage the floods and droughts that are severely impacting agricultural productivity and infrastructure.

As affluent countries get more energy-efficient, demand for energy is falling, while in the less energy-efficient emerging economies, demand for energy is rising. Supply, meanwhile, is static or falling. Countries round the world are gradually attempting to make the move towards renewable energy, to address the limited availability of fossil fuels and the climate change that has occurred due to extensive fossil fuel usage. This transformation in energy generation is accompanied by changes in energy transmission, distribution and consumption. Newer business models and grids are emerging as the flow of energy becomes bi-directional from the traditionally unidirectional. Unlike in the past when power companies would provide electricity to factories, now factories also produce power through generators and renewables that are then supplied to the factory and to power companies. Energy storage too is getting redefined with the availability of micro-scale graphene-based super-capacitors which recharge laptops in seconds and electric cars in minutes, and which can also be used to store energy generated by wind turbines and solar panels. Automobiles, big consumers of fossil fuels, now have hybrid and electric variants.

Extreme weather events across the globe are being intensified by climate change leading to significant impacts across food production, infrastructure, energy use, insurance and supply chains. The collision of these macro-forces means that, firstly, the current model of capitalism is coming up against limits on many fronts. This is also increasingly adding to corporate risk as extreme climate events such as floods, droughts, earthquakes and extreme temperatures are affecting business continuity and productivity.

These risks and impacts are intensified in developing countries where the resources to meet these challenges are limited. India, by and large, jumped onto the industrial revolution bandwagon only after Independence in 1947. In the mid '90s, with the western world looking east for new growth markets, India's growth trajectory made a huge leap. India's model of industrialisation was much like the one followed in the rest of the world—it sourced natural resources and modified them to create products. In the early 2000s, services were added to India's production mix with it becoming the central hub of software services for the rest of the world. This created a burgeoning middle-class, flush with cash and a hunger to consume. While much is said about India's growth numbers, it is equally true that this growth has not been inclusive. India, the emerging economic giant, is equally the land of the impoverished, home to about 360 million people[6] living below the poverty line,[7] while fifty-seven of its billionaires own as much as two-thirds of what the population does.

When Al Gore talked about sustainability and climate change in his 2006 book and movie, *An Inconvenient Truth*, much of what he was talking about seemed to apply very far into the future. But the book (and movie) did create an urgency about the seriousness of the situation. By looking at the devastating consequences of rising temperatures, increased soil moisture evaporation which would result in drier land, fast-melting glaciers and rising ocean levels, it highlighted the interconnectedness of economic growth and environmental impact and more importantly, the need to act fast.

Every year, world leaders gather for the United Nations Climate Change Conference. Ever since the 1997 meeting that led to the Kyoto protocol, this meeting has gained prominence. The twenty-first edition of the meeting in 2015 led to the signing of the Paris Agreement that highlighted the urgency to take action against growing climate change perils. Today, even though India has ratified the Paris Agreement (see *TN 8: The Paris Accord*) and vowed to cut emissions by 30 per cent, we find ourselves where we are. Delhi, the national capital now has the distinction of being the most polluted city in the world. India has, of course, committed to reducing its carbon emission intensity by up to 33-35 per cent over fifteen years, as compared to its 2005 levels. The country also plans to produce 40 per cent of its installed electricity capacity by 2030 from non-fossil fuels. But how will any of this be achievable if one is to go by the current trend?

Delhi is not the only city suffering from high levels of pollution. Most urban centres across the world have similar problems. Long-term solutions to improve the air quality include revamping coal-fuelled power plants and increasing the reach and usage of public transport, so as to reduce emissions. This means that all stakeholders that include governments, citizens and corporations need to pull together to solve common problems.

While it is true that the government must be held accountable, what of companies? In the Delhi pollution scare in the winter of 2017, apart from the odd article detailing how corporations were taking steps to protect their employees by installing air purifiers, encouraging them to work from home and providing masks, there was little else done. And herein lies the most disturbing trend—the general apathy of the educated, working class towards sustainable solutions. Not one industry leader stepped up with a long-term solution to reduce toxic emissions, or with a plan to partner with the government and arrive at a solution, or for that matter, with a blueprint to reduce their own carbon footprint.

According to Jonathon Porritt, there are virtually no differences in people's attitudes towards sustainability between developed and developing countries. He says, 'It's true that sustainability means very different things in different parts of the world—and a lot depends on exactly where a country is in terms of its own economic development journey. But there's a widespread assumption that somehow the poorer countries in the world today, still down the economic growth curve, don't really care about sustainability. Our experience tells us that this simply isn't so. Indeed, if you look at some of the surveys about public opinion on environmental and wider sustainability issues, the responses in countries like Brazil, China, India and so on are at least as strong as responses in a country like my own (UK). And that's not surprising: there is now a growing middle-class in many of these countries who are only too aware of the damage being done to their lives and their economy through pollution and misuse of resources. There's even a growing awareness of what we now call "ecosystem services"—the degree to which we depend on a healthy and productive environment to underpin our own economies.'[8]

While there is increasing public awareness about sustainability, much more needs to be done to persuade people, societies and companies to function in more sustainable ways. Public policies need to be designed better to enable these changes. These also need to take into consideration the fast-changing nature of today's world, which is increasingly going digital.

In the connected world responsibility needs redefinition

We are more connected than we have ever been before. Today almost three-quarters of the world's population uses the mobile phone.[9] Our mobile phone is smarter than the supercomputer of twenty years ago. In the digital age, data is being created, aggregated and consumed at a frenetic pace. Almost 90 per cent of the data in the world was generated in the previous two years.[10] Important events, friendships, travels, likes, dislikes and our life's cherished moments—all of which define our identity—are now part of the digital world. Social media is enabling constant exchange of ideas, sharing of content and making connections. In this process, we are giving away information about ourselves and generating data for companies who further map it against our economic profiles, location, education and many, many more areas. We are giving away so much data that there are 52,000 unique attributes that Facebook uses to classify users. Data about us is everywhere—with the company that sold us the smart watch, the search engine we use, the smart car and the navigation system we use, the health data we generate and the e-commerce sites we visit. Digital agents such as Siri and Cortana (personal digital assistants) are getting embedded into our everyday existence. We will soon have to merely ask for web searches to be conducted, appointments to be booked, groceries to be ordered and thus get through many other mundane things, as these digital assistants will not only obey our commands, but also learn from us.

By 2017, over 4.2 billion people had used the internet, thrice the number of people who had done so by 2007.[11] With the arrival of the Internet of Things (IoT), more data and channels are becoming available to businesses for reaching out to their consumers. The IoT is enabling sensors, which, when embedded in devices, allow machines to talk to us. Sensors are being embedded almost everywhere, refrigerators, solar panels, water systems, even clothes—the list is long. Sensors are also transforming industries such as healthcare by tracking health data, enabling better prevention and access to just-in-time medical interventions. According to a Gartner report, there will be twenty-one billion devices on the IoT by 2020.[12] The current digital age is being called the Fourth Industrial Revolution[13] by the World Economic Forum. A world which will be driven by a proliferation of devices and software algorithms, which will do many of the things we take for granted. These developments in financial services, robotics, artificial intelligence, electro-mobility and biotechnology are likely to fundamentally change the nature of work. Anything that can be automated will be. Software-based systems that learn on their own will drive most of the services in banking, telecom, manufacturing, transportation and retail.

With more data being available and collected, everyone stands to gain from greater transparency, more convenience and better monitoring, but this also throws up the challenge of data privacy and data security. The digital ads that we see are explicitly targeted to our online personas. It all began rather simply with click-through ads that progressed onto search engine marketing and re-targeting. However, what began as an online extension of television or print marketing to increase product sales has now morphed into something a bit more worrying. Doubts are being expressed about how the re-configuring of newsfeeds to personal profiles has possibly helped influence decision-making around elections in the largest democracy of the world. This is done by using personal profiles to target advertisements and fake news stories to individuals to induce them to vote in a particular manner during the elections. Thus, the minds of people can be manipulated to make them act in ways that were previously not even thought of. The recent controversy about peddling of fake news that enabled the alleged Russian manipulation of American voters is a case in point. Despite these concerns, the march towards digitisation and digital aggregation of data is continuing unabated and is likely to gather steam. In a world that is moving at breakneck speed to digitising everything and connecting all these diverse data points, data is being spoken of as 'the new oil'. This information gives enormous power to aggregators of information. This data can, and is, being used to influence decisions. However, most frameworks around responsibility don't yet address this issue of information asymmetry. The fact that large corporations know large parts of our lives and can potentially exercise significant control needs deep introspection.

Governments and Investors are mandating sustainability disclosures and CSR spends

Globalisation and interconnectivity mean that the world's finances, people and knowledge are inextricably linked, as evidenced by the global financial crisis. In the wake of the crisis, the desire to promote financial stability and sustainable development by better linking investment decisions, corporate behaviour and reporting has become global. One of the most significant impacts of technology has been transparency. Companies can no longer hide the impact they have on natural resources and the communities they operate in. The demand for accountability from critical stakeholders, coupled with technology-enabled transparency are the driving forces for improved sustainability disclosures.

Conventional stock valuation models (based on physical assets) are giving way to ratings tools that quantify intangibles that determine whether or not a company will be profitable not just now but also in the future. The key drivers of this shift are the rating agencies, flow of information and the feedback loop in the equity market. Today, intangible assets play a more prominent role in the valuation of a company than a couple of decades ago. Investors are understanding the need to capture the value of intangibles in order to efficiently allocate funds and drive decision-making. This has led to the development of reporting frameworks that incorporate non-financial aspects such as environmental, social and governance (ESG) into conventional corporate reporting.

Figure 1.2: ESG reporting

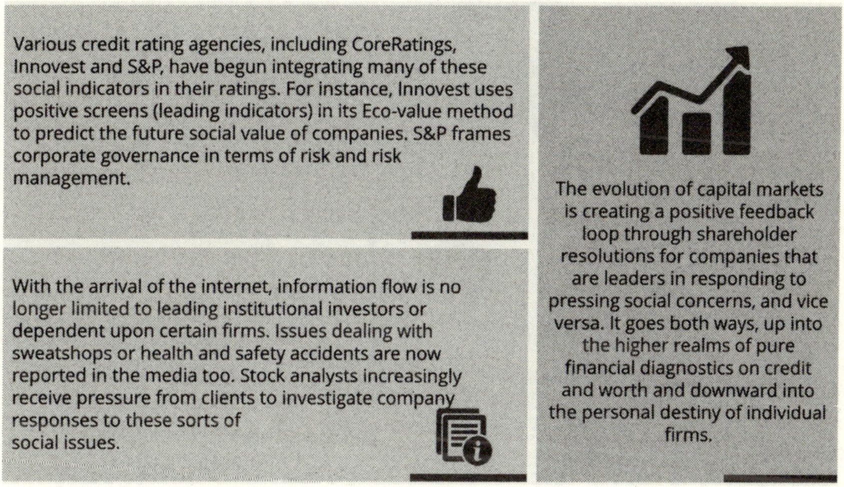

Global Reporting Initiative (GRI) and Integrated Reporting (IR) are two such reporting formats that have emerged as recognition has dawned that financial reporting is not enough. Traditional annual reports look at historical data and are largely focused on the financials of the company. Today's world, though, is far more complex and investors need to understand how a company relates to its environment, society and its investments in intellectual property and research. About 30 per cent of India's top companies have a sustainability report. In February 2017, a circular was released by the Securities Exchange Board of India (SEBI) that encourages the top 500 publicly listed companies to use IR as a framework to improve the quality and relevance of the information.[14] This is a huge change not just in

Figure 1.3: CSR requirements across the world

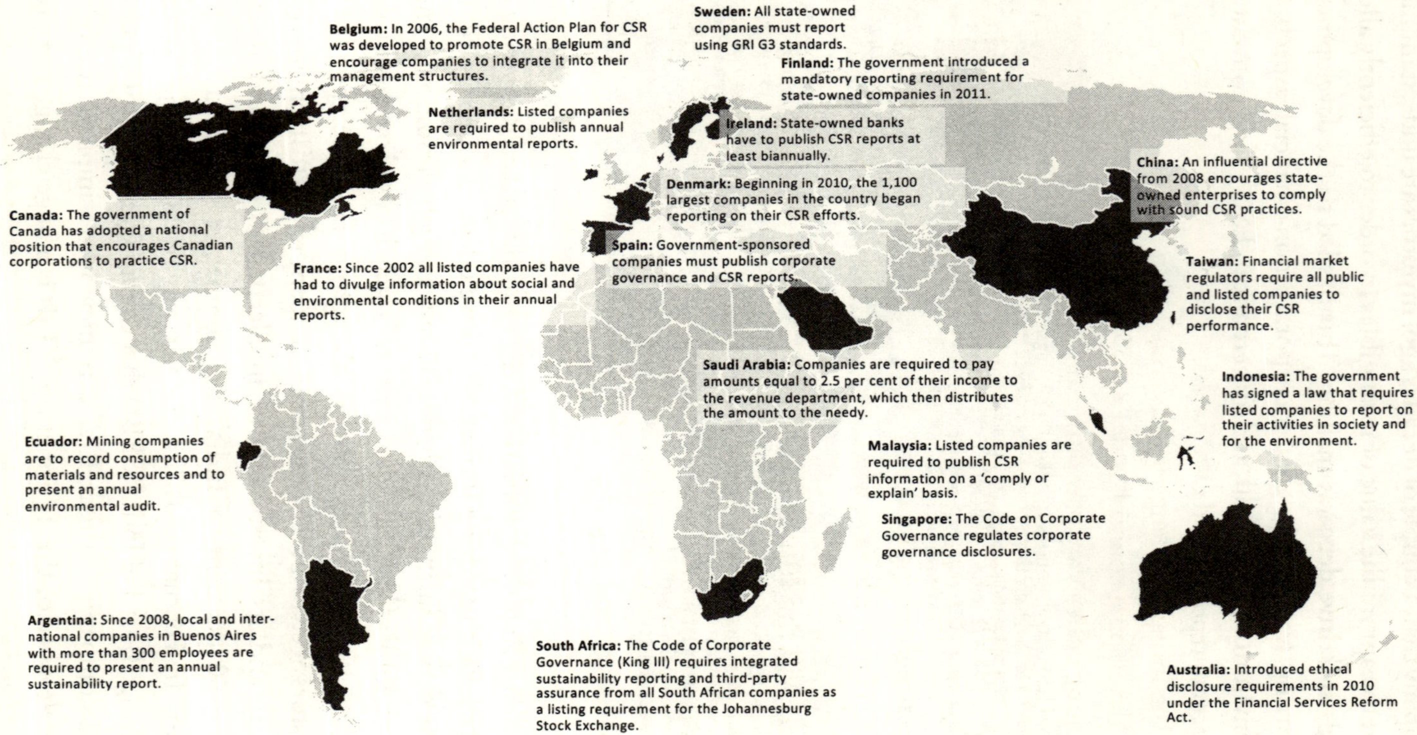

terms of reporting but also reflects on how companies need to think about responsible growth. Integrated reporting requires companies to internalise interdependencies between business and sustainability to make business reporting more clear and relevant. Long-term thinking and reporting on multiple forms of capital enables companies to understand, adopt and execute responsible business practices.

The Indian challenge in this context, and, indeed, the problem of any developing country, is complex. While good governance and far-reaching policies are part of the answer, much more needs to be done. India's new Companies Act has asked corporate India to step in to help with the provision that companies invest 2 per cent of their net profits in CSR. Not just India, but governments across the world are increasingly asking for corporate disclosures around sustainability and CSR. Here is a look at what some of them are asking for:

What will the future look like?

As we get more and more connected, the challenges that we anticipate in the twenty-first century need a new model of responsible and balanced growth, one that values humanity. One that does not trade on decency and one that keeps in mind that merely adding to the number of customers cannot possibly be the only yardstick to measure growth. The older models of growth were merely economic models, not taking into consideration how we need to live our lives. What gets measured, gets done, is an age-old corporate dictum. However, the reality is that the twentieth century model of business didn't quantify wastage of materials, air pollution, water pollution and as a result, we have ended up trashing the planet. It didn't measure diversity and so we ended up with a huge imbalance within corporations. It didn't value children's and women's safety and as a consequence, the internet is littered with porn. These challenges exist today and are likely to magnify in the digital world that we are headed towards. For the brave new companies of tomorrow, we need a framework of responsible growth and not one where the basic tenets of humanity and human existence have no value. One, where the soul of the corporation is etched in empathy and not in an algorithm. Should we continue to do business as we have been doing, the twenty-first century corporation will perpetuate the existing damage caused.

The need of the hour, thus, is a strong focus on, and a dedicated effort towards achieving sustainable and balanced growth and not mere economic growth which is non-inclusive in nature. It has to encompass the inter-linkages of five systems, viz., economic (the world economy), social (the global society), environmental (earth's physical environment), digital (technology and data), and governance (both government and corporate) and create a comprehensive framework.

Figure 1.4: The circle of systems

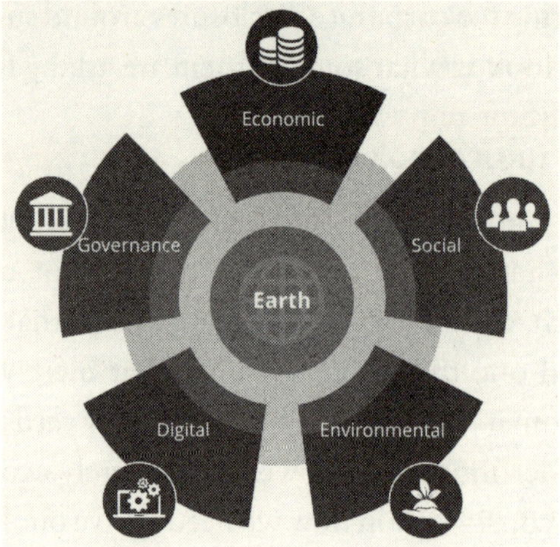

An integrated approach to development and future planning is called systems thinking, which helps in understanding the structure and dynamics of the complex systems that we live in, from organisational change to climate change, from physiology to financial markets. Systems thinking, when applied to sustainability, is a potent force since it focuses on not just doing 'less bad', but also on doing 'more right'. Systems thinking applies to, and benefits almost every aspect of a business—product/service designing, manufacturing, distribution, finance and marketing. However, opportunities to create or preserve the most value vary greatly among industries. An extractive services company, for instance, could significantly reduce its costs through better management of energy and water, whereas a retail company could reduce its resource intensity and costs by revamping its supply chain. According to Adam Elman of Marks & Spencer, 'These conversations about the need for change will be helped by the simple reality of environmental and social harm that are unfolding before us. Air pollution from forest fires in Indonesia and coal burning and vehicles in China and India are harming people's health. Drought and flood from California to Cumbria to Chennai are devastating lives and the economy. We will always be cautious about attributing particular weather events to climate change, but many, many lives are being affected now around the world, and this will grow.'[15] He also highlights the need to engage the financial sector in making significant improvements in the quality of our lives, 'And after a decade of ambivalence, the finance sector seems to have spotted the substantial risks that are now being baked (literally) into the system that funds the economy today and tomorrow. Having been a bystander for much of the past decade, mainstream financial markets will become a significant source of pressure on business to change, to manage risk and seize opportunity.'

The ability to innovate, manage risk and address sustainability and social issues is increasingly becoming important for companies. The belief is that large corporations are no longer too big to fail. The larger they are, the more susceptible they are to risks from environmental changes, community-based challenges and digital disruption. Fundamental changes in how we work, communicate and interact are slowly changing the very fabric of society and culture. Already, corporations that define the future do not have a single go-to place. Companies like Cisco, IBM and Accenture now advocate for employees to work out of any location, while being constantly connected to the network. This helps bring down costs and increases productivity as employees do not have to undergo the stress of battling peak-hour traffic and have the option of spending quality time with their families when they desire. Organisations will also get increasingly flatter as they compete in the ever-changing, fast-moving world, where connectedness will drive constant availability of information, requiring quicker response times.

How will responsibility and balance then be defined?

CASE STUDY

TOYOTA KIRLOSKAR MOTORS: BUILDING A RESPONSIBLE BUSINESS STRATEGY[16]

Established in 1997, Toyota Kirloskar Motor Pvt. Ltd. (TKM) is a subsidiary of Toyota Motor Corporation. A young and vibrant company, Toyota's constant aim has been to innovate continuously and to play a major role in the development of the automotive industry.

TKM's plants located in Bidadi, Karnataka, are spread across 432 acres and have a capacity of 310,000 vehicles per annum. The first plant manufactures the Toyota Innova and the Fortuner and has a production capacity of 100,000 vehicles per annum. TKM's second manufacturing plant has a capacity of 210,000 vehicles per annum. The second plant manufactures Corolla Altis, Etios, Etios Liva and Camry. TKM employs around 7,000 people.

Guiding principles at TKM

TKM had adopted the guiding principles of Toyota Motor Corporation which include:

- Honour the language and spirit of the law of every nation and undertake open and fair business activities to be a good corporate citizen of the world.
- Respect the culture and customs of every nation and contribute to economic and social development through corporate activities in their respective communities.
- Dedicate its business to providing clean and safe products and to enhancing the quality of life everywhere through all of its activities.
- Create and develop advanced technologies and provide outstanding products and services that fulfil the needs of customers worldwide.
- Foster a corporate culture that enhances both individual creativity and the value of teamwork, while honouring mutual trust and respect between labour and management.

- Pursue growth through harmony with the global community via innovative management.
- Work with business partners in research and manufacturing to achieve stable, long-term growth and mutual benefits, while keeping itself open to new partnerships.

The Toyota way

With the rapid growth, diversification and globalisation of Toyota in the past decade, values and the business methods that had been passed on as implicit knowledge were identified and defined in 2001 as the 'Toyota Way'.

The Toyota Way has two broad principles:

- Respect for people – This fosters teamwork.
- Continuous improvement – This has three components:
  - » Challenge
  - » Kaizen (continuous improvement)
  - » Genchi Genbutsu (go and see for yourself)

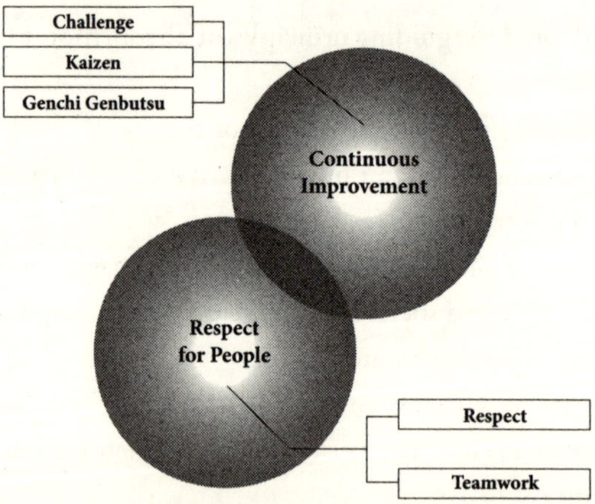

Source: Reproduced with permission from Toyota Kirloskar

Responsible business at TKM

Toyota has continuously striven to contribute to the sustainable development of society through the manufacture and provision of innovative and quality products and services that lead the times. Motor vehicles greatly expand the freedom of mobility, but impact society and the environment in various ways.

TKM believes that sustainability and CSR are as important as business profits. CSR activities are close to its CEO, Akito Tachibana's heart and he takes a keen interest in promoting them. TKM's priority areas are education, health and hygiene, environment, road safety and skill development. TKM focuses on a few areas and tries to ensure that they do things right in those areas. They also aim to perfect their activities on a small scale at first and when they are confident, try and scale them up. For them the approach is that of a pyramid.

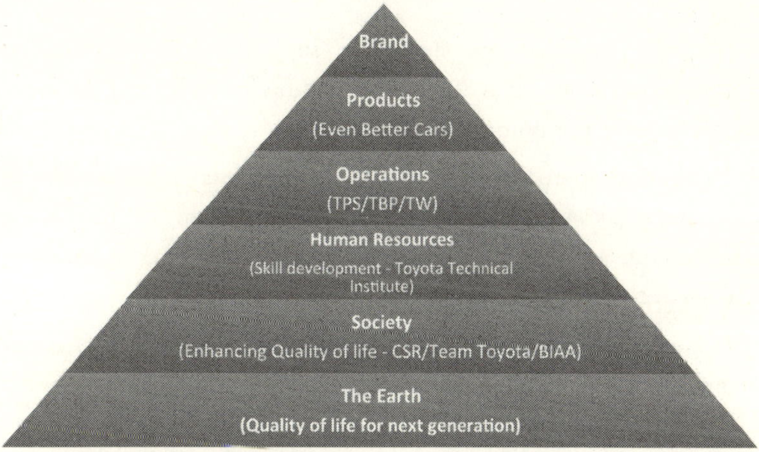

TPS: Toyota Production System **TBP:** Toyota Business Practice
TW: Toyota way **BIAA:** Bidadi Industrial Area Association

Source: Reproduced with permission from Toyota Kirloskar

At the top is the Toyota brand, which is supported by its products. Their operations teams are responsible for turning out quality cars; the human resources team takes care of the people who come from the society around the factory. Their products represent quality that encompasses all their activities, and it is this that helps them in bringing out a sustainable product. Their human resources are honed at the Toyota

Technical Training Institute that inculcates a sense of sustainability and social responsiveness. Their 'Ecozone' project under the environment wing (that promotes biodiversity and nature) is what they give back to the earth.

They value their supply chain (dealers and suppliers) and respect the fundamentals of their relationship through teamwork and pass on these Toyota values across all their operations. At Toyota, they practise the 'Customer First' approach by listening to the customer. Projects like 'Best in Town' dealerships aim to bring excellence in their service to meet the ever-changing customer expectation.

Their business responsibility has a four-step approach: Reactive, Proactive, Predictive, and one that Influences.

A **Reactive** approach is one where support with donations or compensation is offered as a one-time solution for addressing the social issue. However, this is not sustainable.

A **Preventive** approach aims to solve the societal requirements by proactively taking steps to eradicate the problem by developing infrastructure such as school buildings, sanitation facilities and more.

A **Predictive** approach is a sustainable approach where the focus is on education and behavioural aspects. For example, the 'Behaviour Change Demonstration' programme under the sanitation programme, which is hugely successful.

Influence plays a critical role in changing social behaviour. Influence of children in open defecation free (ODF) villages is a classic case in the social movement under the Swachh Bharat initiative in the community.

Based on the Toyota way, they believe that a predictive approach works best for them. Their focus on quality enables them to apply the same principle of 'Kaizen' to sustainability practices. The key challenge for Toyota is, how to integrate the various elements of the pyramid into their sustainability and CSR activities with quality being the central focus.

THE TOYOTA ENVIRONMENTAL ACTION PLAN

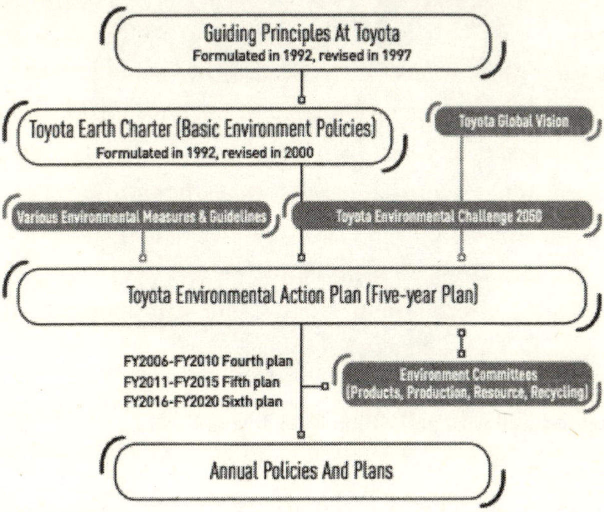

Source: Reproduced with permission from Toyota Kirloskar

The Toyota Environmental Challenge 2050

The Toyota Environmental Challenge 2050 aims to have new vehicles with zero carbon-dioxide (CO_2) emissions during its life cycle; plants with zero CO_2; to minimise and optimise water usage; to establish a recycling-based society and systems; and a future society in harmony with nature. These are definitely challenging, but Toyota expects that continued attention will provide an opportunity to achieve success. Although TKM had originally set up a target of 2050, they are well within achieving a significant part of the target by 2020.

The critical challenge for them was in ensuring that many of the changes that they wish to bring about actually get implemented. Not everything was in their control. There are several spheres where they need to operate in.

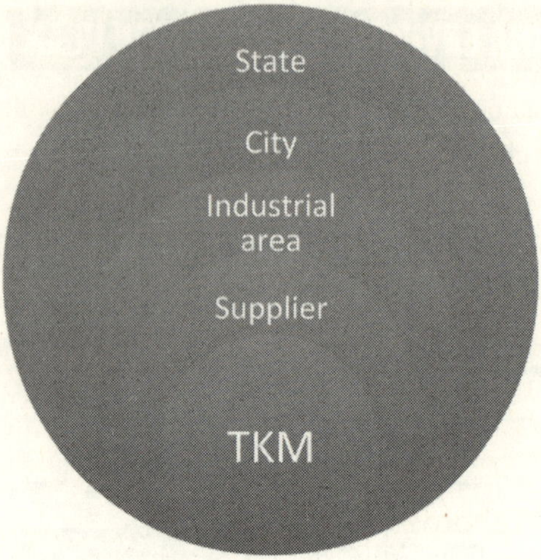

Source: Reproduced with permission from Toyota Kirloskar

Their sphere of influence is the strongest within TKM and weakest at the level of the state. They therefore adopted a simple approach. TKM tries to implement its ideas within the organisation first. These success stories are then used to showcase to their suppliers, who are encouraged to adopt them. They, in turn, become examples of success and motivation to move to the next level.

TKM is creating an eco-park to promote eco-awareness and wants to showcase to all stakeholders its commitment to dealing with environmental challenges. The expectation is that industrial areas will pick up success stories of TKM or stakeholders and join in. An example was their water supply work in villages in Bidadi, which has influenced several other factories to join in. This has created a tremendous amount of goodwill for Toyota as villagers come from far flung areas to collect clean, RO-processed water. Influencing the city and the state were the hardest. TKM believed that the effect of demonstration could work here too.

Their ABCD (A Behavioural Change Demonstration) programme, a step in this direction, fights against open defecation. They had already started this initiative, and it had gained momentum when the Swachh Bharat campaign was announced. Children learn about issues of open defecation at schools sponsored by TKM. These children become ambassadors of change as they influence their parents to build toilets. This influences the neighbours and communities to change. Gradually, the change is picked up by the local bodies. Thus, the cycle of change continues.

They celebrate the 'environment month' in June each year and invite external parties to attend, learn from them and implement in their own settings.

TKM and stakeholders

Each link of the value chain is important to TKM. Stakeholders are involved in all aspects of its business. They look at the company, its suppliers and its dealers as a team. They believe that good teamwork leads to success. TKM influences its dealers and suppliers through the Toyota way using elements of 'Kaizen', TPS and TBP to help integrate the value chain. For TKM the quality of life is important and they believe that the quality of life can be improved through safety measures. When the safety practices at its premises are cultivated in the staff, it will influence their families to adopt safety measures too. For instance, when a staff-member comes to a crossroad in the plant premises, TKM trains them to look in each direction and say *yosh* (all clear or no danger) for each direction and proceed. This gets ingrained into people's mind-set, they do not then have to spend energy or make an effort and everyone's safety is guaranteed. They value safety and embed its significance in everything that they do. Dealers are trained to provide safety training and explain safety features in their vehicles.

Holistic approach to sustainability

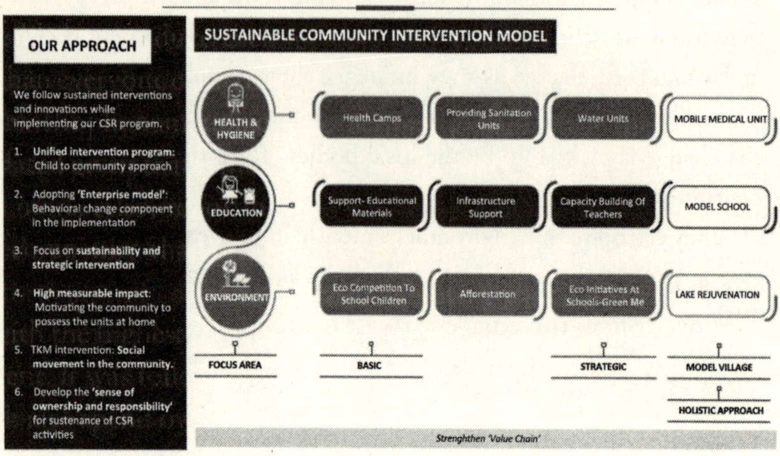

Source: Reproduced with permission from Toyota Kirloskar

The outcomes

The application of structured frameworks enables Toyota to build programmes with lasting value. Bringing together the stakeholders provides an ability to imbibe sustainability across the value chain. Adopting the Toyota way enables the company to continuously improve and bring in stakeholder participation.

CHAPTER 2

Corporate India Gears Up

In 2014, Bellandur lake in Bangalore developed so much froth that it spilled over on to the adjacent road, making it difficult for vehicular traffic to ply. A few months later, the same lake caught fire. This has happened many times since 2014. Now, can you imagine a lake *on fire*? The residents of the area became so seriously concerned about the health of their loved ones that the NGLT (National Green Law Tribunal), acting on their pleas, ordered the closure of a large number of industries in the vicinity of the lake as it was found that they were polluting the lake with their effluent discharge.

This was industrial disaster brought home to a big city, a city that had not too long ago prided itself on being green. But clearly, spiralling growth has proved disastrous for its environment.

That India is a land of paradoxes has been repeated many times over, and this is reflected in corporate India as well, especially when it comes to responsible growth. While, on the one hand, there are manufacturing plants with zero environmental impact, on the other, there are factories that have relentlessly destroyed the water systems and air quality of the very area that they are located in. There are companies that have social responsibility as a key decision point across all aspects of the value chain and yet there are some who simply don't see why they should focus on anything other than profitability.

The challenge, it seems, is multi-fold. At one level, disclosures are weak, as sustainability reporting is extremely inadequate in India. This is especially true about the manufacturing industry.

The Responsible Business Rankings Study 2018 showed that under a third of the companies of the 220 companies studied release sustainability reports, and even fewer are externally certified.[1] Both the release of sustainability reports and external verification is highly variable across industries. Even when sustainability reports are released, the reality is that most Indian companies don't focus on what really matters. For instance, FMCG companies don't really focus on the plastic packaging their products generate. Only a small fraction of funds is spent by car companies on road safety. Apparel companies studiously ignore the impact that synthetic apparel and shoes that can't be recycled have on the environment. This is possibly because few companies really look at business responsibility at a strategic level.

The diagram below illustrates the three pillars of responsible business from the perspective of corporate India. Mandatory Spending, Sustainable Development Goals (SDGs) and Governance are three pillars on which business responsibility rests. The issues around each of the pillars are discussed throughout the chapter.

Figure 2.1: Three pillars of responsible business

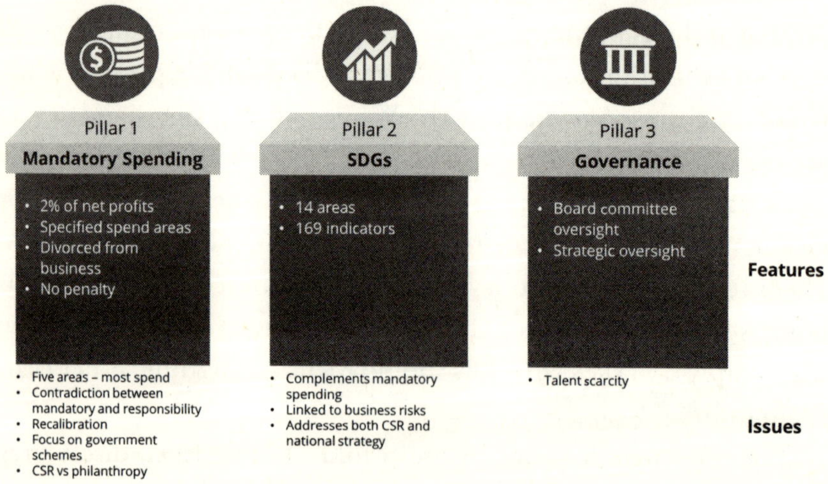

Sectoral Issues

Almost every sector in India has a significant number of issues that need to be addressed urgently.

Cement Sector: Cement is the major ingredient of concrete, which is the second-most consumed material on the planet. Cement production can severely damage the environment if it is not managed properly. By 2016, India had become the second-largest cement-producing country in the world. Almost all states in India produced some quantities of limestone, a significant component of cement, but about 75 per cent of the total production came from the states of Madhya Pradesh, Chhattisgarh, Andhra Pradesh, Rajasthan, Gujarat, and Karnataka. Cement's role in the Indian economy is critical because it employs more than a million people. It is also anticipated that the demand for cement will grow to 550–600 million tons per year by the year 2025.[2]

Cement manufacturing involves four major steps: quarrying, crushing, clinkerisation, and grinding. Like all industrial activities, cement production can harm the environment if not managed properly. Many of the features of cement production make it environmentally unfriendly. Limestone, a key raw material, is extracted through mining, and the output results in dust and particulate matter emissions if systems are inadequately designed. Some mines are located near agricultural land, wasteland, or forests; therefore, mining could change the land-use pattern of an entire region. Cement is also an energy-intensive industry and manufacturing it leads to large-scale emissions. Finally, water is a critical resource for any cement-manufacturing company. It is required for cooling, dust suppression, and domestic needs. Thus, water conservation has become a significant sustainability opportunity for cement companies.

Automobile Sector: An increase in pollution levels in most urban centres around the world has heightened the focus on automobiles in recent times. Emissions from vehicles are a huge source of particulate emissions and pose health risks like respiratory problems and eye irritations. In several Indian cities, these exceed the air quality standards set by the Central Pollution Control Board (CPCB). Sulphur dioxide, ammonia and suspended particulates in the air are higher than the CPCB standards. Also, India's diesel-powered vehicles pump out exhaust gases with ten times the carcinogenic particles found in petrol exhaust. While the industry is being urged to move towards electric cars and other cleaner fuels, currently, most vehicles run on diesel or petrol.

The automotive industry is also a significant consumer of water for its various production processes. According to some estimates, producing a single car takes over 39,000 gallons of water.[3] Primary water uses in automotive manufacturing include surface treatment and coating, paint spray booths, washing, rinsing, hosing, cooling, air-conditioning systems and boilers. The component-manufacturing segment has its own list of water-intensive processes. The painting process uses the highest volume of water as paints and coatings need to be regularly cleaned with water. The industry is being urged to move towards the manufacture of electric vehicles that have fewer parts and are expected to be less polluting.

Oil and Gas Sector: The conversation around sustainability has, at its core, the oil and gas industry, for this industry provides over half of the world's energy sources and is responsible for significant amounts of harmful emissions. Energy is an integral part of everyday life and plays an indispensable role in cooking food, providing electricity and lighting, transportation, manufacturing and several other industries that are heavily dependent on the energy generated by oil and gas companies. The oil and gas industry uses vast amounts of energy and water to manufacture its end use products such as petrol, oil, gas and diesel. Besides, the exploration and mining of oil in itself degrades the environment.

The sectoral impacts are therefore immense. With the industry's high impact on greenhouse gas (GHG) emissions and climate change, oil and gas companies need to move towards a product mix that consists of renewables. Strategic decision-making is necessary to build a long-term framework which focuses on genuine change, product innovation and new avenues of growth with reduced environmental impact.

Telecom Sector: The telecom revolution changed India's landscape. From a country where one had to book a telephone and then wait for months, sometimes years, for it to be 'allotted' and then installed, we are now a nation where access to a phone is almost a given. Phone purchases are frequent and telecom transmission infrastructure too has reached the far interiors of the country. This transmission infrastructure has a significant impact on the environment. Telecom towers now dot the urban landscape. Not only do these towers use substantial amounts of diesel for power, they also emit harmful radiation. The data centres that are an integral part of telecom companies are also energy guzzlers and require significant power for cooling. There are other impacts on the ecology too—not only are humans affected by radiation from towers, but it also affects birds, bees and other species that live nearby by hampering their ability to navigate.

Telecom products also generate mountains of e-waste. The 'seconds' market often repurposes phones, SIM cards, wires, batteries and assorted equipment but many find their way into landfills or are taken apart by untrained people in unsafe ways. These devices include heavy metals such as lead, cadmium, mercury and arsenic. If not handled properly, they can poison our environment and threaten the health of individuals and communities.

Mining and Metals Sector: The mining sector in India (taking into account atomic, major and minor minerals and fuel) made up about 2.4 per cent of the GDP in 2014-2015.[4] The country produces eighty-eight minerals including, four fuel minerals, three atomic minerals, twenty-six metallic and non-metallic minerals and fifty-five minor minerals (including building and other materials).

India possesses considerable reserves of the top five or six commodities, iron ore and thermal coal among others. Sustainability is a key issue in this sector because, though the mining operations may occur on a relatively small land area, the associated infrastructure and the pollution from their activities have the potential to affect the health of ecosystems around them. The sector's direct impacts on the environment include massive energy consumption and associated GHG emissions, land erosion, formation of sinkholes, loss of biodiversity, and contamination of soil, groundwater and surface water. Indirectly, it impacts the environment through transportation and other supply chain processes.

Besides the manufacturing sector, the service sector also needs to be paid attention to and its activities viewed through the lens of sustainability. A large part of the service sector is the financial industry, comprising both banking and non-banking activities. Another important sector in the service industry is the information technology sector.

Banking and Financial Services Sector: The banking industry throws up an interesting conundrum. Unlike the manufacturing sector it does not naturally cause emissions. However, the world of finance impacts almost everything in the modern world. A critical ingredient for a bank's well-being is its customers and society. Due to increasing linkages between banks and other parts of the financial system, risk moves quickly from banks to the financial system as a whole. Banks are also increasingly losing their brick-and-mortar character. With a significant portion of banking activity now being online and on the cloud, security risks are becoming prominent. With fintech gaining prominence and tools like artificial intelligence, machine learning and blockchain coming into widespread usage, the banking sector needs to be on its guard to protect its existence while ensuring that customer privacy, data security, and minimising the risk of misuse are given paramount importance. Given the current spate of irregularities at banks leading to swindling of large amounts by greedy business people, banks need to put their systems in place so that depositors, their key stakeholders, are cared for.

Information Technology Sector: Like the banking sector, the information technology sector also doesn't cause emissions. But with the world increasingly becoming digital, the information technology sector has to worry about many things. Safety and privacy of its customers and users is primary. Recent hacking attacks have shown that large corporations are extremely vulnerable, as demonstrated by the recent WannaCry ransomware attacks.[5] The attack exposed the vulnerability of major companies across the globe. The IT sector's responsibility is to build systems that minimise vulnerabilities. This sector also generates large amounts of electronic waste. Careful disposal and recycling efforts are the key to the sector's social responsibility. The sector also connects customers and users to large server farms. Maintaining and running these farms involves the use of large amounts of electricity. IT companies need to consider minimising energy consumption as well as moving towards renewables.

Grave as the situation might seem, it is steadily improving. Of the top 200 companies in India, about one-third have begun their responsibility journey. This has been brought about by some policy and regulatory changes such as India's mandatory CSR law as well as India's ratification of the Paris Agreement. However, these regulations have led to the creation of an artificial divide between CSR and sustainability. One way of looking at CSR is by looking at actions that companies take to benefit communities and their sustainability initiatives that protect the environment (waste disposal, water and energy). Take the case of water conservation. While it is part of sustainability, it also helps communities by providing greater access to water. In India, this distinction is muddied by the regulatory requirement that CSR activities should not be related to a firm's business activities.

The need for mandatory CSR

Since ancient times, merchants and guilds have, apart from developing their trade, contributed to the well-being of society. Paropkar (or charity) was considered to be an essential virtue. During good times they would cater to the well-being of the community through construction of wells and tanks to provide water security, build bathing ghats for sanitation, create animal welfare centres and plant trees by the roadside to provide shade and shelter to itinerant traders. They also built rest houses (dharamshalas) for wayfarers and pilgrims and donated liberally for healthcare and festivals. Underprivileged girls were helped by providing for their marriage expenses. During times of drought and famines, they often provided food and money to the needy. The practice of CSR is, in a sense, an attempt to continue this old habit of doing good.

In a way, social responsibility has been inherent in the Indian business ethos and has carried into the present times as CSR. Some of this consciousness came from the religious scriptures that promoted giving (daan) as a means of achieving virtuousness (punya). At the time of independence, many large business houses were known for their philanthropic activities. The Tatas, the Birlas, the Wadias and the Sarabhais were all well-regarded for their charitable acts. Early on in the post-independence phase, high tax rates left little money for charity. This continued till liberalisation led to the entry of multinationals, which provided an impetus to social responsibility, and a more benign tax policy that left a surplus with companies to spend on charity.

Some business groups such as the Birlas, Tatas, Bajajs and Dalmias were influenced heavily by Gandhi's concept of 'trusteeship'. Under this principle, surplus wealth was proposed to be kept in a trust for the common good and welfare of others. It also specified that everything one did had to be economically viable as well as ethical while at the same time making sure that sustainable livelihoods were created for all.

Take the case of the Tata Group, where its founder, Jamsetji Tata famously said, 'In a free enterprise, the community is not just another stakeholder in business, but is in fact the very purpose of its existence.[6]

This implies that businesses cannot survive in a society that fails, and that corporations have a responsibility to concern themselves with the quality of life of the communities they serve. If the community that constitutes customers, suppliers and lenders is not successful, it is highly unlikely that the corporation that serves them will survive. The heirs of Jamsetji Tata not only executed the vision of the founder, but also left lasting legacies of their own. Their decision to leave their wealth to charity reinforced the philanthropic activities of the organisation and also resulted in the creation of a trusteeship model in the Tata Group. The two trusts created by the sons of the founder—Sir Ratan Tata Trust and Dorab Tata Trust—are among India's largest private charities giving away amounts well in excess of 100 million US dollars a year. They also hold equity in Tata Sons (the holding company), and the dividends received by the trusts are reinvested in philanthropic activities. The group embodies this unique model of capitalism where responsibility is integral to the way of doing business and the company is held by trusts that are essentially focused on doing good. A later Chairman of the Tata Group, J.R.D. Tata, said, 'The wealth gathered by Jamsetji Tata and his sons is held in trust for the people and used exclusively for their benefit. The cycle is thus complete—what came from the people, goes back to the people many times over.'[7]

Therein lies the key to what works in business—people who make the community identify their interests with those of the company and these shared interests in business success help in creating long-term sustainable, profitable growth for all. The Tata Group also has a sustainability policy that commits it to certain environmental standards and social responsibility. CSR is embedded in the Tata code of conduct and the company has made it a mission to improve the quality of life of the communities they serve. Tata companies disclose their work through reporting formats including the new emerging Integrated Reporting (IR) format.

The trusteeship framework adopted by the Tata Group is, however, an exception. India's current model of industrialisation, like that of the rest of the world, is based on sourcing natural resources and modifying them to create consumer products. As stated previously, it is a fact that India's growth has not been inclusive. India, the emerging economic giant, is equally the land of the impoverished, home to about 360 million people living below the poverty line.[8] With close to 12 million youth joining the workforce every year, there is a crying need to create opportunities for livelihood creation. These challenges will get further compounded as India becomes the most populous country in the world by 2030. More than 1.5 billion people will then need food, nutrition, water, energy, education and health security. Already, environmental resources are under tremendous stress, given the fact that, with 17 per cent of the world's population, India has only 2.4 per cent of the world's land, 4 per cent of global water and 1 per cent of global forest resources. The need to create sustainable livelihoods and replenish our environmental resources has never been more urgent.

Indian companies have so far, for the most part, adopted the make-waste-trash model of growth without completely understanding the problems that would emerge from such a model. The irony, however, is that India has, in fact, all along had the trusteeship framework that Gandhi had proposed, as a framework of reference. Unfortunately, Indian corporations did not give this much importance. This model was debated in the '40s and '50s, but had no real takers for most of the twentieth century. However, the challenges thrown up by the twenty-first century, such as economic collapse, the absence of values and problems of sustainable growth, necessitate another look at trusteeship. The mandatory CSR law is perhaps a way for the Indian Government, perennially short of resources, to get companies to start thinking about giving back to society. (See *TN 7: Guide to the new CSR Rules*)

Mandatory CSR in India – the compliance perspective

The passage of the Companies Act 2013 brought about a dramatic shift in the way companies looked at CSR. Before the enactment of the Act, companies chose what to do for CSR. Some of what they did was philanthropy, and some were doing work on the ground to improve the livelihoods of communities. With the passage of the Act, now, companies (meeting specific criteria) are required to spend 2 per cent of their average net profits of the past three years on CSR. The Act has also listed out areas in which communities could spend, for their CSR activities to be recognised. Although the requirement to spend is mandatory, no provisions have been made for levying a penalty for non-compliance. Companies are required to set up separate board-level committees to plan and monitor the CSR activities of the company. Companies are also required to report their project-wise spending on CSR activities.

Section 135 of the Companies Act 2013 mandates

Every company having a net worth of Rs 500 crores or more, or turnover of Rs 1,000 crores or more or a net profit of Rs 5 crore or more during any of the three preceding financial years shall constitute a CSR committee of the Board consisting of three or more directors of which at least one director shall be an independent director.

The Board of every such company shall ensure that the company spends, in every financial year, at least 2 per cent of the average net profits of the company during the three immediately preceding financial years, in pursuance of its CSR policy.

The implementation of the mandatory CSR requirements has brought about several benefits:

- Greater focus on CSR activities: Companies now have dedicated departments and teams that look after CSR activities.
- More efficient spending: Given the requirement to report publicly. Controls through Board-level committees impose greater discipline on spending.
- Greater support to civil bodies (like NGOs): With more money being available, NGOs are able to do far more work than they used to.
- Increased requirement for manpower: Companies are now looking at trained manpower to undertake their CSR activities.

At the same time, the Act has had some negative consequences too:

- Artificial divide between business-related and non-business-related activities: This may cause companies to take a step back on some of the main sustainability-related initiatives.
- Limiting the kind of work that companies can do by making them adhere to the prescribed list and mandating that activities not be linked to business restricts corporate actions.

The mandatory CSR law was hotly debated and came under tremendous fire from businesses. Many said that the law is a type of tax. The argument that the government is getting companies to do what they should be doing in the first place, added to the debate. Another argument was that 'mandatory' placed alongside 'responsibility' is a contradiction in terms. The law also made a distinction that activities covered under CSR could not be part of the 'ordinary course of business'. Industry bodies vehemently opposed this, highlighting that CSR ought to be part of the core capabilities of the company. However, the government stood firm, saying that if a company conducted CSR activities in areas that were close to its business interests, the government would not be able to distinguish business activities from the company's contribution to society over and above its business activities.

The Act is now a law and one should look at this legislation holistically, considering both its pros and cons. The first benefit has been that the law has succeeded in elevating the discourse around CSR in corporate India. Earlier, CSR would be relegated to the margins of a company and funds would be deployed by owners and senior executives, with CSR managers having little say in decision-making. Also, funds would vary considerably from one year to the next. The fact that eligible companies have now set up CSR committees overseen by the Board ensures that CSR has now entered boardroom discussions. Serious questions are being asked about the spending of CSR allocations and the efficiency of the outcomes delivered. Board members are also now getting a better sense of the communities that the companies operate in. Mandatory CSR reporting has ensured greater transparency and opens up the company to greater public scrutiny as compared to the past. The time when CSR projects were done for feel-good reasons and budgets were erratic, guided by the whims of a few, are now slowly receding. The CSR legislation is fast beginning to incentivise collaboration between corporations who are now using the provision for pooling of CSR funds. For many corporations, this is a space where expertise can be shared without fear of losing competitive advantage. Also, over time, as more information gets shared, more corporations will seek economies of scale and better utilisation of assets.

As with any legislation, there are some risks and loopholes which are being exploited. In some cases, the government is accused of diverting these funds to their favourite schemes and projects. It is also possible for corporations not to spend on CSR by exploiting the loophole in the law that suggests that they need not spend on CSR, provided they disclose this information to the government and state their reasons for doing so. Further, discussions are on with the government to revise the rules specially, in the areas of volunteering and allowing greater flexibility in choosing projects. However, all said and done, Indian companies are becoming far more sensitive to the responsibility they carry towards the communities they serve. As the world moves towards a serious environmental crisis, this sensitivity and the collaboration this legislation has ensured will stand them in good stead.

The CSR law in India is largely focused around charitable contributions towards the under-privileged, but an important caveat is that this needs to be distinct from 'the ordinary course of business'. However, many strategic frameworks followed by international companies talk about combining the company's core competence with charitable efforts. Some of the large multinationals who have global mandates around CSR and sustainability have then needed to reconfigure their business responsibility practices in response to the recent Indian laws.

CSR projects undertaken by companies have largely followed three routes:

1. **Inhouse** – The company forms a foundation or trust and has dedicated full-time staff for execution.
2. **Outsourced** – The project implementation is outsourced to NGOs and monitoring is done through specialist third-party monitoring agencies. The corporate or its foundation/trust then merely acts as a funding agency.
3. **Joint execution** – The company partners with NGOs, government bodies or other corporations to execute social programmes. The company brings in funds, employee volunteers and specialised resources. The NGO provides field strength, knowledge and scale.

The big questions today in CSR departments include what causes to support, how to scale up their activities and how to implement without losing focus. While some companies have chosen to work with external NGOs, others like Dalmia Bharat have set up a foundation which acts on behalf of the company. The Dalmia Bharat Foundation engages in a number of activities around creating sustainable environments through soil, water and energy; providing skills to create livelihoods; and developing societies through education and health. Similarly, the Mukul Madhav Foundation acts as a CSR arm of Finolex Ltd. While the company undertakes all sustainability activities in and around its factory premises, it disburses funds to the foundation to undertake CSR activities. Over the years the foundation has established deep expertise in healthcare- and education-led projects and partners many companies and institutions in implementing them.

Industry partnerships and new platforms are also emerging. Piramal Sarvajal manages a network of community-level decentralised drinking water purification and vending solutions. Sarvajal partners with local entrepreneurs, government bodies, corporate CSR agencies and other philanthropic organisations to deploy customised safe drinking water outlets in villages, slums, schools, hospitals, public spaces and institutional setups.

Social projects need long-term financial commitment, in ground work and, in many cases, behaviour change, and this has been a big ask. Hero MotoCorp, a large two-wheeler manufacturer, focuses primarily on safe driving programs as part of its CSR initiatives. The safe driving programs are conceived and implemented by the company under three key planks of behaviour change, formal education on safe driving and awareness generation.

Also, most corporate initiatives are not connected to each other. Possibly because each corporate is working, albeit in many cases with utmost sincerity, in little unconnected pockets across the country. While they may be impacting individual lives in the areas that they are operating in, there is no clear-cut roadmap to eradicate the same problem in different parts of the country. Corporate boardrooms should be deliberating whether they can collectively fund efforts to solve common problems. Together, these corporations can leverage the kind of scale and longevity needed to address these deep-rooted problems.

For many corporations, this strategic shift has been challenging, and has been compounded by the scarcity of CSR talent to create scalable long-term strategy and implement it. While several opportunities have been created because of the mandatory CSR law, several CSR jobs at all levels lie vacant. Moreover, there is the other main thing being asked these days: 'After four years of mandatory CSR spending, what impact have we achieved?' Harnessing the funds released because of the new law will require educated and motivated individuals to provide leadership across all sectors of the economy. Not only will corporate executives need to be trained and sensitised, business school and postgraduate curricula will also need to be reworked to take on board the new opportunities and challenges brought on by the twin mandate of social good and economic growth. The 2 per cent requirement is merely a nudge from the government to corporate India to do good and then report these actions. For Indian brands, this is an opportunity to begin switching gears on their business strategy in favour of the long term, and integrating sustainability and CSR into their brand promise. If done strategically, rather than as a standalone activity, CSR can yield substantial results. While the risks of poor implementation are real, for every company that may struggle through this mandate, there will be others who will raise the bar with on-ground learning, strategic thought and innovative solutions.

Compared to the US, where companies account for about 5 per cent of the not-for-profit sector's budget, in India this percentage has gone up to 10 per cent mainly on account of the regulatory change. Although it was believed that large NGOs would easily be able to fill the gap in social spending by companies, it has been stymied by the fact that the NGO sector in India is highly fragmented. This leads to a problem of managing social projects on a large scale. Also, in terms of capability, NGOs in India need to build management systems that they, often, sorely lack. They are usually good at the work that they do but lack marketing skills, their documentation is often shoddy, the establishing and maintaining of Key Performance Indicators is weak and scaling up poses significant challenges. The lack of a cultural fit between companies and NGOs also creates problems in managing projects.

Often, companies choose activities that are easy to undertake. Creating physical assets like toilets, supplying solar lanterns and running health camps are seemingly easy choices. Rather than pick up fancy projects that look good on annual reports they need to focus on actions that actually impact the society around them. Companies should look at projects that resonate with their stakeholders. How would their actions impact the customers or their suppliers? Does the company feel good about what it is doing? Does it represent the values that the company attaches to the way it runs its businesses? Every company should aim to move the needle in the area of social change that it picks up.

Like the example of Sarvajal that we quoted earlier, companies need to actively collaborate to succeed in their social ventures. India is a large country and addressing problems in a limited area creates islands of success but doesn't really percolate downwards to the fullest extent. Collaboration among companies is one way to bring about effective and efficient social change.

India could also look at social innovation to manage social change. In a country as large, as diverse and as complex as India, the role of social innovation and social entrepreneurship is critical. Companies should focus on building and supporting these capabilities. Creation of innovation labs and supporting social entrepreneurship through equity infusion and mentorship could go a long way in building social change capabilities.

Action Agenda for CSR in India

- Companies need to focus on core areas rather than fancy projects which they are not able to implement or scale.
- Select NGOs that count as a good project as well as cultural fit.
- Focus on capacity building so that projects can scale.
- Projects need to move away from a charity-based approach to a self-sustaining one. Chequc book philanthropy is unsustainable.
- A collaborative approach is required.

CSR spends

While Indian law has mandated CSR spends in some key areas such as poverty alleviation, health, education, water, energy, capacity building and many more, the fact remains that 45 per cent of the spends by India's top companies are focused on just health and education. In contrast, other areas such as eradicating hunger and poverty, support during national calamities, etc. received 1 per cent or less of the total spent amount in 2016–17.

Also, 70 per cent of CSR spend is in five key areas. These areas are common to both manufacturing and services companies and in almost the same order.

Figure 2.2: CSR spend by key areas

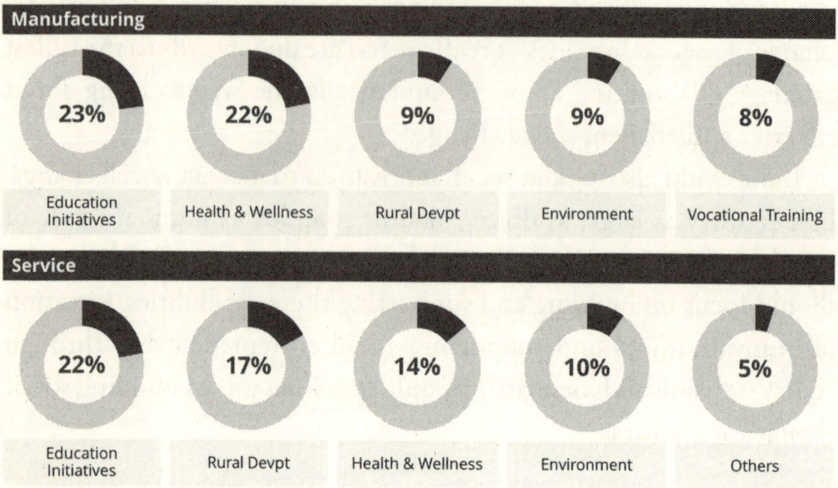

Source: Responsible Business Rankings, 2018.

The percentage of spend also throws up some interesting insights. While the Indian law mandates a spend of 2 per cent or more, the average CSR spend of India's top 166 companies was only 1.8 per cent in 2016–17. This was significantly higher than when it was 1 per cent in 2012–13 (before the mandatory requirement came in). There could be many explanations for this. Standard economics assumes that humans behave rationally. Studies show that, in reality, humans act irrationally in many situations. Daniel Kahneman in his popular book, *Thinking Fast and Slow*, uncovers some of the ways in which humans behave irrationally. One of the irregularities pointed out by Kahneman is 'anchoring'. Anchoring is a cognitive bias that describes the common human tendency to rely too heavily on the first piece of information offered (the 'anchor') when making decisions. To demonstrate anchoring, Kahnemann and Tversky[9] rigged a wheel of fortune. It was marked from 1 to 100 but was rigged to stop at 10 or 65. Students of the University of Oregon participated in the study where they were to note down the result of the wheel spin and answer the following questions:

Is the percentage of African nations among UN members larger or smaller than the number you just wrote?

What is your best guess of the percentage of African nations in the UN?

The wheel of fortune was unlikely to yield any useful information and the students should have simply ignored this piece of data. However, they did not ignore it. The average estimates of those who saw 10 and 65 were 25 per cent and 45 per cent respectively. The heuristics involved appear to be straightforward. Start from an anchoring number, assess whether it is too high or too low, and gradually adjust your estimate by mentally 'moving' from the anchor.

Till 2015, corporations had no minimum requirement for spending on CSR. The Companies Act of 2013 mandated a minimum spend of 2 per cent of the profits on CSR. Hence there was now an anchor point available to corporations to assist in their CSR-spend decision-making. With no anchor, corporations could choose to spend whatever they wished on CSR. With the availability of the anchor point, companies became more likely to curtail their spending when the 2 per cent limit was reached. Alternatively, those who had spent less than 2 per cent aimed to spend at least that amount.

Another mechanism that may be at work is recalibration. Suppose you are driving on a highway where the speed limit is 60 kilometres per hour (kmph). You notice that your speedometer is showing that you are travelling at 40 kmph. You are likely to accelerate to reach near the 60 kmph mark. On the other hand, if you find that you are travelling at 70 kmph, you are likely to slow down to 60 kmph. This is quite like the anchoring discussed earlier. Now, you notice that everyone on the highway is travelling at 70 kmph (they must know something that you don't). So, you will accelerate to a higher speed. Alternatively, you find that everyone else is travelling at 50 kmph (they must know something that you don't) and you are likely to slow down too. This is recalibration.

Companies look at studies like Responsible Business Rankings 2018[10] and get feedback on what everyone else is spending. This enables

Figure 2.3: Average spend by industry

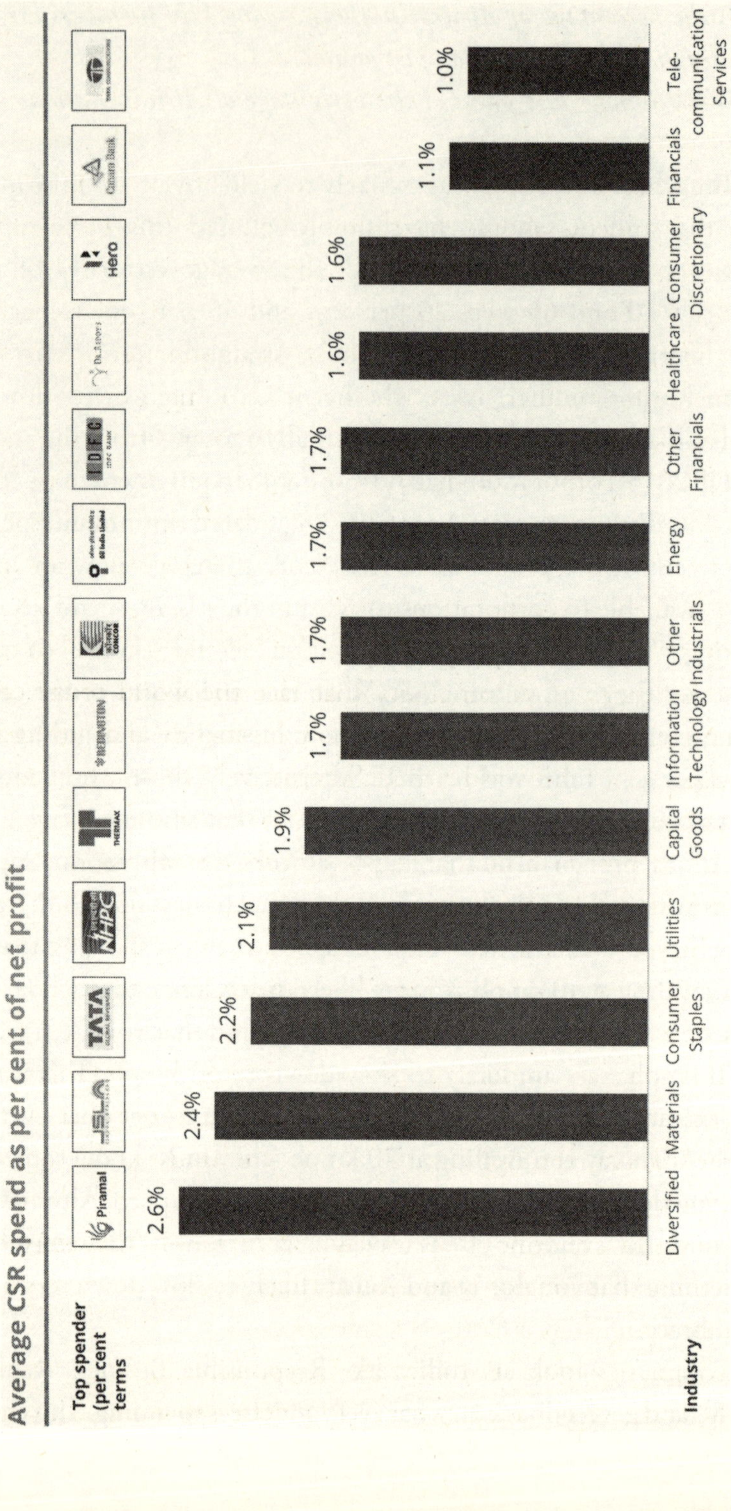

Source: Responsible Business Rankings, 2018.

them to recalibrate their spending. If a company is spending less than everyone else, they are likely to increase their CSR spends. This is like everyone else driving fast and me driving slower. If the company is spending more than everyone else, they are likely to reduce their CSR spending. This is quite like driving faster than everyone else. This should possibly get reflected in the next few years. The phenomenon of anchoring and recalibration appears to be validated given that almost a third of the companies spend 2 per cent or more. Also, reporting of CSR spending is replete with instances of companies that spend precisely the specified percentage.

The diversified industry led the industries with the highest average spend as a percentage of net profit at 2.6 per cent. It was followed by materials, consumer staples, and utilities, which also spend over 2 per cent of their average net profit. Financial companies spent the least.

Sustainable Development Goals and CSR

The challenges of sustainability that face the world today call for collective action and changes in how businesses and governments function across the world. On 25 September 2015, countries adopted a set of goals to end poverty, protect the planet, and ensure prosperity for all, as part of a new sustainable development agenda. Each of these Sustainable Development Goals (SDGs) has specific targets to be achieved over the next fifteen years. For the goals to be reached, everyone needs to do their part, governments, the private sector, civil society and the people.

This was an important development for most multinational corporations and their need for global scalable frameworks of social impact. Today, the opportunity for corporations to develop brand new customer experiences, integrate newer technologies and create a better world is enormous. While companies in India have largely been focused on compliance issues, global corporations have been aligning themselves with international frameworks such as SDGs.

While corporate involvement in previous UN initiatives was limited, the SDGs have been crafted with the understanding that

Figure 2.4: Sustainable Development Goals

Source: United Nations

commercial interests would have to be directly involved in both goal selection as well as specific measures of achievement across time. Businesses and industry are seen as drivers of socio-economic progress, for promoting sustainable commerce and trade and working towards building trust through greater transparency and accountability. The sustainable development goals are a broader canvas than the definitions of philanthropy-driven CSR or environmental sustainability. Instead, they focus on areas where urgent interventions are needed to create a better world.

The civil foundation of any society is driven by corporate action that, in turn, influence norms, conventions, customs and laws. 'Corporate Choice' is therefore an important component—companies can either pick the initiatives that they undertake, or they can simply meet their legal and compliance benchmarks. We must keep in mind that norms and customs get codified and eventually become laws. The game changer however, is that corporations can also innovate and these activities can be either strategic or structural.

Table 2.1: CSR spend and SDGs related

SDGs	Areas of spend specified by CSR rules
Goal 1 No Poverty; Goal 2 Zero Hunger; Goal 3 Good Health and Well-being; Goal 6 Clean Water and Sanitation	i) Eradicating hunger, poverty and malnutrition, promoting preventative health care and sanitation and making available safe drinking water;
Goal 4 Quality Education; Goal 8 Decent Work and Economic Growth; Goal 10 Reduced Inequality	ii) Promoting education including special education, and employment-enhancing vocation skills especially among children, women, elderly, and the differently-abled and livelihood enhancement projects.
Goal 5 Gender Equality; Goal 10 Reduced Inequality	iii) Promoting gender equality, empowering women, setting up homes and hostels for women and orphans; setting up old age homes, day care centres and other such facilities for senior citizens and measures to reduce inequalities faced by socially and economically backward groups;
Goal 7 Affordable and Clean Energy; Goal 11 Sustainable Cities and Communities	iv) Ensuring environmental sustainability, ecological balance, protections of flora and fauna, animal welfare, agroforestry, conversation of natural resources and maintaining quality of soil, air and water;
Goal 11 Sustainable Cities and Communities	v) Protection of national heritage, art and culture including restoration of buildings and sites of historical importance and works of art; setting up public libraries; promotion and development of traditional arts and handicrafts.'
Goal 10 Reduced Inequality; Goal 10 Reduced Inequality; Goal 10 Reduced Inequality	vi) Measures for the benefit of armed forces veterans, war widows and their dependents vii) Training to promote rural sports, regionally recognised sports, Paralympics sports viii) Contribution to the Prime Minister's National Relief Fund or any other fund set up by the Central Government for socio-economic development and relief and welfare of the Scheduled Castes, the Scheduled Tribes, other backward classes, minorities and women;
Goal 9 Industry, Innovation and Infrastructure	ix) Contributions or funds provided by technology incubators located within academic institutions which are approved by the Central Government;
Goal 1 No Poverty; Goal 2 Zero Hunger; Goal 10 Reduced Inequality; Goal 11 Sustainable Cities and Communities	x) Rural development projects

A strategic activity is one that encompasses doing both social good as well as increasing shareholder value. These actions are valuable to corporations. A structural action is one which focuses on doing only social good. These actions are rather expensive and impact company revenue and often cannot succeed without the support of multiple companies within an industry. Strategic actions ensure that the corporation remains competitive and is not bogged down by higher cost structures and lower revenues.

India is ranked 116 out of 157 nations in 2017 on a global index that assesses the performance of countries towards achieving the SDGs.[11] While SDGs are country-level indicators, corporate performance under the SDGs can shine a light on the glaring gaps that exist in India and how companies can gear up to address them. Also, there are significant overlaps between the SDGs and the areas outlined by the Indian CSR law. (Details on SDGs are available in *TN 9: Sustainable Development Goals*)

CSR as a development framework

The active involvement of corporates in the creation of SDGs has shown that they are interested in CSR in the form of 'development' and not just 'charity', the big difference being that companies now want to be involved in social impact projects that are strategic, measurable and scalable. This is best illustrated by the way the Tata Group attempts to implement projects derived from the SDGs.[12]

The Tata Group sees the SDGs as an excellent framework to build resilience into their respective businesses, founded in the belief that communities are the very reason for their existence. Tata Sons is the principal investment holding company and the promoter of Tata companies. There are twenty-nine publicly-listed Tata enterprises with a combined market capitalisation of about US$144.79 billion (as on 28 March 2018). Tata companies with significant scale include Tata Steel, Tata Motors, Tata Consultancy Services, Tata Power, Tata Chemicals, Tata Global Beverages, Tata Teleservices, Titan, Tata Communications and Indian Hotels.

How do the Tatas make SDGs work better for the group? Based on global experiences, some tried-and-tested approaches are given below that all the companies of the Tata Group follow.

Step 1: Examine SDGs from a business risks perspective

All companies are required to go through all the SDGs and identify:

- If there are any goals or targets that the operations of the company can adversely or negatively impact.
- If there are, what steps has the company taken or plans to take that can mitigate these impacts.

Step 2: Determine which SDGs are relevant to the company's core business

Not all 17 goals and 169 targets are equally applicable to all companies, hence the companies need to determine which ones are. They need to prioritise them and the flowchart below suggests a process for this:

Figure 2.5

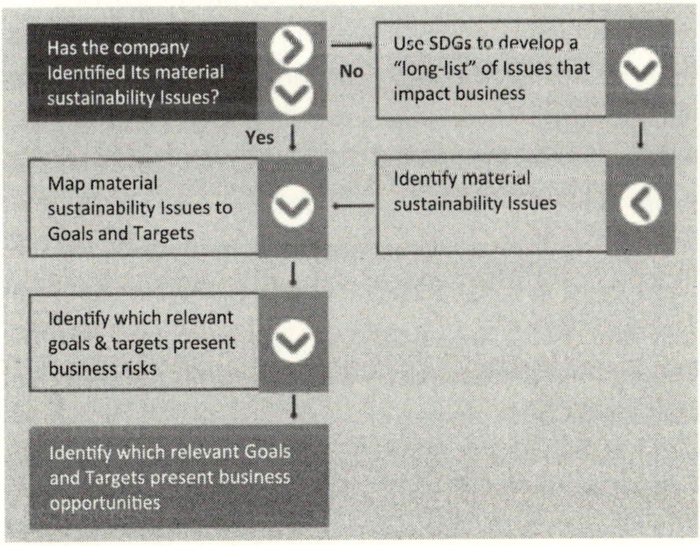

Source: Reproduced with permission from the Tata Group

Step 3: Determine which SDGs are relevant to each company's CSR activities

A company's CSR activities are designed to meet the development needs of the communities that it serves. The goals and targets provide an excellent framework to determine this. Here is how:

- Where a company has a clearly defined CSR strategy with goals and targets, the company should determine which SDGs and targets this strategy is designed to address and ensure that its KPIs and targets are aligned with the SDGs. This will make it easier to report the company's contribution to the specific goals and targets.
- Where a company's CSR strategy is still under development, the company can refer to the SDG framework which provides a set of goals and targets and, subsequently, activities that the company can contribute to. In the case of companies operating in India, care must be taken, of course, to ensure that these activities also align with Schedule 7 of the Companies Act.

The systematic implementation by the Tata Group could serve as a guide for others who want to undertake a similar exercise.

The definition of common goals in the SDGs has enabled the availability of finance through collaborative efforts to drive change. This interest from the corporate world has emerged because non-financial aspects are increasingly becoming the drivers of corporate reputation. Trust, transparency and quality amongst all other social parameters are indicators of corporate risk at one level and reliability at another. Corporate social responsibility is also being used as a tool to help companies motivate employees and build better teams.

All in all, a business strategy with CSR at its core is not just good for society; it's good business too!

CASE STUDY

NESTLÉ INDIA: CREATING SHARED VALUE

Nestlé's association with India began in 1912 when it started trading as The Nestlé Anglo-Swiss Condensed Milk Company (Export) Limited. Nestlé India is one of the largest fast-moving consumer goods (FMCG) companies in the country and is known for its chocolates, milk-based products, instant noodles and a vast range of food and beverages. In 2017, the company reported a revenue of Rs 9,195.3 crores (Rs 91,953 million) and a net profit of Rs 926.5 crores (Rs 9,265 million).[13] Nestlé's stated purpose is enhancing the quality of life and contributing to a healthier future. It wants to help shape a better and healthier world. It also wants to inspire people to live healthier lives. The company has a responsible sourcing programme and a transparent product labelling programme as part of its charter of ethics and responsible behaviour. The company's marketing activities also focus on the themes of nutritional education and awareness.

Nestlé India has carried forward the global Creating Shared Value (CSV) framework into its functioning in India and, additionally, worked extensively on CSR-related initiatives. CSV remains the fundamental guiding principle for how Nestlé does business. It is the strategy tool that Nestlé uses to operationalise and manage all the actions it takes to ensure it creates value for shareholders and for its work in society. This is how Nestlé brings its purpose to life—to enhance quality of life and contribute to a healthier future.

For long-term investors mainly, CSV was vital as it supported the long-term health of the company. With its emphasis on both shareholders and society, the CSV approach to business helps Nestlé define which products and services are in line with the expectations of society. Furthermore, Nestlé activity participates in CSR activities which do not have any direct relation with day-to-day business.

The company's focus areas are firmly embedded in its purpose. Individuals and families, its communities and the planet as a whole are seen to be interconnected, and the company's efforts in each of these areas are supported through its transparent 2020 public commitments. These commitments are aimed at enabling Nestlé to meet its ambitions for 2030 in line with the timescale of the SDGs (see Figure 1).

Figure 1: Nestlé Focus Areas

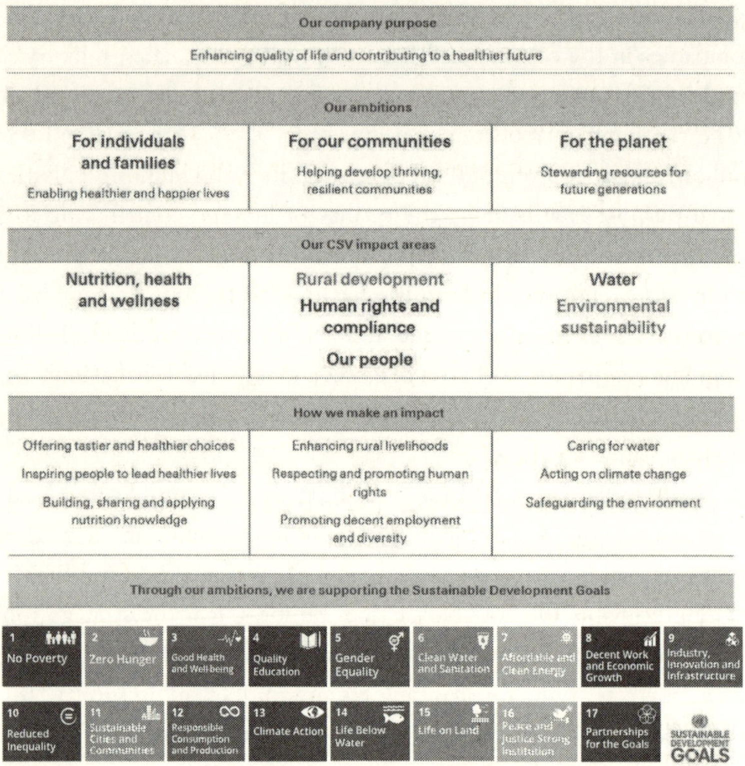

Source: Reproduced with permission from Nestlé India.

The key areas in which Nestlé works for society:

1) **Nutrition-based education:** This is a core element of Nestlé's social responsibility programmes in India. This is because India is home to a large population suffering from nutritional deficiencies. Large income disparities within the country lead to a unique situation where, on the one hand,

the poor suffer from severe malnutrition, and on the other, the prosperous are increasingly becoming obese.

Nestlé's work in society is in line with its commitment to enable healthier and happier lives for individuals and families. Nestlé, because of its extensive work in health and nutrition, working along with experts, created extensive programmes for health and nutrition awareness and behaviour change towards improved health outcomes for adolescents, young couples and caregivers.

Nestlé knew that just education was not enough in a large country like India. They have also launched a range of fortified products, including a taste enhancer called *Maggi Masala-ae-Magic*, which has been fortified with iron, vitamin A and iodine to help counter three big micronutrient deficiencies in the country.

2) **Water:** This is an important focus area. Nestlé has realised that clean drinking water and sanitation are huge issues in schools and villages around its factories and is committed to creating access to water and sanitation across schools in the country. The company has also chalked out a comprehensive plan on water education for farmers and schoolchildren.

   Nestlé is committed to improving its water footprint. Through its constant efforts, over the last fifteen years, the company has achieved a 53 per cent reduction in water consumption per tonne of production. They have used advanced technology to improve their capacity to produce more from fewer resources, as well as reduce waste generation. In 2016, Nestlé initiated twenty-eight water reduction projects across its factories.

3) **Rural development:** Another core area and a good example of CSV was when the company began working with farmers and dairy suppliers and developed a programme to help them

increase the quality and yield of their products. For instance, in the Moga district in Punjab, the company assisted farmers in caring for cattle, advising them on feed quality and keeping them updated with the latest developments in dairy farming. Similar activities were undertaken for coffee farmers in South India and chicory farmers in North India. The unique model created by Nestlé is depicted in Figure 2.

Figure 2: Nestlé's Milk District Model

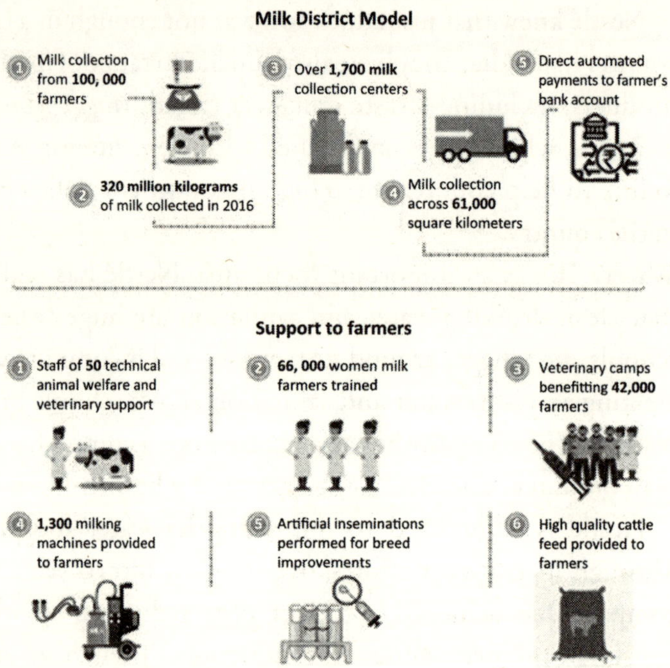

Source: Reproduced with permission from Nestlé India.

Nestlé India's milk factory in Moga has become an international case study[14] on working collaboratively with local communities for creating shared value. What had started as a small operation with only 180 farmers willing to supply milk in 1961 expanded to about 90,000 farmers. Nestlé has worked extensively to help farmers in improving herd management, farm productivity and overall income. This has created long-term sources of income for the community and, at the same time, helped Nestlé create goodwill and establish a continuous supply of milk and milk products.

The 'Nestlé in Society' framework has enabled the company to build a close connection between the company and the communities it operates in. It also fostered the need to work for the betterment of the ecology and environment.

CHAPTER 3

India Rediscovers Its Sustainability Roots

Historically, India has been a country where waste was mostly taboo, and living in harmony with nature, a cherished cultural norm. The ancient scriptures looked upon life as a gift to be celebrated and the earth was seen as something to be praised and worshipped. The Isha Upanishad, a sixth-century Sanskrit text has talked about all life forms living in harmony with the earth system without encroaching upon each other's rights. Ancient wisdom also frowned upon waste and everything in the Indian cities and villages had to be reused and recycled, leading to a highly evolved system of waste collection and disposal. Over the centuries, this philosophy of conservation and love for nature was strengthened further through art, music, scriptures and traditions. In fact, the first recorded measures of conservation anywhere in the world were the edicts issued by Emperor Ashoka in 269 BCE. These edicts carved on stone and iron pillars prohibited the destruction of forests and the killing of animals. Over the years, many tribes and villages began to celebrate certain trees, animals, rivers and ponds as sacred. This environmental thinking became part of the rich cultural heritage of India.[1]

These ancient tenets were, however, forgotten when India decided to move towards an industrialised system, falling in line with modern-day economics. As companies scaled, supply chains became bigger and more complex. The commons, such as forests, rivers and hills, lost their 'sacredness', with large companies viewing them merely as resources that had to be modified and used as inputs. Economic performance was prioritised irrespective of the social cost. Industries could dump sewage in rivers as only their cost of production mattered and treating waste would only add to these costs. Cutting forests was okay to make paper but replanting trees was a cost that the company did not want to bear.

If one were to drive to the Kudremukh National Park in the Western Ghats today, there are still the remnants of a gigantic strip mining operation by the name of the Kudremukh Iron Ore Company Limited (KIOCL). What was once a mining town with residences for the workers and management, teeming with activity, carefree school children and buzzing markets, is now a ghost town, with nothing but dilapidated buildings, storing within them memories of a time gone by. A time that, in hindsight, resulted in severe ecological damage to the region. The mining activity, spread over forty-eight square kilometres in the middle of the park, caused widespread destruction to the Kudremukh National Park, a UNESCO World Heritage Site. Spread over a 630 square kilometre area, the park is a hotbed of biodiversity in the form of mountainous grasslands and tropical rainforests housing many species of animals and plants. It is home to the great pied hornbill, the Malabar civet and the lion-tailed macaque, besides also sheltering a population of tigers. The national park is also the origin-site of the rivers Tunga, Bhadra and Netravathi. All of this fragile ecosystem was under threat because of the operations at KIOCL. A landmark judgement by the Supreme Court in October 2002, finally brought the curtains down on the mining operation and what the court deemed as 'an environmental abomination'.[2]

Sadly, by then, the impact of mining had already gone beyond the actual extraction of ore and dumping of tailings. In the case of Kudremukh, for instance, since the hill range (Aroli–Gangamoola) was inaccessible, a ghat road had to be constructed to reach it. Other roads connected the mini-township that housed the workers and management. These roads were needed to provide access for giant earth-moving machines, and this resulted in cutting through untouched forest land. Also, to allow for the iron ore (in the form of slurry) to reach Mangalore, the closest port city, a sixty-seven kilometre pipeline was laid out which cut right through the forest. This pipe was prone to breakage (in the year 2000, for instance, it broke four times), spilling approximately 4,000 tonnes of concentrated iron ore into the pristine streams that make their way through the mountainous terrain.

The case of KIOCL is but one example of the ill-effects of modern-day industrial systems. Environmental groups the world over are up in arms against the harmful practices of industry and of the irreparable damage they leave behind. Also, consequences of climate change and 'short-termism' become increasingly apparent, it is clear now that ignoring sustainability concerns is dangerous. For the better part of this decade, India has reeled under the impact of floods in several parts of the country, drought in others and extreme pollution in almost all its cities. Extreme weather events have damaged physical infrastructure, disrupted supply chains and impacted business continuity.

In corporate offices, though, there has been confusion about cause and effect. For instance, whose responsibility is air pollution? At one level, there is a realisation that it is everyone's responsibility, but at another level the sustainability manager might well take this view: 'I comply with the law, what more can I do?' The prevailing business frameworks have led managers to focus on the symptoms and not the actual causes. Large sums of money spent on mitigating emissions and discharges haven't really helped since they are only part of the core design of production systems that are immersed in toxic materials and polluting energy sources.

To begin with, companies decided to overlook their responsibility and passed off the problems of pollution and environmental degradation to the government and citizens. The Delhi smog being a case in point. The thick blanket of smog that enveloped Delhi and surrounding areas at the end of September 2017 was the worst in seventeen years and has been compared to the Great Smog of London in 1952 that resulted in 4,000 deaths. Air pollution claims around 10,000 to 30,000 deaths in the national capital every year.[3] With the escalation in pollution levels, all eyes turned to the government and what it could have done, or can still do, to remedy this situation. As a short-term measure, schools were shut down, roads hosed down and construction activity halted. The courts then came down hard upon all levels of government and demanded that they offer more than what they termed an 'ad hoc' and 'unserious' response. Described in the media, social media and other conversations as a 'toxic cocktail', a 'gas chamber' and 'poison gas', amongst other things, air pollution is here to stay unless everyone works together. While Diwali crackers are one reason for the spike in air pollution levels, automobile emissions, refineries, chemical plants, coal-fired power plants, manufacturing of cleaning products, pesticides, degreasers and unchecked crop burning in neighbouring states are some of the other sources of this heightened level of toxic air. To add to the lethal brew, the three landfills of the city also have their own list of lapses. The methane gas produced in these landfills catches fire ever so often, further spiking the pollution indices.

Companies are now slowly beginning to realise that they are indeed part of the problem, which is why the sustainability narrative in India in the past few years has become more nuanced, and the environmental movement has become broader and more professional. Indian businesses are also facing international regulatory and compliance issues around sustainability and emissions. Sustainability challenges have been dovetailed with global concerns on climate change, ozone depletion and the loss of biodiversity. The alarming consequences of excessive overuse of natural resources is being seen as we reach Earth Overshoot Day[4] faster each year. In 2017, we reached it by August, which points to the fact that we had consumed what the earth could replenish in only *eight* months. The environment is a global issue and the world is coming together to address these challenges. The increasing incidence of man-made disasters such as the Chennai floods and Uttarakhand floods are, therefore, forcing corporate leaders to emerge and speak up for change.

This trend is only likely to gather momentum in the light of the Paris Agreement of 2015. Governments the world over, after more than two decades of intense negotiations and debate, finally came to a legally binding agreement that aimed at containing the increase in the global average temperature to 'well below 2°C above pre-industrial levels, and to pursue efforts to limit the temperature increase to 1.5°C above pre-industrial levels'—a more ambitious goal than had been expected. The implications of the Paris Agreement are not just in terms of the new business environment but are also about the larger impacts on how businesses will have to be run five, ten and fifteen years from now. The cost of environmental damage can no longer just be passed on to the community. Businesses will increasingly be expected to bear this cost and, in fact, undo the damage. The Paris Agreement has had significant impact on climate finance as well as enabling technology. Inter-governmental initiatives like COP21[5] and Sustainable Development Goals (SDGs) are platforms that are helping companies find common ground and encouraging them to align together for greater impact on specific targets.

The move towards sustainability in India is also being assisted by a spate of legislations to clean up rivers, manage waste and protect the environment. India's 'E-Waste Management and Handling Rules of 2016' are one reason companies are looking at how they are disposing of their electronic waste. Electronic waste is hazardous to health and the environment, and the new 2016 rules have recommended

Figure 3.1: Sustainability in India

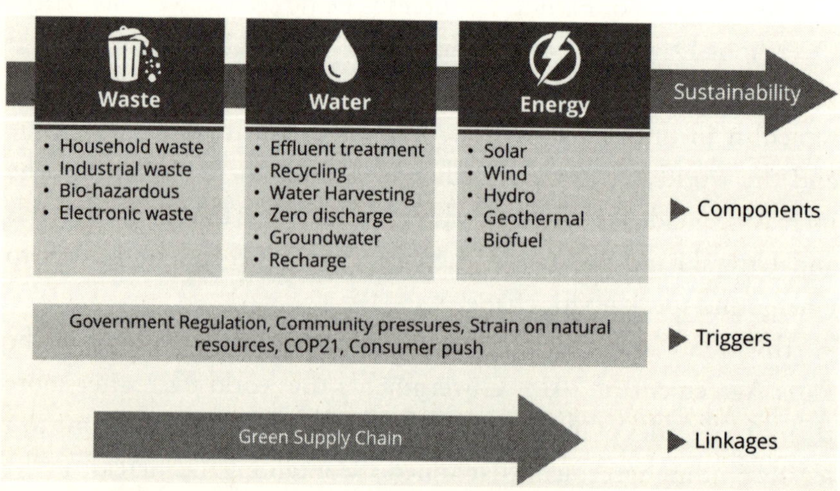

the setting up of a Producer Responsibility Organisation (PRO). Stringent norms and checks are being set in place so that organisations are made responsible for managing the end-of-cycle of electronic waste generated by their products. (See *TN 10: India's Waste Management Laws*, which discusses the details of the laws.)

Sustainability momentum builds up

In 2011, India introduced the national voluntary guidelines that asked companies to report on a variety of governance and sustainability issues through an annual Business Responsibility Report (BRR). While it was initially restricted to the top 100 companies, in 2016 the mandate was extended to include the 500 top listed companies.[6]

From our 2018 study[7] of 218 companies' sustainability reports (SR) and annual reports, we find that 30 per cent more companies now generate sustainability reports and 56 per cent more companies generate BRR reports as compared to 2017. Several companies also do risk assessments and highlight sustainability as being a key component of corporate risk.

Figure 3.2: Sustainability reporting in India

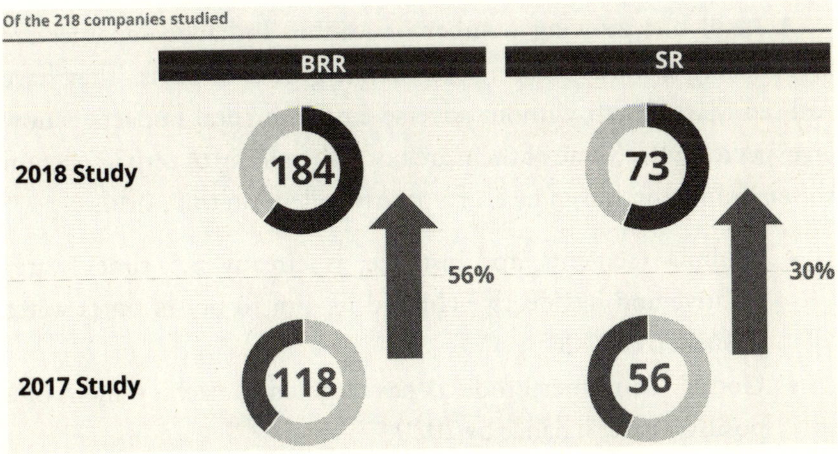

The *Responsible Business Rankings 2018* study[8] analyses various sustainability parameters of these top companies. These include factors such as waste, water and energy, targets to reduce impact, sustainable products and services, sustainable supply chains and sustainable logistics. Overall, there has been a steady increase in corporate performance over the years. The figure below indicates the percentage change in the overall scores over the years.

Figure 3.3: Sustainability scores are increasing

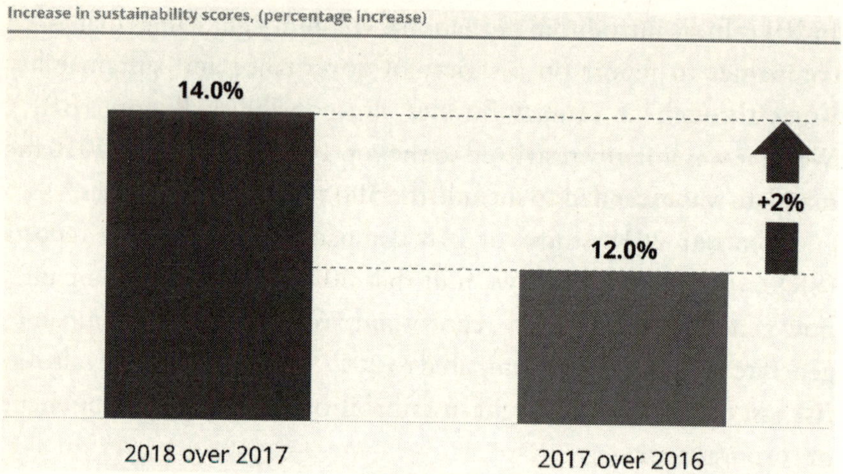

Source: Responsible Business Rankings 2018

A small but growing number of leading Indian companies are also moving towards creating sustainable growth models. They have realised that growth without adverse environmental impacts is now an expected goal. Some of them are not only talking of zero impact on the environment, but in fact, of a positive effect on the world.

- Ambuja Cements, for instance, is already 5.5 times water positive and has nearly achieved its aim to be six times water positive by 2030.[9]
- Godrej Consumer Products has targeted the achievement of a positive water balance by 2020.[10]
- ITC has been carbon positive for over thirteen years, water positive for sixteen years and solid-waste-recycling positive for eleven years.[11]

The Tata Group has gone a step further, as it is one among fifty leading global companies to pilot the Natural Capital Protocol across four group companies—Tata Power, Tata Steel, Tata Chemicals and Jaguar Land Rover. Dr Mukund Rajan, member, Group Executive Council, and brand custodian, Tata Sons, said, 'The Tata Group believes that our business should identify, measure and value their impacts and dependencies on natural capital, so that they can strengthen their decision-making, address risks and identify opportunities, while at the same time protect the increasingly scarce natural capital to enable a better future for subsequent generations. This is why valuation of natural capital is one of the commitments we undertake under the Tata Sustainability Policy and why four Tata Group companies have piloted the draft protocol and provided inputs to the Natural Capital Coalition.'[12] (see *TN 11: Natural Capital Protocol*)

The march towards renewables

Carbon emissions are a significant cause of worry for India and the world. Carbon emissions impact not only the air we breathe but also result in changes in weather: more storms, floods and unexpected climate events. India is going ahead with initiatives to develop climate-resilient infrastructure, as well as focusing on efforts to enhance climate resilience and reduce vulnerability to climate change. The participation of both the companies as well as the government is critical in achieving these ambitious climate goals. Globally, after years of purchasing renewable energy credits (RECs),[13] governments and companies are increasingly tilting towards renewables. This is founded on the belief that accelerating the scale-up of renewable energy will help deliver a better, healthier and more sustainable world. Currently, renewable energy forms only a small proportion of the total energy consumed in operations across sectors. However, to push the country and the corporate sector towards renewables the Indian government, in 2017, cancelled 14 gigawatts of planned coal power projects and has targeted 175 gigawatts of renewable energy capacity by 2022 (including 100 gigawatts of solar power). The government expects non-conventional sources to account for 40 per cent of total generation capacity by 2027, three years ahead of the time set by the Paris Agreement.

The disclosure about the shift to renewables is scanty and fragmented in the companies' sustainability reports. In fact, the targets for renewable energy are not even disclosed across most companies, though most have disclosed programmes and plans for solar and wind projects in their operations. The telecom sector leads the adoption of renewable energy in operations, followed by IT and energy. This does not come as much of a surprise as the telecom sector is a massive consumer of grid electricity and diesel. The financial sector is a laggard with very few banks and non-banking financial companies (NBFCs) disclosing renewable energy initiatives. While many companies have developed captive capacities for solar and wind energy, they will also need to procure additional energy through Power Purchase Agreements.

Table 3.1: Renewable sources of energy

	Top 2 renewable energy sources used (per cent companies studied)		
Sector	**Solar**	**Wind**	**Biofuel**
Capital goods	69%		31%
Consumer Staples	67%		53%
Energy	70%	60%	
Healthcare	80%		60%
Materials	73%	37%	
Utilities	83%		42%
Telecom	80%	80%	
IT	78%	22%	22%
Financials	41%	6%	
Auto	89%	56%	

Source: Responsible Business Rankings, 2018

Amongst the renewable energy sources, solar and wind are the most commonly deployed by companies. Solar is the most widely adopted renewable energy source across most sectors, and it leads the second-most deployed renewable energy source by a wide margin. Solar is preferred probably because it is not as geography-specific as wind and hydro projects and the up-front costs involved too are relatively less. Telecom and IT sectors lead the adoption of solar, however, the scale of operations is quite small.

Apart from solar, we find that some renewable energy sources are preferred in some industries by virtue of their operations. For instance wind in the energy sector, hydel-power in utility companies, waste-heat-recovery in cement companies and biofuel in consumer staples.

Table 3.2: Sector-wise solar capacities

2016–17

Sector	Solar capacity (KW) (captive)	Captive capacity (KW) (Renewable energy)
Financials	100-255300	100- 65200
Telecom	193-17500	25-17500
IT	10-15200	10-15200
Other Industrials	625-1500	625-6000
Energy	60-20000	60-188000
Automotive	1200-13500	1500-21950
Other Consumer discretionary	168.7-1300	168.7-1300
Capital goods	100-11500	1030-14900
Consumer Staples	130-300	130-271000
Diversified	50-8500	50-27000
Healthcare	30000	30000
Materials	10-16000	10-274000
Utilities	55-933000	55-1391000

Source: Responsible Business Rankings, 2018

Given the push from the government, several Indian states are chalking out programmes for renewable energy. Private companies are also pledging their commitment to setting up renewable energy projects for their own use or are promising to source 100 per cent of their consumption needs from green sources.

Companies have instituted renewable energy programmes for their supply chains. ONGC, for instance, has started the concept of 'greening the vendor' in its entire value chain. Through this policy, ONGC is seeking to promote efforts that lower carbon footprint not only within ONGC but also amongst its stakeholders across the vendors' chain (business partners). Similarly, Hero Motor Corp conducted energy audits in a number of supplier units to establish actual energy consumption. Considerable saving of electrical energy was achieved. Larsen & Toubro is developing a system to monitor their suppliers' environmental and social footprints, and this would be reported from 2018 onwards. P&G has implemented a supplier sustainability scorecard, which assesses the environmental footprint of their suppliers, enabling it to partner with the greenest of companies and help reduce the environmental impact along the supply chain.

ABB is another case in point. ABB has defined a specific goal of being recognised as a world leader in sustainability by 2020. Its Indian subsidiary, ABB India Ltd, has been manufacturing in India for more than sixty years and has been present in India for a whole century. ABB's technologies range from airports to massive solar parks, from remote, rural microgrids to rooftops. More than 50 per cent of solar energy in India currently passes through ABB equipment. By mid-2017, ABB had surpassed a portfolio of 4.5 gigawatts' renewable capacity with delivery of over 2,000 units of power generators in India.

Water management initiatives

India has 4 per cent of the world's freshwater resources and a whopping 16 per cent of the world's population, and is ranked a dismal 120 out of 122 nations in terms of water quality, according to a UN report.[14] It is predicted that by 2030, 40 per cent of the people in India will not have water to drink.[15] Although rivers are considered sacred and holy in India, we are in what can only be termed an unholy mess today! The Central Pollution Control Board estimates that almost half of India's 445 rivers are unsafe for consumption on account of pollution, and there is not even one from which water can be consumed without extensive treatment. Several northern Indian states have exceeded their surface irrigation potential, and farmers in these areas have now set their sights on groundwater resources. It is estimated that there are 25 million groundwater pump sets in the country, making states like Punjab, Haryana and Rajasthan water-stressed zones, where the withdrawal of water has exceeded or will soon exceed the rate of groundwater recharging.

Shifting rainfall patterns on account of climate change have meant that India is either coping with drought or dealing with floods at any given point of time. Of the total water available in India, 85 per cent is dependent on rains and the rest is fed by melting snow. Rainfall patterns have become extremely erratic and unreliable now, and this means water replenishment happens in a very haphazard manner. It is therefore imperative that India manages its water and water storage more efficiently. Climate change has seen an increased rate of melting glaciers that have caused flash floods and widespread devastation. It has also meant that there is inadequate water during the dry season. Moreover, with increased temperatures overall due to climate change, both crops and human population need more water than before to cope with the heat.

The National Water Mission has targeted the reduction of water consumption by 20 per cent in all sectors by 2030. Many policy-level initiatives have been taken and higher allocations made to water-based projects in the 2017–18 budget. Some policy changes put in place are:

a) The mandate of a zero-liquid discharge system for some industries.
b) The issuance of the 'green order' by the Supreme Court in February 2017.[16]
c) Reuse of treated water in nearby thermal power plants.
d) The purchase of recycled water by Indian Railways.

In addition to policy changes and their enforcement, governments (both Central and state) have taken measures to invest in infrastructure for water and waste-water management. In 2017, India collaborated with Israel and Hungary on water management technology and has awarded projects to private companies for the setting up of sewage treatment infrastructure to keep the Ganges clean.[17]

Separately, other stakeholder groups have opined about the impending water crisis. Water and legal experts suggest that the government separate land rights from water rights. Earlier in 2017, the Ganga and its main tributary, the Yamuna, were accorded the status of living human entities with human rights by an Indian High Court. According to the report of an expert committee for framing India's future water management policy,[18] industries consuming large amounts of water must calculate and declare their water footprint in their annual reports. They must take steps to progressively bring down this footprint every year and state this progress in their annual reports. They should, ideally, use only recycled water. Use of groundwater for industrial purposes must be authorised by the government.

Figure 3.4: Water management initiatives

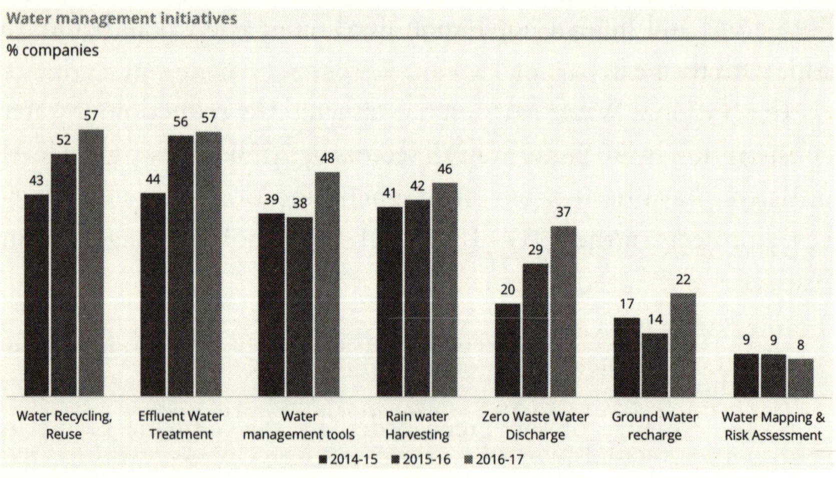

Source: Responsible Business Rankings, 2018

Our research finds that 91 per cent of manufacturing companies (86 per cent in 2017) have programmes and targets to reduce water consumption as compared to 56 per cent (52 per cent in 2017) of services companies.[19] Effluent water treatment and water recycling/reuse are the most widely deployed programmes as they help reduce fresh water intake. In line with the government mandate, the proportion of companies having zero wastewater plants, too, has gone up in the year, as compared to the previous year.

Stepping up to manage waste

Indian cities are drowning in garbage. Over 62 million tonnes of waste is generated in India annually. While over 80 per cent of the waste is collected, only 28 per cent of it gets processed in any form. Most of the collected waste lies in huge landfills, polluting the land it rests on and is prone to frequent fires that pollute the air too.

The government's 'Swachh Bharat' (Clean India) programme has set specific targets for waste management and primarily focuses on segregation of waste at source. The revised waste management rules listed in 2016—both Solid Waste Management Rules and E-Waste Management Rules—extend the ownership of non-biodegradable waste to their producers. The producers of electrical and electronic goods, too, have been made responsible for the collection of e-waste and its exchange as part of 'Extended Producer Responsibility' under the new E-Waste Rules.

While services firms outpace manufacturing firms in e-waste management initiatives, we find that only a few IT companies such as Cisco have extended their e-waste management programmes to customers and spread awareness about the same. The financial services industry lags significantly behind in e-waste management programmes despite the rapid digitisation of the industry.

The industry's new focus is on recyclable plastic packaging, given rising environmental concerns over waste management and the revised rules. The revised Plastic Waste Management Rules 2016 mandates the phasing out of the manufacture and use of non-recyclable multi-layered plastic in two years' time. The brand owners are required to collect back the non-biodegradable packaging waste generated due to their production. Also, all manufacturers of disposable products

Figure 3.5: E-waste management programmes

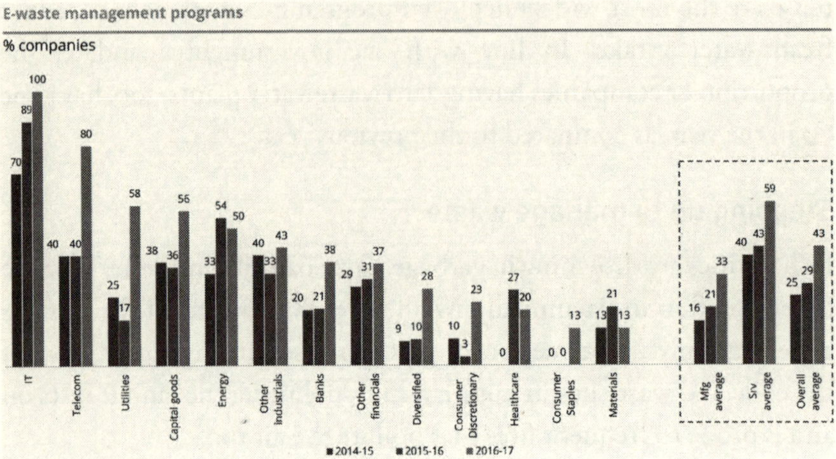

Source: Responsible Business Rankings, 2018

such as tin, glass, plastic packaging, or brand owners who introduce such products in the market are required to provide necessary financial assistance to local authorities for the establishment of a waste management system.

- Nestle India is looking to collaborate with Indian start-ups to make alternatives to PET bottles for packaged drinking water. Their goal is to incorporate more recycled plastics and/or bioplastics made from renewable materials into their packaging.
- Hindustan Unilever stated in 2015 that it had implemented innovative ways of reducing the resources used for packaging by focusing on using lighter, stronger and better materials that have a lower environmental impact. Unilever aims to move to 100 per cent recyclable plastic packaging by 2025 globally.

Our study found that the consumer staples industry leads green packaging initiatives, followed by the capital goods and consumer discretionary sectors, as shown in the graph below. Overall, only a few companies (19 per cent) disclosed their green packaging initiatives.

Figure 3.6: Packaging initiatives

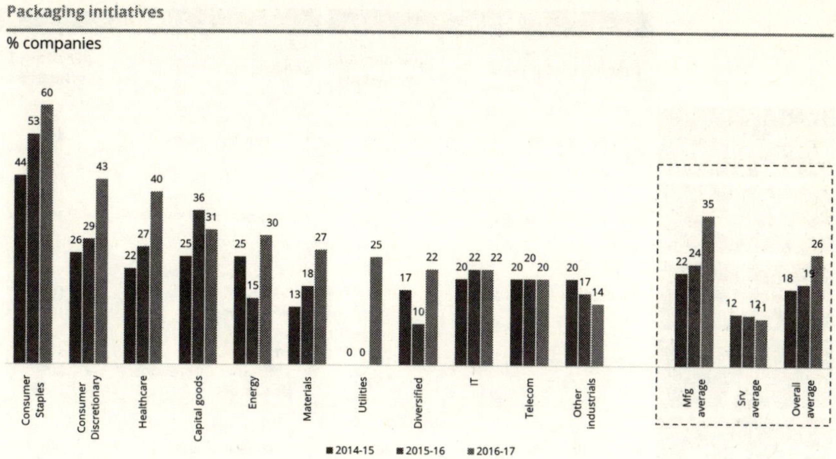

Source: Responsible Business Rankings, 2018

In 2016–17, we find that companies are focusing more on using recyclable packaging. Use of sustainable packaging material, too, witnessed higher adoption in the year. Table 3.3 below illustrates the packaging initiatives by companies highlighting the percentage within the industry that adopt a particular initiative. Although companies are taking these initiatives, the adoption rate definitely needs to increase.

Corporate India is cognizant of this challenge and many like Cummins India have taken the responsibility of not just eliminating waste from their own manufacturing but also of lending a helping hand to the cities their offices and factories are located in. In a city like Pune (today, an industrial and educational hub), with a population of over 4.1 million people and growing at an alarming rate, the increasing population has resulted in straining the infrastructure, limiting the availability of resources in the city and thus calling for effective waste management. Until recently, the civic authorities were handling garbage collection and dumping a portion of the garbage at a landfill located close to Pune. Cummins undertook a 'Zero Garbage' project in Pune, which converts biodegradable waste into biogas that is then used to produce electricity.

Table 3.3: Leading companies with packaging programmes

	2015-16		2016-17	
	Leading sector (s)	per cent of companies	Leading sector (s)	per cent of companies
Choice of sustainable packaging materials	• Capital goods	29%	• Consumer staples	40%
Reduce size of the package	• Consumer staples	27%	• Healthcare	30%
Redesigning product to reduce packaging	• Consumer staples	27%	• Consumer Staples • Energy • Healthcare	13% 10% 10%
Reuse of packaging (e.g.: refills)	• Consumer Discretionary • Healthcare	19% 18%	• Energy • Consumer Discretionary • Healthcare	30% 20% 20%
Recycling	• Consumer staples	40%	• Consumer staples	40%

Source: Responsible Business Rankings, 2018

The electricity produced from waste is used to power street lights. The recyclable non-biodegradable waste is recycled reducing the amount of garbage going to landfill. The zero-garbage model adopts an innovative approach towards solid waste management in which citizens pay a nominal fee to the waste pickers for collection of waste at the door step.

Green supply chain

Corporate supply chains have been opaque for a long time. This is now changing with greater focus on traceability. Coupled with companies becoming more transparent, supply chains are getting the right attention. So, what is traceability? Traceability is the ability to verify the history and location of products and services in the supply chain. This involves building supply chains that are transparent and able to provide an easy way to assess where contamination is occurring. Traceability improves product sourcing, reduces costs and ensures a healthy output. This is not new. For instance, companies have been tracking agricultural commodities and forest products for years. With growth in technology, newer tools and techniques such as sensors and data analytics are enabling companies to more efficiently and affordably account for the environmental and social impacts of their materials and products. Thus traceability is spread through the whole chain, right from farms, forests and mines to individual factories. The growth of third-party verification is another factor. Professionals are now readily available to verify the provenance of products and raw materials. This makes it very difficult for companies to escape by feigning ignorance. Worldwide, many food and beverage companies are partnering with their growers and other agricultural partners to push for sustainable business practices.

We find significant improvement in the proportion of companies with programmes for their supply chain in 2016–17 as compared to the previous year.[20] However, the percentage continues to be low by most measures. Interestingly, the average proportion of companies with supply chain programmes are marginally higher for manufacturing compared to service industries in 2016–17.

Sustainable sourcing is a key focus for many companies. The consumer staples industry has various industry-specific initiatives for this such as Trustea,[21] and the Roundtable on Sustainable Palm Oil sourcing (RSPO).[22]

Our study finds that 50 per cent of the manufacturing companies studied give specific targets to their suppliers for reduction of carbon footprint and 43 per cent conduct environmental audits of new suppliers before they are brought on board or conduct ongoing periodic audits of existing suppliers on their environmental impact.[23] The table below shows the percentage of companies within a sector (manufacturing or service) who are adopting a green supply chain initiative. There is an increasing trend towards green supply chain initiatives. Still, a lot more companies need to join the bandwagon as more than half the companies still do not participate.

Figure 3.7: Green supply initiatives

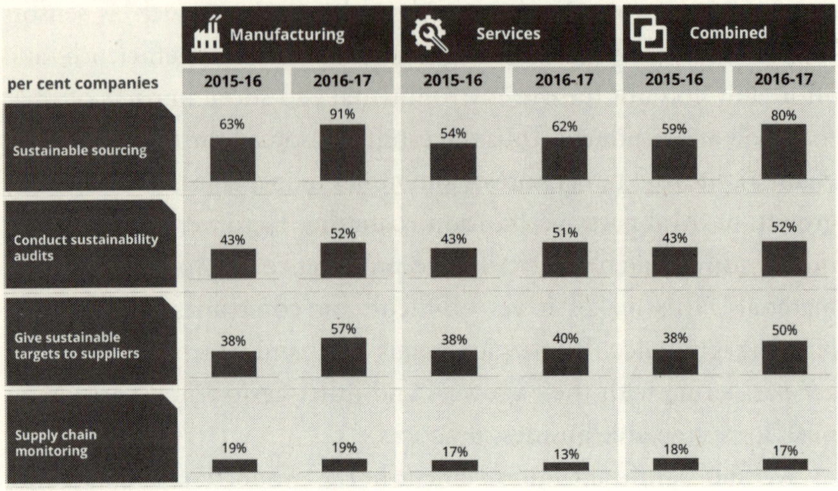

Source: Responsible Business Rankings, 2018

Only a few top-scoring companies ensure that suppliers meet the same environmental and social standards—including disclosure of goals and performance metrics—as those companies have set for their internal operations. Some also take the initiative to create sustainability awareness and train the employees of suppliers.

Figure 3.8: Supply chain initiatives in manufacturing industries

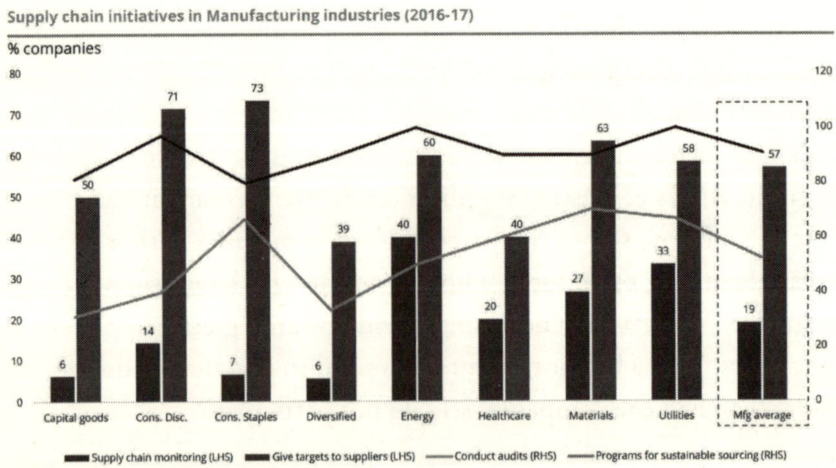

Source: Responsible Business Rankings, 2018

- Bosch India, for instance, identifies and eliminates waste across the suppliers' value streams by using project-specific tools.
- Coca-Cola India worked with its bottlers and direct suppliers to understand and mitigate human rights risks across the supply chain.
- Dr Reddy's Laboratories' supply chain initiatives include reworking packaging design to reduce its carbon footprint, and inculcating a culture of resource conservation among local and small producers.
- Tata Power, through its unique programme on energy and resource conservation called 'Tata Power Club Enerji', is generating customer awareness on energy conservation and environmental management. The programme is spearheaded by school children and helped citizens across the country to save Rs 100 crores in FY 15–16.

Increasingly, companies are looking at establishing sustainable supply chains towards reduced environmental impact. More resilient supply chains, greater diversity and higher flexibility are no more long-term goals but urgent requirements that need immediate investments.

Greening a company's transportation systems provides one of the best opportunities to reduce GHG emissions. A sustainable transportation and logistics strategy includes an analysis and monitoring of both owned and third-party operated fleet and logistics, as well as the type of fuel used. 43 per cent (31 per cent in previous year) of India's top companies have programmes for sustainable logistics, though only 17 per cent (16 per cent earlier) of the companies studied disclose information related to emissions from logistics.

The move towards lower emission-based transportation of goods is also being promoted by the Indian government, which is keen to promote electric vehicles. Separately, the Cabinet approved an MoU between India and Bangladesh in 2017 for the fairway development along the India–Bangladesh protocol route by undertaking joint dredging. This will expedite the process of using the Brahmaputra and

Barak rivers as viable inland water routes. This emerges as the most viable alternative to road transport, and the river route is expected to bring down the road transport cost.

Industries vary in their approach to green logistics. The energy sector looks at expanding pipelines, auto companies emphasise vendor hubs, and consumer staples firms try to optimally utilise the space in existing transport to reduce the number of trips and shift load from road to rail. Some metals and mining companies use the conveyor system to ferry metals from mines to plants. Ambuja Cements (ACL) uses Over Land Belt Conveyor (OLBC) systems for transportation of limestone from mines to the cement plant stockpile. A seemingly impossible 3.5 km conveyor belt was installed through three hills to not only reduce the distance between the mines and the plant at the Darlaghat in Himachal Pradesh but to also protect the landscape of the region from road transportation traffic and emissions.

Figure 3.9: Green logistics in manufacturing industries

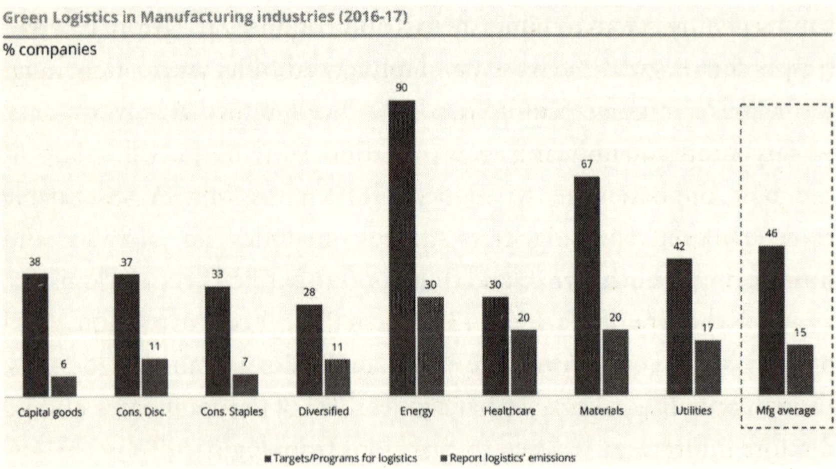

Source: Responsible Business Rankings, 2018

A long road ahead

Is this enough to transform the business responsibility landscape? Sadly, no! Many of these changes are incremental and don't really hit at the heart of the way we do business. This is not just true of India but of the rest of the world too. It is a reality that the polar ice caps are melting, sea levels are rising and biodiversity across the world is diminishing at a distressing pace. Business as usual with incremental changes won't exactly do the trick. While we are discussing ways to create closed-loop systems to eliminate waste, one does not see the large-scale industry collaborations that will enable these systems to be created. If you look closely, you will find that the prices of most manufactured products are going down. The economies of scale are definitely delivering, but they are not factoring in the costs of carbon, destruction of ecosystems, water and more. Also, businesses such as bottled water are still valued by consumers. Consumers are not willing to pay extra for sustainability, which is why organic products are still niche.

When companies are faced with challenges around sustainability and social responsibility, many of them simply begin outsourcing. The fashion and branded apparel industry has been guilty of this for many years. To balance the demand and supply, apparel companies have relied on outsourcing materials and production. Recent horrific tragedies in Bangladesh have only highlighted what many have known for years. Several factories have people working for subsistence-level wages, unsafe and unhealthy working conditions, use of child labour is rampant, and basics such as fire and safety checks are routinely given a miss. Many activists and writers have taken up these issues, and brands have had to gear up to increase their responsibilities in areas from where they source and sell their products. In addition to the safety and health of workers, serious questions have arisen on social issues, with racism, body image and gender politics taking centre stage. A growing number of industry insiders are pushing designers and manufacturers to be more aware of, and accountable for, the decisions they make on everything from the models that are sent down the runway to how and where their garments are manufactured.

The focus must not only be on reducing harmful operations but on innovations and design that can fundamentally alter the way things function together. This implies a cross-functional approach that requires integrated planning across business departments, such as product or service design, manufacture, distribution, finance and marketing. The businesses of the future should move from resource efficiency to resource neutrality.

Take the example of Ikea. The company is looking to increase recycling and eliminate waste by 2030. They are looking at initiatives to support customers to care for and repair, rent, share, bring back, donate and resell their products to prolong product life. The company has pledged to design for circularity so that products are more durable, can be reused and can be easily separated when disposed off. New ways to turn waste into raw materials and converting packaging material into new products are being explored.

Not too long ago, Switzerland became the first country to vote on the need to implement a green economy. The country's constitution already recognises the need to live harmoniously with nature. The green economy ballot was aimed at giving a further boost to resource efficiency and the implementation of a circular economy by 2050. It is indeed historic that a country held such a vote where as many as 36 per cent of voters cast a 'yes' in favour of the country becoming a green economy. Sweden has set the bar high with its ongoing recycling revolution. Less than one per cent of the household waste in Sweden finds its way to a rubbish dump as the rest of it is recycled in various ways. Incineration plants burn household waste and it is turned into energy. Today, thirty-two incineration plants produce heat for 810,000 households and electricity for 250,000 private houses. Even though Sweden emits three times more waste than it did in 1985, its heavy metal emissions have reduced by an incredible 99 per cent since then. Sweden even imports 700,000 tonnes of waste from other countries.

WRAP (Waste & Resources Action Programme), a not-for-profit organisation registered in 2000, has been established in the United Kingdom with the vision of creating a world where resources are used sustainably. WRAP works with governments, businesses and communities to deliver practical solutions to improve resource efficiency. WRAP is looking at reinventing how products are designed, produced and sold. The mission is to rethink how we use and consume products and redefine what is possible through reuse and recycling.

The connected world, used to moving things and information, has no automatic way of managing discarded products. Which is why our landfills are showing no signs of reducing and possibly never will, unless we start thinking of ourselves as part of a system that needs to be redesigned. The malaise of reductionist thinking extends to our companies too. Managers, directors and CEOs routinely think of immediate targets that impact profitability, rather than long-term consequences. Which is why companies that are moving towards the path of creating responsible business need a deeper understanding of what sustainability means to them. Reduction in emissions, an urgent focus on waste and proper management of water are some important concerns. The flows of value—not just of materials, but of data, of knowledge and of participation need to drive a radical new design of business. The bigger challenge is that we are in an age where large multinational corporations are themselves being disrupted by new challengers who have digital skills at their very core.

What does sustainability, social responsibility and, indeed, responsible growth mean for the twenty-first century corporation?

CASE STUDY

HINDUSTAN UNILEVER: THE SUSTAINABLE LIVING PLAN

Hindustan Unilever Limited (HUL) is India's largest Fast Moving Consumer Goods (FMCG) company. The company has been present in India for over eighty years and has more than thirty-five brands spanning twenty distinct categories such as soaps, detergents, shampoos, skin care, toothpastes, deodorants, cosmetics, tea, coffee, packaged foods, ice cream and water purifiers. Its portfolio includes leading household brands such as Lux, Lifebuoy, Surf Excel, Rin, Wheel, Fair & Lovely, Pond's, Vaseline, Lakmé, Dove, Clinic Plus, Sunsilk, Pepsodent, Closeup, Axe, Brooke Bond, Bru, Knorr, Kissan, Kwality Wall's and Pureit. The company has about 18,000 employees and had a turnover of Rs 33,895 crores during the financial year 2016–17. HUL is a subsidiary of Unilever, one of the world's leading FMCG companies with sales in over 190 countries. Unilever has over 67 per cent shareholding in HUL.

Unilever has a simple but clear purpose, 'to make sustainable living commonplace', and a vision to grow the business whilst decoupling our environmental footprint and increasing positive social impact. Through the Unilever Sustainable Living Plan (USLP), the company endeavours to realise this vision and purpose.

The Plan, launched in 2010, has three big global goals.

1	*2*	*3*
By 2020 we will help more than a billion people take action to improve their health and well-being.	By 2030 our goal is to halve the environmental footprint of the making and use of our products as we grow our business.	By 2020 we will enhance the livelihoods of millions of people as we grow our business.

Within each goal, the company has undertaken the below initiatives:

Goal 1: Health and Well-being

Health and Hygiene: In the area of health and hygiene, HUL operates through its water, sanitation and hygiene (WASH) initiatives and focuses on behaviour change programmes. Some of its home and personal care brands like Lifebuoy (handwashing programme), Domex (improved sanitation) and Pureit (providing safe drinking water) spearhead these behaviour change programmes across India. HUL's 'Swachh Aadat, Swachh Bharat' (SASB) programme in line with the Government of India's Swachh Bharat Abhiyan aims to promote good health and hygiene practices by adopting three clean habits (washing hands with soap at key occasions, drinking safe water, and using a toilet and keeping it clean). In 2016, HUL set up a first-of-its-kind urban water, hygiene and sanitation community centre called 'Suvidha' at one of Mumbai's largest slums in Ghatkopar. HUL's efforts in the area of health and hygiene have so far reached over 130 million people in India.

Improving nutrition: The company continuously works to improve the taste and nutritional quality of our products using globally recognised dietary standards. In 2016, 46 per cent of its total food and refreshment portfolio in India met the highest nutritional standards.

The company focuses on reduction in salt levels, removing trans fat, removing sugar and reducing calories in ice creams. It is also committed to including energy per portion on the front of the pack and details of eight key nutrients. HUL is also committed to declaring the percentage of Guideline Daily Amounts (GDA) for five nutrients on the back of the pack.

Global Alliance for Improved Nutrition (GAIN) and Unilever have signed an agreement that seeks to improve the lives of 2.5 million farmers and their families globally. It seeks to improve the health and nutrition of smallholder farmers and farm workers in Unilever's supply chain, through it's Nutrition Intervention Programme. The first programme was implemented in India with the aim of benefitting more than 40,000 farming families (200,000 people) in Unilever's business supply chain.

Goal 2: Reducing environmental impact

Greenhouse gases: In 2016, HUL reduced carbon dioxide emissions per tonne of production by 49 per cent, as compared to 2008. This reduction was achieved through initiatives such as enhanced usage of biomass based fuels, installation of equipment for utilisation of process waste from factories, like spent coffee, tea, etc. and use of hot-air generators. The company also focuses on reducing greenhouse gas emissions from its transportation activities, refrigeration and energy consumption in offices.

Water: In its manufacturing operations, water usage (cubic meter per tonne of production) was reduced by 53 per cent compared to the 2008 baseline. Initiatives like captive rainwater harvesting and use in processes and utilities, increase in condensate recoveries, and reduction of water losses from the boiler and cooling tower contributed to this reduction.

Rainwater consumption and usage increased as more factories joined the list of units consuming it for various processes and utilities. Water abstraction from natural resources was further reduced as the company piloted the latest effluent treatment technologies in their manufacturing units.

Waste: Total waste generated from the factories reduced by 45 per cent in 2016 as compared to 2008. Factories identified newer avenues for re-use and energy recovery from waste, in addition to the current reduction and recycling streams, within the purview of statutory guidelines of waste disposals. The company maintained the status of 'zero non-hazardous waste to landfill' from all factories and offices. All of the factory and office-generated non-hazardous waste was recycled in environment-friendly ways.

Reduce packaging: Innovations in packaging have led to a reduction in the use of plastic by the company. HUL substituted commodity polymers with performance-based polymers, optimised the packaging designs and changed the packaging formats of their products to consume less plastic. As a result, HUL reduced waste generated due to polymer by 1,400 tonnes in 2016.

In addition to this, HUL also saved 7,000 tonnes of paper across categories and 50 tonnes of glass in the foods category through material usage optimisation. Along with material waste reduction, packaging process optimisation led to 350 tonnes of reduction in CO_2 emission in the cosmetics category in 2016.

Recycle packaging: The company is working in partnership with industries, governments and NGOs to increase recycling and recovery rates in their packaging. HUL uses r-PET (80 per cent recycled PET[27]) in blister packs for personal care brands like Pepsodent toothbrush and Fair & Lovely. This ensures that there is an application for newly available r-PET resin in the market thereby establishing circular economy thinking.[28]

Reusable packaging: HUL provides its consumers with refill packs in its home and personal care portfolio to make it convenient for consumers to reuse the primary pack. The company has deployed the reuse of secondary packaging systems by bringing packaging material from suppliers to factories.

Sustainable sourcing: In 2016, Unilever refreshed its Palm Oil Policy and brought forward the target for purchasing 100 per cent physically certified palm oil from 2020 to 2019. As of 2015, all HUL palm derivatives were backed by RSPO (Roundtable on Sustainable Palm Oil) certificates. HUL has signed multiple partnerships to drive market transformation and traceability of the supply chain. The company has steadied its volumes of sustainably sourced paper and board for packing its products at 99 per cent in 2016. Over 46 per cent of the tea was sourced from sustainable sources in India for Unilever's brands in 2016. This is a substantial increase from 28 per cent in 2015. HUL continues to source 100 per cent of the tomatoes used in Kissan ketchup sustainably.

Goal 3: Enhancing livelihoods

Fairness in workplace: The company implements the UN's guiding principles on business and human rights[29] throughout its operations and reports on progress publicly. Its Code of Business Principles upholds the principles of human rights and fair treatment. It ensures that HUL conducts its operations with honesty, integrity and openness, and with respect for human rights and the interests of employees.

Opportunities for women: HUL was recognised as one of the 'Top 10 Best Companies for Women in India' by *The Best Companies for Women in India (BCWI) Study 2016*, instituted by Working Mother in partnership with the AVTAR Group. The company undertakes many initiatives to build gender-balanced organisations, like career break policies, maternity and paternity support programmes, inclusive leadership, etc.

The USLP is unique as it addresses social, economic and environmental challenges. All HUL products and brands are included as part of USLP. The Plan also covers the entire value chain—from sourcing of raw materials to their disposal. With thousands of products that are used by nine out of ten households in India, HUL is uniquely placed to make a meaningful difference.

CHAPTER 4

Creating a Responsibility Strategy and Driving Change

In most industries, it is fast becoming imperative to understand and actively manage actions that impact environmental sustainability and social responsibility. Consumer goods companies are under pressure to create sustainable supply chains and to reduce plastics in their packaging. Automotive companies are moving away from fossil fuels and combustion engines towards electric vehicles. Consumer goods and technology companies are increasingly looking at recycling as a key concern. Apparel and electronics companies are being put in the spotlight for equitable standards in labour and human rights. The list is endless.

These sustainability challenges are impacting business operations and risk and changing the nature of value creation. Scaling up in a resource-constrained world does not merely mean resource aggregation and transformation. This also involves companies analysing supply chains, pinpointing where the raw materials come from and calculating how much energy is expended to make their products. Companies also do a thorough analysis of internal and external aspects: What resources do we depend on? Will we be able to source these over time? What are the risks? What waste do we create during production? How is it disposed of? How are customers, communities, suppliers and other stakeholders impacted through our services and policies? A business that can answer questions such as these and look at eliminating or reducing possible harmful effects, can then force itself to innovate, become more sustainable and thereby more resilient.

Sustainability-led innovations are also helping companies become more efficient, more innovative, more connected, more profitable, and more competitive. Managing efficient use of natural resources such as water and electricity, has had a positive impact on company profitability. Similarly, using a more abundant raw material rather than a scarce raw material, whose prices will invariably rise due to shortages, will also usually lead to higher profitability. One area where a business can realise cost savings, that might not be as readily apparent, is when they reduce costs associated with employee turnover; this is because many people want to work for a business that aligns with their values.

Progressive business leaders are beginning to think strategically and see sustainability as a catalyst for new business models. Apple, the technology giant, says on its website, 'To ask less of the planet, we ask more of ourselves'. The company has set itself various goals in this context and asks itself some key questions on the resources it utilises: 'Can we power a global business with the sun, wind, and water? Can we get 100 per cent of our supply chain to move to 100 per cent renewable energy? Can we one day stop mining the earth altogether? Can we use only 100 per cent recycled and responsibly sourced paper in our packaging? Can we improve on the world's best materials?'

Clearly, thinking about people, planet and profit, which is termed as triple bottom line thinking, is inevitable. If you are a business leader, these are your choices:

- Start to make your companies more efficient or wait until costs rise.
- Redesign your products for a more sustainable world or try to play catch up later.
- Wait until your customers and government demand your carbon footprint report or volunteer the same now.

Companies can follow a four-step approach to becoming more responsible:

1. Create strategic frameworks
2. Focus on key issues
3. Build responsible brands
4. Build authenticity

Figure 4.1: The responsibility approach

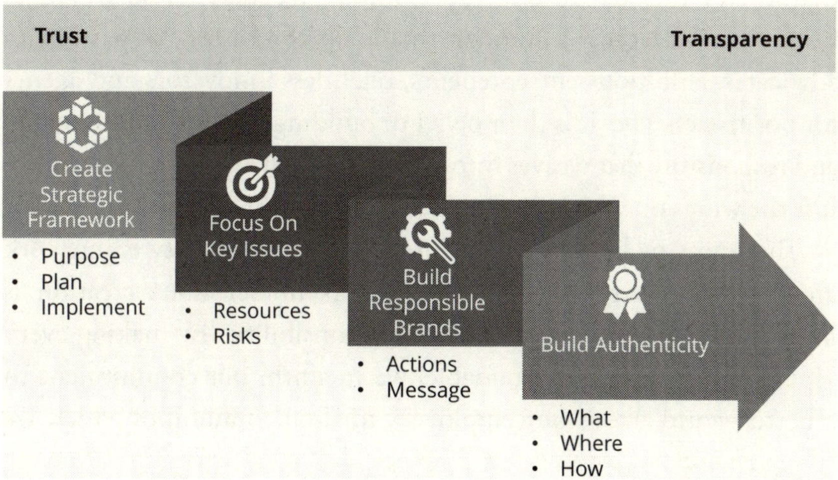

Companies must figure out what they need to do, plan for sustainable actions and implement them on the ground. To do so, they must consider the resources available and the risks that are involved. Merely 'doing' is insufficient. Stakeholders need to be kept informed about what is being done. This can be done both through visible actions as well as by constructing the appropriate message. Both actions as well as the message should have a ring of authenticity to succeed. In doing all this, companies need to keep in mind that trust and transparency are critical to success. The following sections detail these.

Create strategic frameworks

Historically, the role of business has been defined as creating shareholder value. However, the addition of sustainability has resulted in the creation of many new variables for organisations.[1] It could potentially redefine the purpose of an organisation and bring change at a fundamental level. Strategic frameworks are used to give form to a company's business responsibility ambition and ensure long-term planning.

Mahindra, a large diversified Indian conglomerate has created a business philosophy that it calls 'Rise for Good'. Its Integrated Report for the financial year 2016–17 states, 'It's an ambition and an attitude that drives our day-to-day functioning. We take these thoughts from our own legacy; a company made up of a history of passionate advocates, ambitious entrepreneurs, relentless innovators and agents for positive change. It is their belief of building businesses sustainably and responsibly that weaves into the DNA of all aspects of Mahindra. It is the wings on which our businesses take flight.'

The company has created an Integrated Sustainability Framework around this, where shareholder and stakeholder value creation is linked to environmental and social responsibility. 'By making every aspect of our business sustainable, we re-affirm our commitment to a better world. From our employees to the communities which we

Figure 4.2: The Mahindra framework

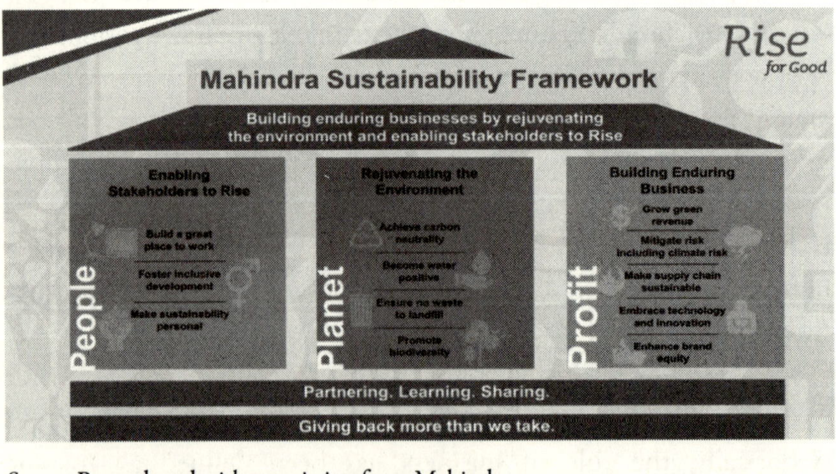

Source: Reproduced with permission from Mahindra.

are a part of, we want to conduct our business conscientiously and responsibly to address the issues of People, Planet and Profit.'

The core purpose of the company is reflected in its brand pillars. 'Accepting No Limits, Alternative Thinking and Driving Positive Change'. The company says that it, 'strives to build not just products and services, but new possibilities for a truly sustainable future'.

Strategic frameworks also help companies in taking difficult decisions with far-reaching implications. Take the case of plastic waste. Plastics are one of the worst products to dispose of, taking hundreds of years to degrade. This is a key issue for the FMCG industry given the scale of usage of plastics in food and drinks packaging, tubes of toothpaste, shampoo bottles and thousands of other everyday things. Realising the need for systemic change, in January 2017, Unilever committed to ensuring that all of its plastic packaging is fully reusable, recyclable or compostable by 2025. [2]

Not just companies, even countries are adapting to this new way of thinking. As stated in the previous chapter, in 2016, Switzerland tried to become the first country to vote on the need to become a green economy. The country's constitution already recognises the need to live harmoniously with nature. Also, as discussed earlier, the green economy ballot was aimed at giving a boost to resource efficiency and the implementation of a circular economy by 2050. The country held such a vote where as many as 36 per cent of voters cast a 'yes' in favour of it becoming a green economy. Clearly, there is increasing awareness amongst people that there needs to be a complete shift in the manner in which natural resources are being used.

In many companies, strategic frameworks are also driven partly by the values of the CEO or the founder and the culture of the organisation. For instance in many family-driven businesses in India, the philosophy of charitable giving was ingrained right from the inception. For Anant Goenka, Managing Director of CEAT Tyres, building a sustainable legacy is key to the social initiatives of the company. 'Our work is about genuinely doing good, but also doing good is always good business since it has a positive rub-off on the brand. We don't advertise our CSR initiatives because for us building a rapport with the communities around our plants, fleet owners, truck drivers and others is what counts.' The company invests significantly in sustainability initiatives even though manufacturing a tyre is a low pollution process contributing barely 10-15 per cent to the total carbon footprint. He says, 'When we examined our carbon footprint we realised that 70 per cent of the impact is in the product which is a combination of rolling resistance and use of unsustainable materials. A key focus for us is to focus on reducing the rolling resistance (RR) of tyres. It helps the customer as well as the environment.'[3] CEAT is the flagship company of RPG Enterprises and is a leading manufacturer of automobile tyres in India. The RPG Foundation acts as the CSR implementing organisation for all RPG group companies. Its vision is to drive 'holistic empowerment' of the community, and the corporate citizenship strategy functions at three levels—at the group level, at the industry level and at the micro-community level.

Action Agenda to create strategic frameworks:

1. Define corporate strategy. What implications does it have for responsible business?
2. Build a five-year plan to address the strategic alternative.
3. Split the five-year plan into annual plans.
4. Set targets for waste, water and energy improvements.
5. Measure progress.
6. Review deviations from target.
7. Take corrective action.

Focus on key issues

Most companies realise that there are limits to what current business strategies can achieve. To create a sustainable model of growth, companies need to map the system they operate in. This implies an end to end analysis of internal and external aspects:

- What resources do we depend on? Materials, Energy, Transport, Land, People
- Will we be able to source these materials over time? What are the risks?
- What waste do we create during production? How is it disposed of?

Finding and mapping these external and internal factors that impact corporate responsibility is helping companies in planning their sustainability initiatives. 'Materiality'[4] or 'relevance' is defined as topics or issues that have a direct or indirect impact on an organisation's ability to create, preserve or erode economic, environmental and social value for itself, its stakeholders and society at large. Materiality issues are mostly context- and industry-specific. Across industries, materiality issues would include waste disposal, biodiversity, energy efficiency, responsible procurement, carbon emission, water, employee diversity, and gender equality among many others. But aspects such as employee motivation strategies, gathering customer feedback or product launches have no place in sustainability reporting. Materiality measurement helps companies to engage in a meaningful manner with the society and environment.

So, how do we figure out what is material to the company? Companies are mostly following a step-by-step approach, where they begin by understanding their stakeholders, identifying material issues and the business risks of the changing environment. They must follow through with adequate capital allocation and enable board oversight on these aspects. Incorporating key sustainability drivers into performance evaluation and compensation programmes and regular corporate disclosures ensure long-term implementation.

Take the example of Dr Reddy's Laboratories, an Indian multinational pharmaceutical company based in Hyderabad, whose long-term thinking has enabled the company to seed an approach called `sustainability by design' which inbuilds sustainability into projects and institutionalises them across the company.

To begin with, Dr Reddy's maps the key challenges, risks and opportunities that are likely to impact its operations and this is followed through with detailed conversations with stakeholders.

After this, Dr Reddy's conducts an in-depth materiality assessment where sector specific issues and stakeholder feedback are examined and evaluated. These are then prioritised and after internal validation the Materiality Matrix is finalised. The company then sets its goals and action plans to address the high-ranking materiality aspects. These issues are further cross-referenced to the SDGs.

Figure 4.3: Materiality Assessment at Dr Reddy's

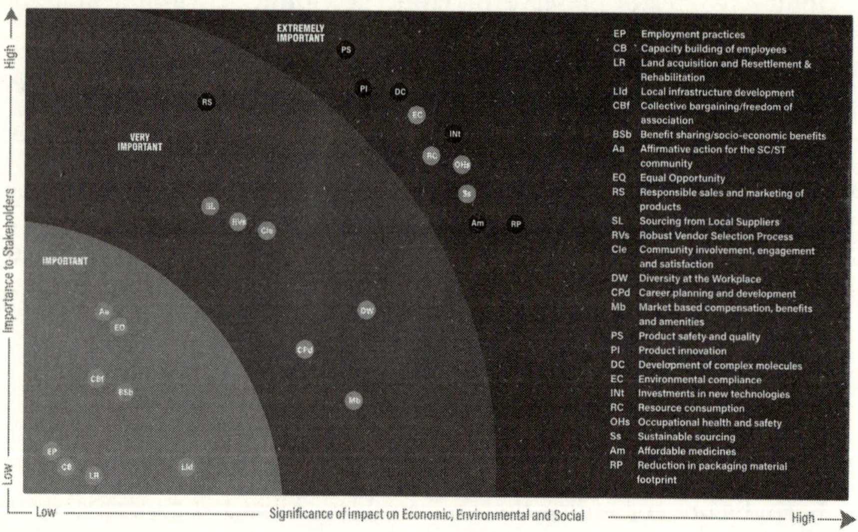

Source: Reproduced with permission from Dr Reddy's

The formal mechanism helps Dr Reddy's gauge stakeholder needs, identify the gaps and risks that it faces and develop programmes that meet stakeholder requirements.

Figure 4.4: Gap identification at Dr Reddy's

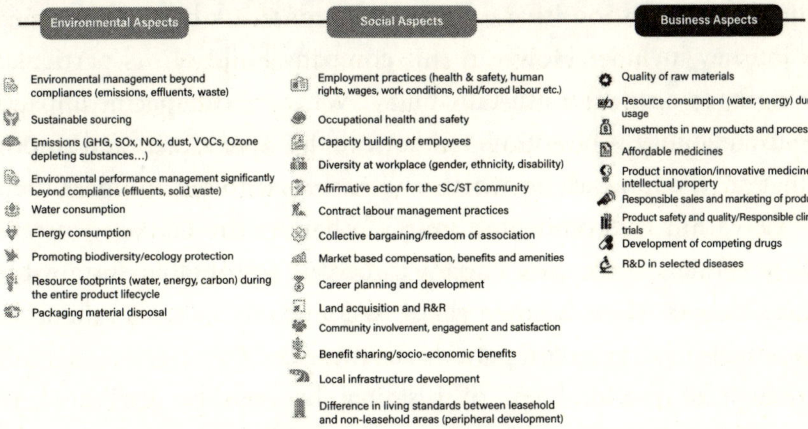

Source: Reproduced with permission from Dr Reddy's

This formal mechanism is conducted annually and helps Dr Reddy's run focused successful programmes.

Action Agenda

1. Define the stakeholders.
2. Define key issues and concerns of the stakeholders.
3. Assess key risks facing the business.
4. Determine material issues.
5. Determine ways to manage the material issues.
6. Measure progress.
7. Take corrective action.

Building responsible brands

While materiality helps define focus, prioritising issues is a genuine challenge. For instance, investors focus more on governance facets than social and environmental aspects. Also, stakeholders may not necessarily take future changes into consideration, instead preferring to focus on short-term issues. Any business that builds scale needs to take the long-term view on where the industry or company is going and how context and, therefore, issues, will evolve in the coming years. The ability to understand how various aspects influence one another within a whole, and the relationship of the whole to the parts is crucial. Some of the questions that a company needs to ask before beginning its journey include: How can this company build on its particular strengths to profit from sustainability? What are the specific impacts of sustainability issues on its markets, supply chain, staff and so on? What are the innovations which will enable customers to meet their needs, within environmental limits? What are the markets, current and potential, where the company can create a profitable, sustainable offer? How must the business shape its context to make sure there is a sustainable base to its competitive advantage?

Much of the problem of sustainability can be attributed to increased consumerism. There were about 3.2 billion people in the middle class at the end of 2016 and this is set to grow by 160 million people per year on an average, through 2030. This is the most rapid expansion of the middle class at a global level that the world has ever seen. Almost 90 per cent of the next billion entrants into the global middle class will be in Asia: 380 million Indians, 350 million Chinese, and 210 million other Asians.[6] Additionally, between 2016 and 2019, global advertising expenditure has been forecast to increase by $69 billion.[7] The US will contribute 28 per cent of this extra expenditure and China will contribute 22 per cent, followed by Indonesia, which will contribute 5 per cent, and India, Japan and the Philippines, which will each contribute 4 per cent. A better standard of living and greater disposable incomes, egged on by marketing, will lead to associated increases in consumption and increase the pressure on land, energy, water, higher carbon emissions and increased waste.

But while consumerism is the cause of non-sustainability, could it also be the solution? All consumption impacts the environment and the economy and therefore, small acts of daily consumption over a long period of time could lead to better impacts. For instance, if one carried one's own bags to the store, the consumption of plastic bags would come down and the plastic load on the environment would reduce. Another way would be to use a bicycle instead of a car for short commutes like going to a park or the grocery store. Or, using less detergent in our daily laundry wash to minimise chemical waste. This could even have a multiplier effect as the consumers who made these choices could in turn influence friends, family and colleagues. Since advertising is so persuasive and pervasive, can it help create a better world?

In the recent past, the trend of connecting causes to people has been catching on. For instance, connecting hand-washing to people's need for better health can be seen as connecting to the cause (better health). Consumers are coming to expect that the products they use meet social requirements or at the very least, that they do not harm people and the environment. Of the more than 400 brands Unilever sells, those with the strongest sustainability credentials—such as Dove, Lifebuoy, Ben & Jerry's and Comfort—have seen sales grow at a high single-digit or double-digit rate over the past three years.[8] The Unilever Consumer Study says that 33 per cent of consumers are now choosing to buy brands that they believe are doing social or environmental good. Worldwide, cause sponsorship was predicted to reach $2.14 billion in 2018, a projected increase of 4.4 per cent over 2017 ($2.32 billion).[9] Brand research teams find that connecting to causes of a strategic nature builds brand trust. It showcases a company's desire to stand for something more than just itself.

While building a consumer connection does explain the trend towards cause marketing, it doesn't really explain why business-to-business (B2B) companies are doing cause-based campaigns. For example, the global mining company, Vedanta, has released commercials with the tagline '75 per cent wealth to social good'. These commercials that speak about the company's products such as zinc, aluminium, iron ore and oil and gas, link each product to a social cause.

Perhaps, the reason is mitigation of social risk. More and more Indian companies have a global footprint today, catering to customers in developed countries as well as those in underexplored markets like Africa and Latin America. Indian companies today own mining rights in Australia, factories in South Africa and telecom networks in Kenya. With expansion in scale and globalisation, unique opportunities have surfaced that carry with them a fair amount of risk. Besides dealing with managing the scale of operations, social risks have come to the forefront as well. These include customers, suppliers, governments, NGOs, communities, employees and media. A social risk can be defined as one which sees four components working in unison—an issue, combined with a stakeholder/s, a negative perception of the corporation and the power to adversely impact the company's perception in the public domain. Truly global Indian companies need to be prepared for this new reality where reputation, responsibility and risk are increasingly interconnected.

The list of companies and sectors that have been impacted by social and sustainability scandals comprises the who's who of the corporate world. Mining, apparel, food, automotive and oil giants have all suffered the loss of reputation because of one or the other issue in the past decade. These controversies have been about product quality, human rights, environmental pollution and many more, but each time, the company and the brands associated with the company have had negative financial impacts, massive employee churn, enhanced scrutiny and regulatory pressures. This is where the importance of responsible branding comes in as it provides a framework for companies to proceed with stakeholder engagement, while at the same time providing information on emerging and current social issues that support the corporate risk agenda, thereby ultimately being a countermeasure for social risk.

Action Agenda

1. Define key corporate actions and communication strategy.
2. Understand the cause.
3. Develop key communication mechanism.
4. Check progress – see what works and what doesn't.
5. Revise approach, where necessary.

Building authenticity

The growth in consumers' access to information has resulted in products available in the market being viewed very differently than in the past. Consumers are not just interested in better quality, they also want to know how products are made. While this is certainly true of food where customers are increasingly interested in knowing where the food they consume is sourced from, it is also true of toys, gadgets, clothes and a whole host of other things where customers want to know if they are responsibly and ethically made. To showcase their sustainability credentials, brands are taking sustainability certifications. Sustainability certifications are generally third-party assessments of products looking at environmental quality, social quality, and economic prosperity. Some of the better known ones are Energy Star, WaterSense, Cradle to Cradle Certified, Green Seal, Certified Organic, Fair Trade Certified, Rainforest Alliance Certified, Forest Stewardship Council (FSC) Certified, and Sustainable Forest Initiative (SFI). Certifications are useful in demonstrating credibility when leading brands both sell to consumers and are interested in developing a network of suppliers.

Building a brand is more than just advertising. While a brand may associate itself with a cause, customers may not readily trust it. Despite the ability of marketers to reach the right profile of customers and the persuasiveness of an argument, customer choice is not always driven by the causes they support or by what is good for the environment. Walk down the supermarket and you will see that customers choose on the basis of price, quality, packaging, placement and a host of other things depending on their lifestyle, family and social signalling. There have been several instances where awareness about a cause or the incentive of a better environmental choice does not result in customer action. The gap between stated intent and actual action is called the 'action gap'. For example, most customers are aware of the problems caused by plastic bags. Plastic bags never really degrade completely, they clog drains causing flooding, get eaten by animals who may eventually choke on them, and end up releasing toxic chemicals into the soil. Yet, the use of plastic bags continues unabated across most of the world. By stopping the use of plastic bags customers could easily impact the environment in a significant way. Yet, they don't. Possibly because customers could trade off their ethical choices against the other attributes of the plastic bag, such as the fact that it is accessible, cheaper and lightweight as compared to other choices.

Merely creating brand communication that aligns itself to causes is therefore not the answer. Business models themselves need to become more sustainable. A dual framework approach where brands are aligned to causes but internal production and practices are not aligned will not take a brand anywhere and is a sure shot recipe for market failure.

Take the case of the healthcare sector. The healthcare industry consists of hospitals, medical devices, clinical trials, outsourcing, telemedicine, medical tourism, health insurance and medical equipment. The context for responsibility is incredibly complex in healthcare, because of the nature of the industry. While the industry sells solutions to illness, the thinking and actions of healthcare players whether in pharma or managed healthcare, need to be oriented towards the betterment of human health and well-being. Since the industry is intrinsically committed to doing public good, society has many expectations of a healthcare firm other than managing environmental impact like any other business. What do consumers expect of the healthcare industry? They expect effective, high quality medicines, attention and care at hospitals, the absence of spurious drugs, ethical dealings and honesty. But is that all? As important as all the other aspects, customers also expect affordable health products and services. Unlike other businesses where price is set by the ability to pay, for the healthcare industry price is at times subservient to public good.

Another instance is the oil and gas industry which sits at the heart of the sustainability debate as it provides more than half of the world's energy sources. The industry is highly energy-intensive and a focus on increasing internal efficiencies while reducing environmental impact should therefore be a key issue for everyone operating in this sector. Oil and natural gas companies generate greenhouse gases (GHGs) in almost every aspect of their work, from the finding, extracting and processing of hydrocarbon resources, to the transforming and delivery of these resources to customers. The direct greenhouse gases are emitted from combustion in stationary and mobile internal combustion engines, gas processing equipment, and from venting, flaring, and fugitive methane. With the industry's high impact on GHG emissions and climate change, oil and gas companies need to move towards a product mix that consists of renewables. However, this is not easy to do. Strategic decision-making is required to build a long-term framework which focuses on genuine change, product innovation and new avenues of growth with reduced environmental impact. What is our current product mix? Should we change it and if yes, how will it change in the next five years? Will we redefine ourselves as an energy company and not just oil and gas? These are the questions that need to be asked.

Companies in the healthcare sector need to balance social good and profitability. Advertising a free health-camp while its doctors follow unethical practices is likely to lead to customer outrage. Similarly, companies in the oil and gas sector need to redefine their product mix. Advertising less-polluting fuel may have a short-term impact but may lead to negligible long-term benefits. An analysis of the CSR and Sustainability reports of over 200 Indian companies over the past four years highlights an insufficient focus on customers. Employees and communities around factories and broad social goals like health and education seem to be grabbing the lion's share of companies' attention. This trend is common across almost all consumer-facing industries.

Senior advertising professional Piyush Pandey talks of two principles when it comes to building brand authenticity while supporting causes:[10]

PRINCIPLE 1—Products are made in factories. Brands are made in hearts.

A lot of decisions are made because we love something. Everything is not 'buy me because of...' You may like me for the things I do and not just for the things you do for me. Hence, brand affinity has a higher life as it is not just functional. Therefore, brands take things that are relevant to society and build it into their communication benefit (for example, cleanliness, women's empowerment etc.). However, communication only changes attitudes and genuine change needs to be part of the brand ambition as the brand will only prosper if society prospers. Defining a common agenda for the brand and its stakeholders helps in narrowing down on the areas of focus and helps in starting the process and staying on course. This is where cause marketing can step in, to communicate the cause, build support and be part of the process that builds a better society.

PRINCIPLE 2—Scale is about belief.

There is talk that business responsibility gives you a license to operate. However, it is only applicable if you operate from an area of difficulty. Business responsibility is an obligation, a belief in a better way, in a different world, a positive contribution to society. This belief helps brands in delivering on their promises not just for the quarterly numbers but for the long term. Delivering on the promise each and every time builds authenticity and therefore such brands scale up faster, whether these are consumer brands or business to business brands. Businesses need to make a lifetime commitment to causes and a better way of functioning before they start communicating.

Action Agenda

1. Be true to the company's responsibility strategy.
2. Maintain coherence between day to day activities and responsibility strategy.
3. Make values-based decisions.

Trust and Transparency should drive the responsibility agenda

Business responsibility is neither just a brand strategy nor is it just a product strategy. It's really about how the company does business over the long-term horizon. At one level companies do realise that environmental sustainability can only be achieved by creating closed loop supply chains. Closed loop supply chains are designed to manage and explicitly consider the reverse and forward supply chain activities over the entire life cycle of the product. This involves recovering the materials used through collection, recycling and recovery through explicit mechanisms that are built and communicated to the end consumer. For instance, if a mobile phone manufacturer decides to collect old phones, chargers and batteries some of the materials may be recovered and used in newer phones, while some parts of the phone may be recycled to produce other products. This process would involve:

- Product returns management including reverse logistics
- Repair, remanufacture and recycle
- Remarking and reuse

Achieving closed loop systems is not exactly easy. It may take several years to achieve it and some industries may never really manage it.

This approach to managing all the impacts of all material flows during economic actions has been termed as the creation of circular systems. Circular systems however, are not that easy to create. They need significant efforts from stakeholders and the commitment to make a change. The corporate world functions as a part of global supply chains. Take the car example mentioned in Chapter 1, whose components are made in countries as diverse as Japan, China, Taiwan, Korea and Mexico. Each component in turn, is composed of materials sourced from various locations. These components then go to factories in the US, Japan, Germany and Australia for assembly. To create a circular system for the automotive sector would mean a realignment of all factories and suppliers in all these countries. A dramatic shift would need to take place in the entire chain.

Also, the time horizon around responsibility and sustainability issues diverges amongst stakeholders. CEOs today have relatively short tenures, while the decisions they take may have long-term impacts. At the same time, the general public or shareholders can hold the company accountable any time in the future. Sustainability defines the company's focus beyond shareholder value and in business longevity and its relationship with society, thereby forcing it to look at the system it operates in. This is why corporate governance has a significant role to play in the creation of a sustainability strategy that will go beyond the paper it's written on, and into every aspect of the business. While business functions can manage critical issues that are linked to company goals, long-term strategic thinking is needed to manage external factors.

Take the case of the food industry, where several recent events have put the spotlight on concerns regarding what we eat. Nothing seems to be above board—fruit, vegetables, meat, poultry and packaged food all seem to be sub-par. Fresh fruits and vegetables seem to be increasingly pesticide-laden and packaged foods seem to have excess sugar, sodium, salt and other high impact ingredients. Milk allergies are seen to be on the rise, as are gluten and egg allergies. These can be attributed to two factors—lifestyle changes and ingredients that are now used as a result of food processing practices. Food producers clearly have a responsibility to ensure that stringent tests are conducted on all inputs at all stages after the food items enter the value chain. Moreover, this push needs to focus on two key areas—trust and traceability. Trust is to be confident that one's consumption is safe. Traceability is to be able to verify the history and location of the food chain. This involves building supply chains that are transparent and provide an easy way to assess where contamination is occurring. Traceability improves product sourcing, reduces costs and ensures a healthy output. However, food labelling and packaging is an equally important yet unfulfilled promise by most companies. Food labels hide more than they disclose and packaging increasingly factors in plastic and non-biodegradable material. The Indian consumers' increased focus on health and wellness requires that food labels focus intensely on nutrition and increased product safety.

Business responsibility is also closely linked to employee behaviour. Within corporate premises and outside, employee behaviour plays a significant role in building the corporate brand. Companies are expected to maintain a high standard. The bigger the company, the higher the expectation. Safety, behaviour, data protection, privacy are some of the obvious blindspots. Employees need to be the flag-bearers of these higher standards. In the event of an incident involving an employee or otherwise, it is now almost impossible for the company name to be hidden. PR activities are not enough to keep reputations intact. A culture of socially responsible behaviour needs to be the norm rather than the exception, which is how responsibility will actually become ingrained within a company's DNA.

Employee behaviour further impacts how employees deal with customers. Take the case of personal information. It is a reality that it is available everywhere—with the pizza company, the e-commerce company, the utility provider or even the courier who brings documents and products home. The risks are many—identity theft, fraudulent credit card purchases, misusing your identity details and many more. Customer data protection and security becomes critical in a range of industries that acquire and manage customer personal information and most often, it is employees and faulty processes that cause data breaches. Women's safety, children's safety, data protection, personal privacy, responsible driving and so on, are all ways in which corporations can set standards for employees and the way they interact with customers.

Technology pervades everything from health to transport, manufacturing and agriculture. Mobile phones have connected everyone and tons of data are being generated every second. Could this power be harnessed for social good? Can the power of location, mobile, crowdsourcing and large data be used to flatten the interface between the citizen, the consumer, the company and the authorities? Trust grows within the system because services, people and the providers are all interlinked in an ever-evolving harmonious stream.

Corporate responsibility begins with simplifying the customer experience and creating safeguards at every step where the customer takes centre stage. A materiality assessment which includes a customer-centric view would help companies in creating a responsibility strategy which is both effective and impactful. Brands that survive in this century will need to be trusted and social responsibility is integral to their actions. Trust, Materiality and Responsibility can be a powerful combination in creating power brands of the twenty-first century. By making these central, responsibility as we know it can drive growth without doing harm.

CASE STUDY

ITC: TRIPLE BOTTOM LINE STRATEGY

In 1996, when Mr Y C Deveshwar assumed office as Chairman, he articulated a new vision for ITC—to be an engine of growth for the Indian economy but by making societal value creation a centre-piece of its corporate strategy. The inspiration was to create an enterprise that would serve larger national priorities. Thus evolved ITC's credo of 'Putting India First'—a pledge to put Country before Corporation and the Institution before the Individual.

This vision spurred innovation in business models that aimed not only to attain international competitiveness in each of its businesses but also in a manner that replenished environmental resources as well as generated sustainable livelihoods.

This vision was based on three critical insights. First, there was increasing realisation across the world that economic development did not necessarily ensure sustainable development. Second, it was ITC's strong belief that business can bring about transformational change in society. The third insight was that corporate contribution to sustainable and inclusive growth can be much larger and meaningful if strategic CSR interventions are delivered in the context of its businesses. ITC recognised that businesses will not be able to succeed in societies that fail. Therefore, it was imperative that corporate strategy not only focused on building extreme competitiveness of the organisation but also in creating environmental and social capital for its stakeholders.

ITC has created a paradigm of growth called 'Responsible Competitiveness'. This enables meaningful triple bottom line outcomes together with competitiveness of its businesses.

Triple Bottom Line Performance: Major Outcomes

Over the past two decades, ITC evolved from a single product company to a multi-business corporation, with market leadership in several segments. ITC, today, has a significant presence across all the three sectors of the economy—agriculture, manufacturing and services.

Since 1996, ITC's Total Shareholder Returns grew rapidly at a compounded growth rate of 22.4 per cent per annum. During this period ITC's non-cigarette revenue rose and now accounts for 59 per cent of its total revenue. The transformed character is visible in the fact that over 80 per cent of ITC's operating capital employed and 90 per cent of its employee base is today in the non-cigarette business.

In just over a decade, ITC has built twenty-five world-class mother brands. Several of the company's brands have already assumed market leadership. These brands help create, capture and retain value in the Indian economy. Such powerful brands also serve as market anchors to enhance the competitiveness of the entire value chain, including that of farmers and rural communities.

ITC is today, carbon-positive (thirteen years in a row), water-positive (sixteen consecutive years) and solid waste recycling positive (for the last eleven years). In India, where livelihood generation is an urgent priority, ITC's businesses and value chains have created sustainable livelihoods for over six million people, embracing the weakest in society. Over 43 per cent of the total energy consumed in ITC is from renewable sources. ITC started the green building movement early in India, with twenty-three of its buildings being certified at the highest LEED Platinum level. ITC's premium luxury hotels also have the unique distinction of being LEED Platinum certified.

The following interventions depict ITC's approach in simultaneously creating economic, environmental and social capital as a unified strategy.

Triple Bottom Line in practice—Tree to Textbook Value Chain

Two decades ago, ITC's paperboards business was in trouble and faced imminent closure. Restrictions on cutting trees made it difficult to obtain pulp and scale up operations. It was tempting to import pulp given a regime of near zero import duties. However, in ITC's view importing pulp meant export of jobs to other countries at a time when

Indian farmers needed livelihood opportunities. Therefore, ITC put an intensive research and development programme in place to develop clonal saplings that would grow in wastelands owned by small farmers and poor tribals. Subsequently, ITC worked with hundreds of farmers and forest user groups to grow these plantations. Till now, ITC's Social and Farm Forestry initiative has greened over 6,80,000 acres, and generated 125 million person-days of employment. While farmers are free to sell their produce to whoever they wish to, ITC stands as a willing buyer. This empowers the farmers. Given that land is limited and there is conflicting demand on land for food, fuel, fodder, fibre and factories, ITC also developed an agroforestry model to mix tree growing with traditional crop production, thereby augmenting farmer incomes. This holistic model demonstrates a unique strategy and action plan to deliver triple bottom line performance—ITC Paperboards is now the country's largest and most profitable, it is also known for its environmental stewardship given its green fibre strategy and has created significant livelihood opportunities.

Triple Bottom Line in practice—the ITC e-Choupal eco-system

Agriculture is the lifeline of India's economy, engaging more than half of the country's workforce. However, it is also a sector besieged by myriad challenges. ITC's e-Choupal, launched in the year 2000, leverages the power of information technology to create an innovative model. This model empowers farmers by enabling market access, as well as provide critical information relating to weather, quality agricultural inputs and know-how to enhance agri-productivity. Complementing this digital infrastructure is the Choupal Pradarshan Khet—customised agri-extension services that promote best practices and assist farmers enhance productivity as well as diversify crop portfolios. The ITC e-Choupal initiative has empowered over 4 million farmers till date. Recognising the imperative need to raise farmer incomes further, the ITC e-Choupal's initiative to contribute to '*Baareh Mahine Hariyali*' (maximising farm utilisation over twelve months of the year) has led to the introduction of a comprehensive package of solutions that has been rolled out to nearly ten lakh farmers. Encouraging results have been achieved with thousands of farmers reporting substantial increases in income, with some who have experienced a doubling of income.

Recognising that farmers are most vulnerable to climate change and that agriculture is already severely water stressed, ITC worked with local communities to create a large-scale Integrated Watershed Development Programme bringing soil and moisture conservation to over 8,75,000 acres. This has led to making agriculture more climate resilient besides enabling improved productivity and multiple crops. This helps raise farmer incomes. The e-Choupal eco-system together with ITC's Social Investment Programme helps strengthen current livelihoods whilst creating opportunities for the future. The Animal Husbandry programme, for example, provides services to nearly 17,00,000 milch animals, augmenting farmer incomes.

Triple Bottom Line in practice—Enabling Livelihoods

ITC's businesses and value chains create over six million sustainable livelihoods. The company's women empowerment programmes have provided livelihood opportunities to over 60,000 rural women, whilst vocational training programmes have benefitted over 55,000 youth. ITC's primary education programme has also covered 5,60,000 children till date. ITC has also built over 30,000 low cost sanitary units as part of its health and sanitation programme, and its Well-being-out-of-waste programme covers ten states and 77 lakh citizens. These social investment programmes also contribute meaningfully to the United Nation's Sustainable Development Goals.

'*Sab Saath Badhein*'—Promoting the Triple Bottom Line Approach

To promote sustainability strategy and practice, ITC joined hands with the Confederation of Indian Industry to establish the Centre of Excellence for Sustainable Development which is today the country's leading organisation in this area. ITC has also promoted the Triple

Bottom Line philosophy through a unique television campaign titled '*Sab Saath Badhein*' to bring focus on the need for an inclusive approach to sustainable development. ITC's contribution to societal goals can potentially help make the planet more secure and also ensure that future progress is more sustainable and inclusive.

CHAPTER 5

Measuring Responsibility

At regular intervals, companies need to figure out how they are performing—good, bad or indifferent. In 1494, Paolo Luca set forth the principles of double entry book-keeping through which the concept of performance measurement took root. Until almost the end of the twentieth century, performance measurement was focussed on measuring the profits of a company. Around the late Nineties was when corporate responsibility started to gain traction and came to be seen as a means of gaining competitive advantage rather than being merely an operational cost or a restriction imposed by the law. The linkage to competitive advantage brought to the fore the need to measure responsibility. Measuring responsibility, however, is a complicated process due to the economic, legal, ethical and social issues involved.

Measurement is at the heart of governance

The governance model for companies is seeing a shift from the narrower focus on business risk to include environmental and social risk. This risk then gets incorporated into the corporate strategy and therefore, reporting combines emerging trends, challenges and opportunities.

Board members will need to pay close attention to social and environmental issues as a growing number of events and scandals involving ESG issues have affected many companies worldwide. Take the case of the blow out of BP's oil well in the Gulf of Mexico in 2010 which led to the world's largest oil spill that caused the death of hundreds of birds and massive loss of marine life. The aftereffects are still visible. The company not only had to pay a hefty fine but suffered a deep reputational loss. Such incidents can translate not only into reputational risks, but also into compliance and financial risks. These risks need to be monitored by the board and tracked on a regular basis. Monitoring and tracking are only possible when activities and actions are measured. Boards often meet every quarter and hence attention can be paid to the progress on a regular basis.

At the same time, investors and stakeholders have started pushing companies for increased disclosure and transparency regarding CSR and sustainability activities, governance practices, and measuring and reporting material impacts. A study of the Dow Jones Sustainability Index (DJSI) has shown that:

- More than one-third applied some sort of social figures in their variable senior management remuneration system—primarily around health, safety and employee well-being; and
- About one-fourth applied environmental success metrics and addressed issues such as emissions, resource efficiency or environmental compliance.

This is indicative of the seriousness with which social and sustainability issues are being tackled by companies. This also helps companies mitigate any adverse short-term negative event as the investors clearly see long-term strategic intent.

Understanding measurement

Corporate financial performance is relatively easy to measure as inputs and outputs are clearly identifiable. Sales and costs are easy to measure. On the other hand, there could be several ways of viewing sustainability performance measurement.

Figure 5.1: Levels of Responsibility Measurement

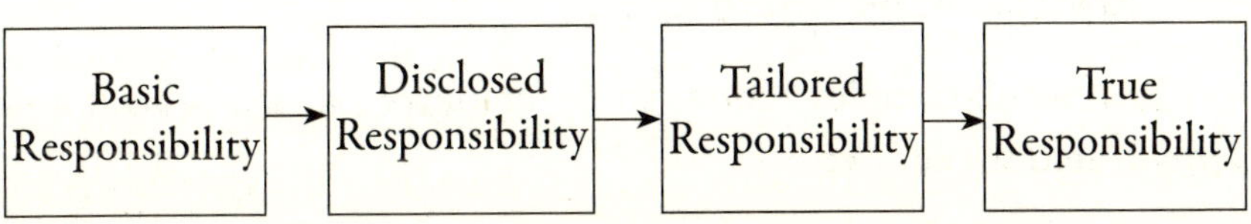

Basic performance measurement is all about what companies put out in their sustainability reports or annual reports. Disclosed responsibility measurement is provided by various studies that newspapers often publish that look at responsibility performance of companies (like our study!). Tailored responsibility performance is customised performance reports that various consulting firms provide companies to account for their unique situations. True responsibility performance is the ideal responsibility performance that is impossible to measure.

Determining what to put in sustainability reports and how to quantify performance of social or environmental actions is very complicated. The complexity arises on many counts. Social and sustainability performance is based on outcomes which are relatively harder to identify. For example, how does reduced smoking among people translate into numbers? Perhaps through increased output. But, can that be quantified? The extra output that has a direct connection with reduced smoking is what: longer life, perhaps? But how much longer does one live because of quitting smoking? This brings to the fore the practical realities of measuring responsibility. And, when one attempts this over a large population across various forms of action, the complexities are compounded.

Much of the work undertaken in the form of environmental action is in the nature of:

- A substitution of non-renewable natural resources with renewable ones.
- Efficiency in the non-renewable and renewable natural resources.
- Restriction of emissions and discharges from the economy to be within their assimilative capacity.
- Restriction on land-use changes so that the life-support capacity of the landscape is maintained.

These are all complex actions with outcomes that are difficult and complicated to measure.

Cost of measurement: To begin with, it is important to understand if companies have the resources to measure these complex actions. These often require them to get the prices of positive and negative externalities right (see *TN 1: Externalities and Their Implications* for a detailed explanation of externalities); extricating the impact of subsidies on unsustainable choices; and making action choices to deal with the problem at hand. Thus, measuring externalities is costly. Greater accuracy of measurement comes at a cost (more data collection, more time spent in evaluation etc.) and hence a tradeoff is required between higher cost of accuracy and lower cost with low accuracy.

Complex layering of data: A large number of stakeholders require information at various levels of detail. Thus government, regulators, international agencies, rating agencies and shareholders all require information in different formats and with different details. This adds a layer of complexity to the communication of responsibility measurement.

Inadequate measurement tools: Reporting apart, there are other practical issues. Are the tools needed to measure water conservation the same as tools required to measure carbon dioxide emission? Clearly, not. How does one integrate different measurement systems? How does one maintain different measurement systems within an integrated system? How does one measure performance when the outcomes are linked to actions by other entities? Take the case of road safety. A company undertakes a road safety programme. They engage residents of a locality or city in promoting safe driving or safe pedestrian behaviour. The residents of the city do show a change in behaviour and begin to undertake safe driving actions. However, an out-of-city person, untrained in safe driving, driving rashly causes an accident. Due to lack of control over such incidents measurement of performance becomes tricky.

Several measurement systems have developed over a period of time. Some of these are shown in Table 5.1.

Table 5.1: Various measurement systems

SDGs	Areas of spend specified by CSR Rules
B impact assessment	Standards, benchmarks and tools enabling companies to assess, compare and improve their social and environmental impacts over time
Environmental profit and loss (EP&L) statement	Pioneering development of a means of placing a monetary value on the environmental impacts along the supply chain of a business
KPMG True Value	A three-step methodology that enables companies to i) assess their 'true' earnings including externalities, ii) understand future earnings at risk and iii) develop business cases that create both corporate and societal value
Natural capital protocol	A harmonised framework for valuing natural capital in investor decision making
Redefining value	A work programme that aims to help WBCSD (full form?) member firms standardise tools to measure and manage their impact on society and the environment
Shared value	A management strategy focused on creating business value by identifying and addressing social problems
Social return on investment (SROI)	A framework based on generally accepted accounting principles used to help manage and understand an organisation's social, economic and environmental outcomes
Total impact measurement and management (TIMM)	New language to assist companies in understanding the overall impact of their activities
True price	A social enterprise that helps organisations – multinationals, SMEs, NGOs, governments – quantify and evaluate their economic, environmental and social impacts, particularly on a product level

While the above list is neither exhaustive nor complete, it does give one a sense of the difficulties faced in measuring responsible performance. This is a challenge that companies grapple with every day and has no easy answers. Measurements are fraught with choices, biases and complexities. The search for the right measures is a continuous endeavour.

There is little literature to support the preference of companies to adopt a measurement system. Ambuja Cement uses the True Value system extensively while Dalmia Cement uses SROI more often. SROI is a popular measure and is discussed in detail in *TN 2: Social Return on Investment*.

For a company to adopt a measurement system, an evaluation based on several variables is needed. How expensive is adopting a particular mechanism? How relevant is a particular system to address the work being undertaken by the company? Can the underlying reporting system generate information required for decision-making quickly enough to undertake a timely corrective course? Does the system actually measure what it sets out to measure? Does the measurement system enable the company to send out credible signals about the work that it undertakes?

While companies may have the right tools, deploying them to scale may be another challenge altogether. Sustainability and social responsibility projects are usually integrated within company systems in the following manner:

- Climate change projects mostly focus on emissions and disclosure. These are normally integrated via enterprise platforms that are deployed in factories and corporate offices. Though projects around emissions take very long to get off the ground because of the fundamental process changes that are needed many times.
- Waste management is also part of company operations. However, projects that need reverse logistics e.g. take back from customers, recycling and reuse are typically new processes that need measurement, reporting and integration across multiple touchpoints.
- Water management in the plant is part of company operations but India being a water stressed country many corporate foundations also invest in water projects in the vicinity of their operations. Measuring water which is highly changeable natural resource is a very difficult task; enterprise software, IOT and several measurement techniques are used.
- Supply chain traceability is another big challenge. Companies can trace products back to the source when they are produced in factories. In case of food and agricultural products companies have traditionally relied on paper-based certifications. Now tools and techniques are emerging today that are looking at DNA based traceability of textiles, food and much more.
- Most social impact projects lie outside corporate systems and at times rely on third party tools, processes and software. Most companies have put in place custom software or rely on rudimentary tools to measure social impact. At times, social projects never really scale despite having the right tools and measurement techniques because the company is unable to successfully integrate them.

- It may also be that a particular tool works better for measuring performance on water and another tool performs better for measuring waste. Companies often end up choosing the most appropriate tools but integrating them into a common measurement becomes a challenge. The question then becomes whether to use a sub-optimal measure for both or to live with the challenges of integration.

Reporting frameworks

Once the internal tools are set, companies report on their sustainability and social responsibility activities. The three primary reporting frameworks being used in India are the Global Reporting Initiative (GRI) based sustainability reports, Business Responsibility Reports and Integrated Reporting (IR).

GRI-based sustainability reports: The GRI standards were the first standards set out for sustainability reporting. They are seen as global best practices for reporting social, economic and environmental impacts. In India, only a handful of large corporations have adopted GRI-based reporting. Due to the wide nature of standards and auditing requirements, small firms find it difficult to adopt them.

Business Responsibility Reporting: The Securities and Exchange Board of India (SEBI) prescribes that the top 500 companies based on market capitalisation should have a business responsibility report (BRR) as part of their annual report. This is a disclosure of adoption of responsible business practices by a listed company to all its stakeholders.

Task Force on Climate-related Financial Disclosures: The FSB Task Force on Climate-related Financial Disclosures (TCFD) develops voluntary, consistent climate-related financial risk disclosures for use by companies in providing information to investors, lenders, insurers, and other stakeholders.

The Task Force considers the physical, liability and transition risks associated with climate change and what constitutes effective financial disclosures across industries. The work and recommendations of the Task Force will help companies understand what financial markets want in order to measure and respond to climate change risks, and encourage firms to align their disclosures with investors' needs.

Although not a reporting framework per se, it is likely to have a significant influence on reporting climate related activities.

Sustainability Accounting Standards Board: Established in 2011, the Sustainability Accounting Standards Board (SASB) is an independent, private-sector standards setting organisation based in San Francisco, California dedicated to enhancing the efficiency of the capital markets by fostering high-quality disclosure of material sustainability information that meets investor needs. The SASB develops and maintains sustainability accounting standards—for seventy-nine industries in eleven sectors—that help public corporations disclose financially material information to investors in a cost-effective and decision-useful format. The SASB's transparent, inclusive, and rigorous standards-setting process is materiality focused, evidence-based and market informed.

Integrated Reporting: A large number of companies still believe that reporting is a compliance issue and not one that involves a focus on communication to key stakeholders. Integrated reporting seeks to overcome this by bringing together material information about an organisation's strategy, governance, performance and prospects. This is done in a way that reflects the commercial, social and environmental context within which it operates. It provides a mechanism to disclose all kinds of capital that underlies any business—financial capital, manufactured capital, intellectual capital, human capital, social and relationship capital and natural capital.[3]

CFO's are increasingly looking at Sustainability related compliance, reporting and risk issues as part of their core activities. The task of the CFO is now more challenging than ever. In the Indian context, with the launch of the new CSR rules, reporting is a bit more complex. The new

CSR Rules cover only a small aspect of what a company needs to do. In our earlier analysis we've highlighted that CSR spans across various stakeholders of the company—employees, consumers, suppliers and communities. The latest rules circumscribe and limit CSR activities significantly to communities. In addition, GRI requirements too are wider than India's new CSR regulations. Companies that have GRI reports or are intending to create them will have needed to take a wider view of CSR spanning all stakeholders. Non-financial reporting in this case has been at multiple levels, the international standards based GRI report and the India specific reports. SEBI has recently issued an advisory to companies to provide information required by Integrated Reporting that encourages the top 500 BSE listed companies to use Integrated Reporting as a framework to improve the quality and relevance of the information provided.[4] Given this development it appears likely Integrated Reporting is likely to form the foundation of business reports in the near future. (Integrated Reporting is discussed in detail in *TN 3: The Integrated Reporting Framework*).

However, one should be mindful of the fact that companies may still end-up using differing reporting formats stating that the requirements of various stakeholders are different. Though if companies were to report more uniformly, comparison across firms will be far more valuable and greater insights can be drawn.

India's top companies for Sustainability and CSR – Measurement Insights

A lot of data in this book is based upon the Responsible Business Rankings study which is based on the study of sustainability and annual reports of around 1000 companies (cumulatively) over the past five years.

In 2014, we decided to embark upon measuring the responsibility performance of India's top companies. While we had, on numerous occasions in the past, talked about the various agencies ranking companies on their CSR and sustainability activities, a key drawback that we constantly discussed was that companies were being measured on the amount of money they spent on CSR activities. Presumably, the logic was that the larger the spend, the better you were. With our combined experience in academics and industry we knew that argument was flawed. More money spent didn't necessarily result in better outcomes. The question, however, was what the outcomes were and how they could be measured.

We debated whether we should look at twenty-five, fifty or hundred companies. We felt that anything less than fifty was not worthwhile as trends may not be easily discernible and the study would suffer from small sample bias. We ended up studying publicly available sustainability reports, annual reports and websites of hundred companies in the first year of the study. Subsequently, the sample size was more than 200. The other question was which hundred should we study? We found that *The Economic Times* compiled a list of top 500 companies which was well-regarded. The rankings were based on sales which was a metric that was easy to understand. Market capitalisation was another potential metric. We chose to stick with sales as market capitalisation would cause significant changes in the sample year on year.

Having decided on the approach to be followed and the companies to be covered, the crucial question was what to measure. We pored over research and literature and came to the conclusion that four metrics (Governance, Disclosure, Stakeholders, and, Sustainability) could almost wholly describe the CSR and sustainability activities of a company. Governance looks at how well is the governance for responsible business structured? Disclosure looks at how forthcoming are companies with respect to responsible business activities and performance. Stakeholders looks at how well are key stakeholders (employees, community, customers and suppliers) integrated within a company's responsible business framework. And, sustainability looks at how pervasive are sustainability practices (initiatives and targets to manage waste, water, energy, emissions) of companies.

Our research shows five key trends across the years—sustainability has gained momentum and CSR spending is increasing leading to

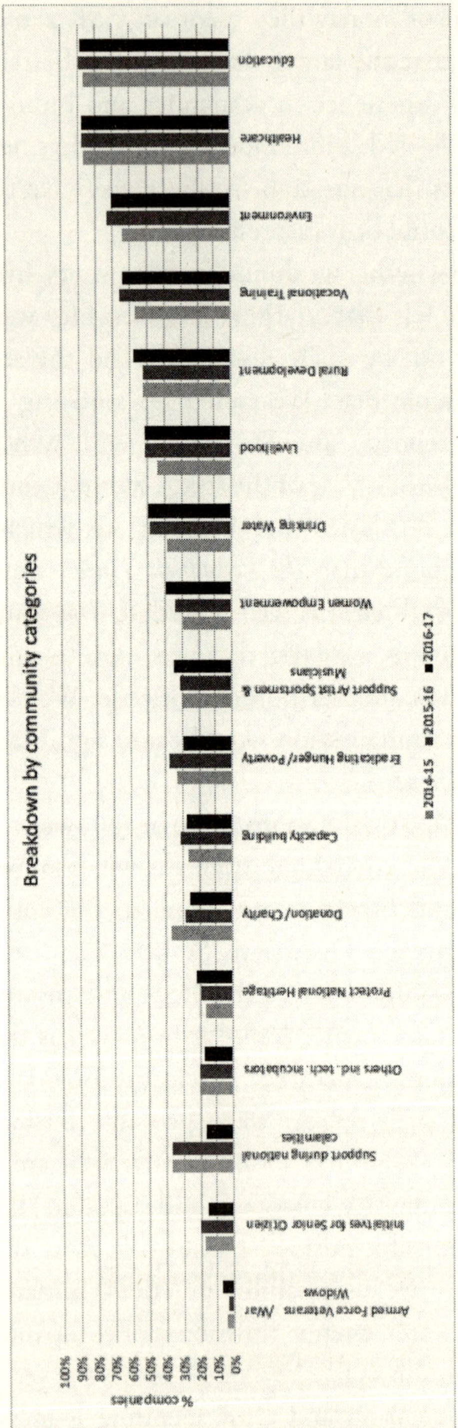

Figure 5.2: Sustainability performance

an improvement in overall scores while at the same time the services sector is a significantly poor performer.

TREND 1: Sustainability gains prominence

On the basis of the four identified criteria (Governance, Disclosure, Stakeholder and Sustainability) over time, companies have improved marginally on governance; improved marginally on disclosure; the stakeholder scores have fluctuated but not changed much; and sustainability is one area where there has been a marked improvement across years. The top-third companies tend to score much better than the remaining two-thirds; manufacturing companies perform better than service companies and private companies perform better than public companies. Both in the case of manufacturing and private companies, sustainability is the primary cause for the difference.

From our study of 218 companies' 2016–17 sustainability reports and annual reports, we find that fifty-five companies had higher sustainability scores (YOY), thirty-five remained the same and only ten witnessed decline. However, we find that the areas which are internal to an organisation—energy, water, waste and products—see participation from a much higher proportion of companies (70 per cent on an average), as compared with programmes for external stakeholders which are limited to only about a third of the companies.

TREND 2: Increased CSR spends

Companies have increased their average spend percentage considerably across years. Also, a greater proportion of companies are spending more than 2 per cent.

Breakdown by spending areas: As per the Companies Act, 2013 the government lists the areas where companies are required to undertake their CSR activities. The bulk of the companies are active in the areas of education, health, vocational training, rural development and livelihood. We also notice that there appears to be a realignment in the activities where companies operate. It keeps shifting across years

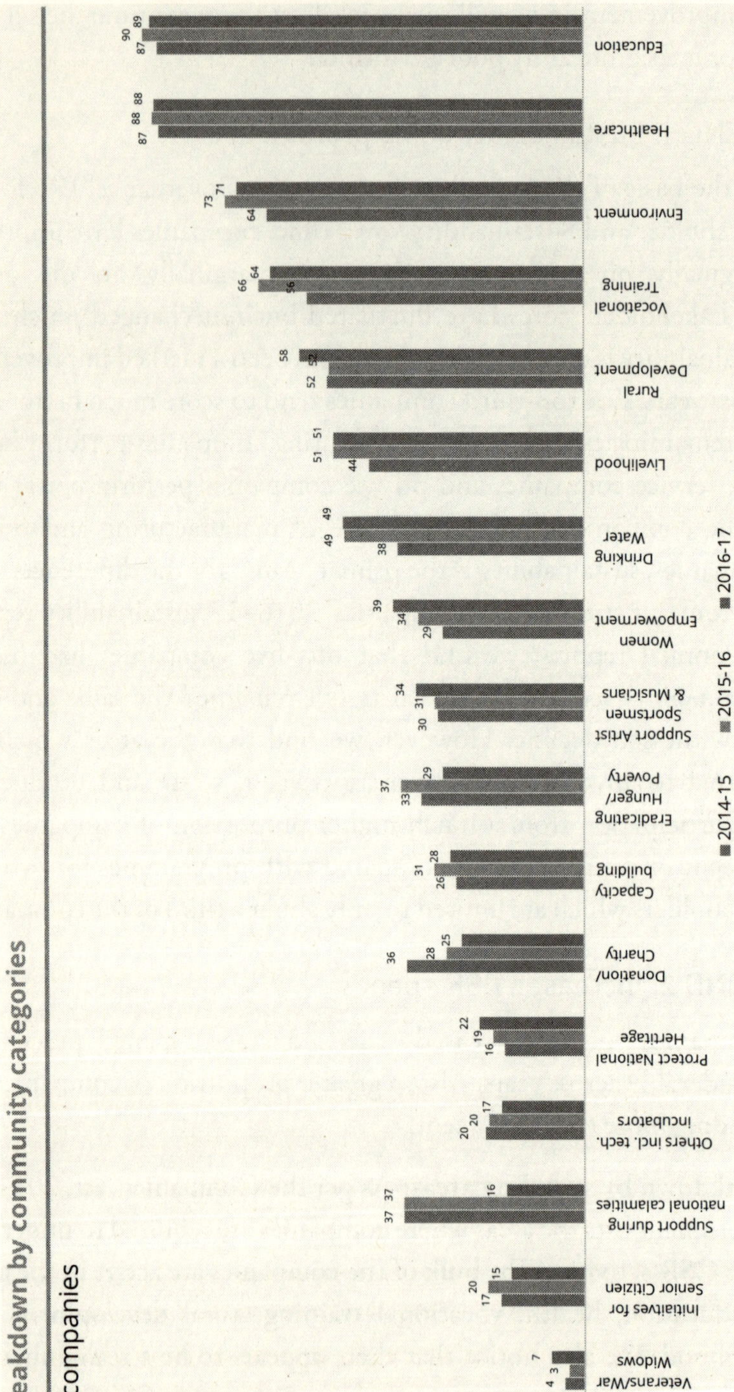

Figure 5.3: Community spend across years

Figure 5.4: Spending trends of companies

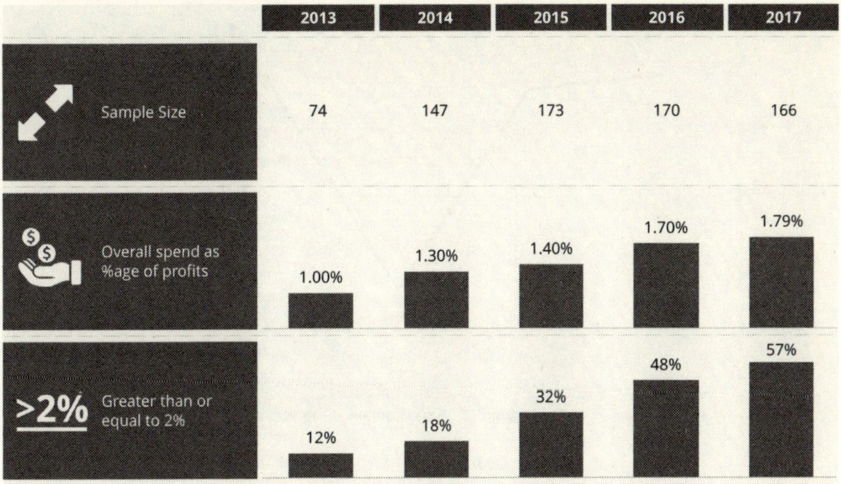

but the bulk of companies continue the focus on the areas where they are most comfortable. Interestingly, donation/charity to entities prescribed by the government has shown a declining trend.

TREND 3: Services sector lags behind

There is something pervasive in measuring performance. It is the bias of all measurement tools and reports that exists towards manufacturing companies. Manufacturing companies either emit smoke, pollute waters or harm the land. These are clearly visible harmful actions. Service companies, on the other hand, display no such outward manifestations of harming the ecology. Given this, actions taken by service companies tend to be very different from that of manufacturing companies. They often invest in LEED-certified green buildings, water recycling within their premises, reducing paper usage and so on. Thus, both comparisons of actions and measuring sustainability performance tends to be difficult.

If one looks at the comparison between manufacturing and services sector, we notice that on all parameters manufacturing sector performs better than the services sector.

Figure 5.5: Manufacturing versus services scores

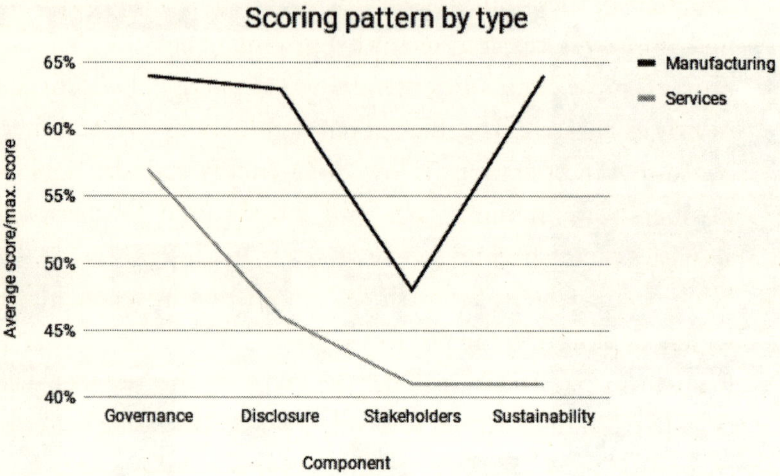

While this could partly be because the metrics for evaluation tend to be more manufacturing-centric, the gap is significantly large to be only attributed to metrics alone.

- Most service companies have formulated and adopted a governance framework around CSR activities.
- Service companies place low emphasis on memberships of global principles/compacts.
- Leading IT companies follow GRI guidelines in their sustainability reports and get them externally certified. The IT sector is export-oriented and hence expected to appear a socially responsible one.
- Telecom companies primarily have BRRs, are inward-looking and are focused on regulatory compliances.
- Banks too are a regulated industry and so the focus is on financial inclusion. Most banks are in the public sector and largely have BRRs.
- Many IT sector companies participate in carbon specific initiatives such as the Carbon Disclosure Project (CDP) and follow GHG accounting and inventory in their reporting. Surprisingly, very few telecom companies participate in CDP

despite being energy intensive. Most service companies are not members of their industry specific sustainability initiatives with no company in telecom sector being a member.

- Though most companies use renewable energy, disclosures are mostly qualitative. The share of renewable energy in total energy consumed in operations is low. Solar energy is under-deployed in operations in most cases and mostly used for peripheral activities or as a backup source.
- Water management programmes are limited in scope and not widely deployed in the services sector.
- E-waste management is under-deployed in the services sector despite rapid digitisation. It mostly involves disposing e-waste to authorised recyclers. A few companies (HCL Infosystems, Cisco etc.) extend it to their customers. The financial sector lags severely in its e-waste practices. Even non-e-waste programmes are mostly limited to reducing/recycling paper (through use of electronic media) and little is said about plastics and other solid wastes.

In conclusion, it is clear that services companies perform relatively weakly on all the parameters. Despite the significant role played by services companies in the economy their weak social and sustainability actions are a puzzle.

TREND 4: Responsibility parameters show improvements

Since we realised that spending alone was not a criterion for the success of a responsible business, we delved deeper to untangle the relationship between spending and the scores that a company received. This was the responsibility matrix—deriving the relationship between spending and performance (Governance, Disclosure, Stakeholders and Sustainability).

Pace setters: These are companies that spend relatively large amounts and have relatively high responsible business scores. These companies have responsible business at the core of their long-term vision with good execution.

Smart utilisers: These companies spend relatively less but have higher scores. They get the best bang for their buck. They spend judiciously and are often able to extract economies of scale and also utilise their experience to the hilt.

Low efficiency: These companies spend a relatively larger amount but have relatively low responsible business scores. These companies focus on complying with regulatory norms. However, they lack in vision and execution. Their approach is more short term.

Starting out: These companies spend relatively less and also have lower responsible business scores. As the name suggests, these companies are still finding their feet. They are still putting their frameworks in place and are struggling to comply with norms. They may take a while to ramp up.

Figure 5.6: Responsibility matrix – trend over years

Spread: Low → High; CSR Spend (Percent of average net profit): High → Low

Low Efficiency (high CSR spend, low spread)

	Avg. Spend %	Avg. Score
2012-13	2.22%	39.6
2013-14	1.80%	34.9
2014-15	2.14%	27.4
2015-16	2.18%	34.3
2016-17	2.23%	41.9

Pace Setters (high CSR spend, high spread)

	Avg. Spend %	Avg. Score
2012-13	1.64%	60.2
2013-14	2.30%	67.1
2014-15	2.09%	65.1
2015-16	2.52%	69.2
2016-17	2.36%	71.9

Starting Out (low CSR spend, low spread)

	Avg. Spend %	Avg. Score
2012-13	0.28%	31.2
2013-14	0.30%	25.4
2014-15	0.57%	23.9
2015-16	0.77%	27.9
2016-17	1.17%	41.2

Smart Utilisers (low CSR spend, high spread)

	Avg. Spend %	Avg. Score
2012-13	0.25%	54.7
2013-14	0.80%	61.6
2014-15	0.93%	63.8
2015-16	1.20%	66.7
2016-17	1.31%	65.5

Pace setters scored high but also spent more. Smart utilisers got the maximum bang for their buck. Companies in the low efficiency quadrant spent a lot but scored relatively poorly whereas those in the starting out quadrant were just finding their feet. They spent less and also scored less. Over the four years, we find that across quadrants, companies are both spending more as well as scoring more. It is a clear sign that corporate India is focussing more on responsible business. India needs more pace setters and smart utilisers to take it to the next frontier

TREND 5: Responsible Business and Stock Market Performance show no correlation

Elsewhere in the book we have argued that undertaking socially responsible actions adds to the company's ability to be competitive. This should result in higher stock market returns for companies that are more socially responsible. Our study has shown that company scores and stock returns are insignificantly correlated. It is almost as if there is no correlation with stock returns. This is no surprise. Earlier studies along similar lines have shown similar results. So, what explains this phenomenon? There are a few explanations.

First and foremost is the assumption that consumers' purchasing decisions are based on a company's responsible actions. Thus, if a company is seen as more socially responsible, the consumers are more likely to purchase the product. Surveys have shown that consumers are socially sensitive and intend to buy socially responsible products. A number of studies have also shown that these intentions don't translate into practice. Thus, purchasing decisions are made on criteria other than the socially responsible nature of the business.

Secondly, stock market returns are not just a measure of socially responsible actions but also that of product-market decisions. Thus, there could be a drowning out of the signalling impact of socially responsible actions.

Thirdly, we find from our conversations and study of equity research reports that investment analysts do not look at the socially responsible actions of a company. This flies contrary to the fact that many of the fund houses undertake socially responsible investments. Perhaps, they do not think that social responsibility is a strong enough factor. This is one area that needs further exploration.

Distance to responsibility needs to be explored

As seen earlier, our research has revealed that we should perhaps have different metrics for manufacturing and service companies. Though that might make comparison across company types difficult.

Still another issue that has vexed us has been that of negative externalities or the social influence of the business carried out by the company. For instance, tobacco, gambling and alcohol are considered social evils. Should these be penalised? The question that arises then is, how does one determine penalties and what activities would attract penalties. For instance, if a company failed to repay loans should they also suffer penalties. Every company may have some negative association and unearthing it would not only be a difficult task but also potentially subject to bias.

Figure 5.7: The Distance to Responsibility

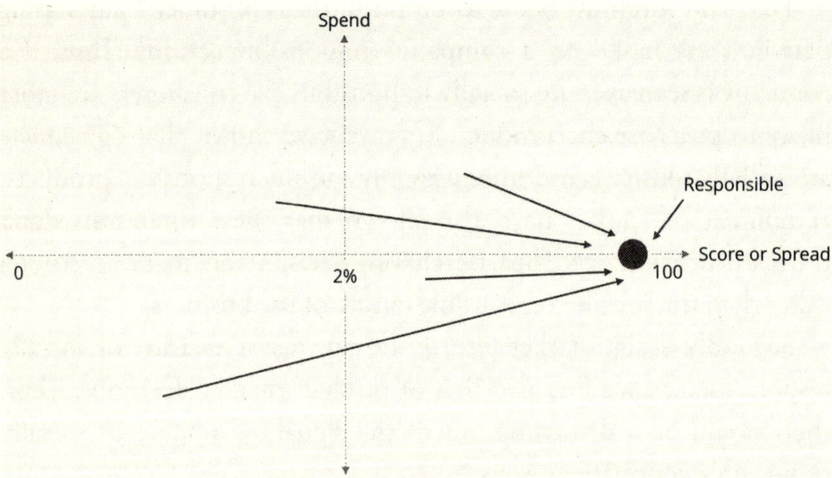

Another way of looking at this is to examine the performance of companies under the 'distance to responsibility' paradigm. Regulation requires companies to spend a minimum of 2 per cent of net profits. Any lower spend percentage is not seen favourably. On our rating scale a company can score a maximum of 100 points. Thus, a company with a spend of 2 per cent and score of 100 points would be the best performing company (responsible). We constructed a measure of distance to optimal[1] that tells a company as to how far away it is from the optimal.

Thus, companies can get a sense of how much they need to do to reach the point of responsibility.

Here we would like to add a word of caution. As we saw the in the earlier section, understanding measurement, responsibility measurement exists at various levels and our analysis is based on disclosed responsibility. True responsibility is immeasurable. We measure what we can and improve with time. Also, the 2 per cent benchmark is based on the government norms. Over time, when everyone starts achieving this norm higher expectation may be imposed on companies. These may change as time goes along—pushing companies to do even better.

People have been trying to measure various things since time immemorial. Responsible business is no different. Unlike accounting that has evolved and measures things in a consistent manner, responsibility reporting is still in its infancy. It is expected that measurement systems will soon start converging. Though there will still be differences, calibration will become relatively easier. As complexities increase measurement systems will need to adapt and provide information that the stakeholders really need.

CASE STUDY

AMBUJA CEMENT: THE MEASUREMENT PROCESS

Ambuja Cement Limited (ACL) is one of the largest cement companies in India. ACL is the Indian company of LafargeHolcim—a global cement conglomerate with a presence in over ninety countries. Since inception, Ambuja Cement has focused on timely, cost-effective and environmentally clean shipments to its customers and has built a captive port with four terminals along India's western coastline. It was possibly the first cement company in India to be certified as *water positive*—saving more water than it used. This was achieved through water saving measures like water harvesting, providing concrete mix designs to masons and modular concrete curing. Apart from water the company works in the areas of skill-based livelihood generation, healthcare, education and women's empowerment.

Ambuja Cement has always believed that sustainability and competitiveness were not mutually exclusive but went together. The company has tied up with many global initiatives like Cement Sustainability Initiative of World Business Council for Sustainable Development to help it push its agenda forward. It has also adopted True Value, the triple bottom-line accounting method which encompass the three pillars of sustainability—people, planet, and profit. The Ambuja Ambition 2030 plan guides its sustainability activities (see Table 1).

Table 1: Ambuja Ambition 2030

Year 2020	*Year 2030*
People & Communities	
Have zero onsite fatality	Have zero onsite fatality
Reduce LTI FR<0.50	Reduce LTI FR<0.20
Reduce TIFR by 30 per cent	Reduce TIFR by 50 per cent
Stakeholder engagement plan at all cement sites	Have 100 per cent of high-risk active suppliers assessed and consequence management in place

Year 2020	*Year 2030*
Develop social programmes to benefit 1.5 million people	
Complete Human Rights assessment at all plant locations	
Water and Nature	
Reduce freshwater withdrawal in cement operations by 7	Reduce fresh water withdrawal in cement operation by 15
Implement WASH pledge at all sites	
Improve water balance index to 5	Improve water balance index to 6
Have a Biodiversity Indicator Reporting System (BIRS) in place at all Active Quarries	Show positive change for biodiversity
Climate	
Reduce net specific carbon dioxide emissions from cement plants by 33 per cent (versus 1990 levels)	Reduce net specific carbon dioxide emissions from cement plants by 40 per cent (versus 1990 levels)
Circular economy	
Use 9 million tonnes of waste-derived resources per year	Use 13.5 million tonnes of waste-derived resources per year

Note: LTI FR = Loss Time Injury Frequency Rate; TIFR = Total Injury Frequency Rate; WASH = Water, Sanitation and Hygiene

Source: Ambuja Sustainability Report 2016

The company engages with varied groups of stakeholders at different levels to understand their expectations. Key stakeholders are determined on the basis of three attributes: (i) peer companies' stakeholders; (ii) relevant stakeholders for Ambuja Cement; and, (iii) interactions with senior management. This structured framework enables the company to course-correct on an on-going basis.

The communication with key stakeholders leads to the mapping of stakeholder concerns and issues. Key topics/concerns raised by different stakeholder groups during the engagement process along with the Company's approach towards these issues are presented in the table below

Table 2: Stakeholder Issues

Customers	*Suppliers*
Affordable product	Supplier/vendor profitability
Brand image	Brand and certification of suppliers
Customer satisfaction	Logistics and distribution costs
Customer education	Support to suppliers as a part of corporate sustainability to reduce risks
Greenhouse gases	Addressing supplier grievances by ACL
Investors	
Profitability	*Dealers*
Demand generation	Brand image
Brand image	Safety
Land acquisition	Suppliers' and dealers' network
Cost savings	Customer satisfaction
Employees	*Government and regulatory agencies*
Health & Safety	Knowledge management
Manpower productivity	Health and safety
Training and development	Product innovation
Regulatory compliance	Regulatory requirements and compliance
Technological up-gradation	
R&D and innovation	
Community and NGOs	
CSR	
Shared value	
Sustainable mining practices	
Quality of supplier/products/ services	
Water consumption	
Relocation and rehabilitation	

Source: Ambuja Cements, Sustainability Report 2016

Having identified stakeholders and their concerns, Ambuja Cements sets about identifying key risk areas for the company. Through stakeholder impact analysis these risks are identified and key impact actions planned.

Finally, the company needs to measure the work that it does. Without a proper measurement system, it is difficult to assess the performance of the company or plan for the future. Ambuja Cement has chosen 'True Value' as a metric of performance. Devised in association with KPMG in 2013, True Value is a tool to understand the value a business creates. Another metric used by Ambuja is Social Return on Investment that relates the outcomes to the resources invested in a particular activity.

True Value methodology allows Ambuja Cement to know where it stands and where it needs to be in the future. It enables the company to collect and present data about the value it creates. Assessing its True Value helps the company to respond to social and environmental challenges.

True Value measurement entailed the following steps:

Step 1 – Assessment: Calculate social and environmental value created – both positive and negative, created.
Step 2 – Analysis: Understand how the key elements of a company's social and environmental actions impact the company's future.
Step 3 - Strategic Response: Find the most cost-effective way to increase the company's True Value.

The use of true value methodology has enabled the company to take concrete steps towards its CSR and sustainability goals. Application of the methodology has enabled it to be probably the only company to be certified as five times water positive; reduce wastage through recycling and make a positive contribution to people's lives.

Local communities are an important stakeholder group for Ambuja. Initiatives in the area of water Resource Management are taken up by a CSR arm of the company known as Ambuja Cement Foundation (ACF). Social Return on Investment (SROI) is used to measure value created by water resource initiatives within the community. SROI is a framework for measuring and accounting for a broad concept of value, taking into account social, economic and environmental factors. It is recognised as a leading method of measurement. It allows us to compare the amount invested in a particular project with the value created, by valuing the different outcomes that have occurred. The SROI framework uses monetary value to represent outcomes. Once these monetary values have been established, a cost-benefit analysis is conducted that includes the notion of social value. Finally, a SROI ratio is produced that shows the social value in currency terms. Ambuja has conducted an exercise in generating SROI for three projects in the area of water resources.

Thus the company manages to evaluate its social performance at the corporate level by using true value methodology and at the project level by applying the SROI approach.

CHAPTER 6

New Challenges are Emerging

Business responsibility matters and so do the frameworks that measure it. Today, it is also important to place business responsibility in the context of the rapid changes that are taking place in the world.

The first industrial revolution took place with the invention of the steam engine and the birth of industrial manufacturing. It occurred between 1700 and 1800.

The second industrial revolution was enabled by the discovery of the internal combustion engine and electricity. It took place between 1800 and 1900.

The third industrial revolution came with the growth of computing and later, the internet. It started in the second half of the twentieth century.

The fourth industrial revolution is happening now! According to a World Economic Forum survey,[1] 75 per cent of the senior executives of the world's leading companies believe that in the next ten years, 10 per cent of the cars will be driverless and we will be using 3D printing for making not just products like cars, but even organs that can then be transplanted.[2] Table 6.1 lists the top twenty technologies of the future.

Today, and increasingly in the future, our resources will not just be materials, water and energy but also technology and knowledge. By 2030, advances in technology powered by leaps in computing and knowledge are likely to solve many of the problems of today. Robots will make dangerous tasks safer, advanced healthcare devices will monitor and remedy health problems and Artificial Intelligence or AI-based algorithms will make decisions faster. Automation will

Table 6.1: Trends in Technology Shifts

No.	Technology Trends	Brief description
1	Implantable Technologies	Devices becoming connected to bodies – Consumable microbots to repair injuries
2	Digital Presence	Individuals increasing their presence in the digital world with computing becoming more accessible
3	New Interfaces – Vision, AR/VR	Eye-gestures, body movements become a means of controlling devices, fully immersive interfaces build up
4	Smart clothing	Technology becomes more personal with clothes that change color or shape and adjust to hot or cold
5	Carbon Sequestration	Programs for injecting large amounts of atmospheric CO_2 into basaltic rock
6	Designer Molecules	Artificial molecules with novel magnetic and chemical properties enabling creation of revolutionary new materials.
7	Storage for All	Massive increases in computing leading to a need for more space. Cheap storage becoming available.
8	The Internet of and for Things	Connecting literally everything to the internet
9	The Connected Home	All home devices and equipment connected to the internet
10	Smart Cities	Connect services, utilities and roads to the internet
11	Big Data for Decisions	Leverage big data to enable better and faster decision-making
12	Driverless Cars	Autonomous vehicles becoming ubiquitous
13	Genetic Computing	Genetronics – self assembling microelectronics and DNA based super computers
14	AI and White-Collar Jobs	AI replaces a range of functions performed today by people
15	Robotics and Services	Robotics influences manufacturing, agriculture, retail and services
16	Bitcoin and the Blockchain	Keeping track of trusted transactions in a distributed fashion
17	The Sharing Economy	Technology-enabled ability for entities (individuals or organizations) to share the use of a physical good/asset, or share/provide a service
18	Cheap solar power	Solar cells with 100% efficiency make solar widely available
19	3D Printing	3D printing for producing consumer products on demand. Bioprinting – recreating body parts.
20	Biometric materials	New materials inspired by living things, self-cleaning clothing, self-repairing buildings

Source: Compiled by the authors.

enable many of the mundane tasks to be done with minimal effort. Aviation, energy, transportation, smart cities, manufacturing, mining, and construction will be transformed in ways that improve peoples' lives. The cost of storage will also reduce, leading to a proliferation of content.

Internet everywhere will help people get better access to public services as governments can ease the general bureaucratic tangles and delays. They will further be able to improve tax collection and provide greater transparency and accountability for public spends.

People will become even more connected with mobile phones which may be implanted into their bodies to monitor location, health and ensure that they are always connected. This trend of high connectivity will be further enabled by gadgets such as the Apple watch and clothes with embedded chips that connect the wearer to the internet. Transportation will shift to cleaner fuels and more efficient technologies. Vehicles that drive themselves will reshape our cities, freeing up space and reducing road fatalities. Personalised medicine and better quality of care will become possible with seamless transfer of data between people, doctors and medical establishments.

In this transforming world, the idea of sustainability and social responsibility needs to be in keeping with human ambition, and should be much greater than the sum of its parts. Human ambition is scaling planetary boundaries and moving into space. On 14 December 2017, Sundar Pichai, the CEO of Google tweeted that NASA and Google had discovered two new planets in a far-away solar system using cutting-edge AI technologies. Google's AI models were trained on 15,000 signals to recognise patterns caused by actual planets as compared to those caused by other objects, and performed with 96 per cent accuracy for planet detection.[3] It was a remarkable feat in more ways than one. NASA's data from previous space missions coupled with the human desire to find more habitable planets had been enabled and powered by a private company—Google.

It's a time of change, but even more so, a time to act. It's time to take actions that not only help in alleviating the visible problems but the ones that go to the very core—the fundamental imbalances that have contributed to where we are today. The one significant learning from the era of industrialisation has been that social equity and the balance of nature are both equally important. The corporation of 2030 therefore will need a new responsibility framework to work for the global good and take on board the modern context that will define 4IR.

Klaus Schwab in his book, *The Fourth Industrial Revolution*[4] states: 'The Fourth Industrial Revolution, finally, will change not only what we do but also who we are. It will affect our identity and all the issues associated with it: our sense of privacy, our notions of ownership, our consumption patterns, the time we devote to work and leisure, and how we develop our careers, cultivate our skills, meet people, and nurture relationships.'

Each industrial revolution saw great disruptions, not just because traditional manufacturing gave way to newer forms of production, but more because entire business models transformed. Local manufacturing gave way to centralised manufacturing hubs driven by economies of scale. Centralised data processing and services gave way to outsourcing to cheaper countries. People acquired new skills and governments made policy changes. Many won, but equally, many lost. The fourth industrial revolution will also lead to great benefits for humanity, but at a price. It is fundamentally different because it is ten times faster and 300 times the scale of the first industrial revolution. However, like all things that are great at one level, this will also bring about newer challenges:

1. As corporations turn digital, data drives value and risks.
2. Algorithms could heighten biases and reduce jobs.
3. Clean Energy will transform but lead to stranded assets and new disruptions.
4. Manufacturing will become decentralised and digital.
5. Finance gets social and sustainable.

CHALLENGE 1
As corporations turn digital, data drives value and risks

India, like the rest of the world, is very much part of the digital revolution. Devices have proliferated and so have online services and platforms. Social media platforms such as Facebook and Twitter have gained a loyal audience that is growing constantly. Indigenous digital platforms such as Paytm and Aadhaar have also gained tremendous ground. Measuring the responsibility of digital service providers is, however, a challenging task. In the physical world, responsibility could easily be defined as the impact of a company on the environment and its relationship with society. In the digital world though, things are not that simple because creation, consumption, sharing and interacting occurs between various technologies which in turn interact with each other. In the physical world, we are governed by geography. In the digital world, space takes on a whole new meaning. Digital actions are governed by the rules embedded in software, which are however defined by the company that owns it. This transformative power of digital technology is changing how business functions. And here is the truth of it—this is just the beginning. Business is going to be quite different from what it has been or what we anticipate it to be. Some of today's most innovative and market-leading companies such as Google, Uber, Airbnb, Facebook and Twitter, did not even exist twenty years ago. But, they are now in almost every part of the world, loved by customers and embraced by advertisers for global access to a worldwide audience.

Most services companies today can be termed as digital companies. They provide services through technology, create large quantities of data and consume information to enhance experiences and engage with customers. This definition covers most internet companies such as Google and Facebook. It also covers banking and financial companies (that are increasingly becoming digital), car rental companies (like Uber and Lyft), e-vehicle companies, and all health companies that are now in the process of building gene editing and genome sequencing platforms.

As the internet has proliferated and become central to our lives, so has our usage of connected devices, sensors and internet platforms. Access to data generated by millions of devices and users across the world has helped create a completely new set of companies. These companies have business models that aggregate customer data and further generate data through the services they provide.

For the better part of the early 2000's the world's most valuable commodity was oil and oil conglomerates dominated the list of most valuable companies. Over time that changed. In Fortune 500's *10 Most Valuable Companies* list (2018), the top five are Apple, Amazon, Alphabet (the parent company of Google), Microsoft and Facebook.[5] Data is the big competitive advantage and is now spoken of in terms of being 'the new oil'. With access to data, companies in one sector can now start businesses in completely different areas. This is quite different from the earlier view of developing core competencies in one area and building scale around it. With the purchase of Whole Foods (an American supermarket chain that specialises in selling organic food products), Amazon can no longer be called just an online portal.[6] The biggest music retailer in India is not a music company but a mobile services provider. Uber, till a few months back, was a car sharing platform but has now added food delivery services to its portfolio.

It's not just online companies that are adding new businesses and lines of revenue, traditional companies too have caught on. GE, now calls itself the 'digital industrial company'[7] where digital services are considered an integral part of the company's operations and customer-facing services. Data is collected through a host of sensors in the products GE sells, and then analysed to increase performance efficiency and cost savings. Financial services companies are also redefining themselves. The fintech revolution driven by technology and big data is now knocking on the doors of traditional banks.[8] Citigroup is accelerating its mobile first digital strategy and its newly formed Citi FinTech unit is spearheading the transformation.[9] Citibank in Asia has entered into a partnership with ride-hailing

Table 6.2: Sources and Uses of data

Sector	Manufacturing	Retail	Financial services	Telecom	Social Media Platforms
How do they collect data	! Social media ! Sensors in products	! Tracking transactions ! Loyalty programmes ! Social Media	! Transactions ! Usage of services ! Social Media	! Transactions ! Usage of services ! Social Media	! User Profiles ! Content generated through usage of platforms ! Usage of third party services on the platform ! Device data
How is it used	! Market research ! Personalisation of products ! Real time insight into product performance	! Customer insights for design, trends, offers ! Boosting customer retention ! Influencing purchases, targeted offers ! Managing stocking and sourcing	! Targeted advertising ! Personalise and automate transactions ! Create new products ! Increase market penetration, cross selling and upselling of products	! Targeted advertising ! Personalise and automate transactions ! Create new products ! Increase market penetration, cross selling and upselling of products	! Targeted advertising ! Targeted content ! Targeted news ! Targeted services ! Recommendations

platform Grab, hospitality pioneer Airbnb and the Lazada Group, a leading online shopping and retailing site.

Data gathered and generated through consumer transactions is a huge revenue source for most companies. Google's mission is to organise the world's information and make it universally accessible. The way consumers search for information online gives it information on what people are looking for, enabling it to deliver relevant advertising. This data is the cornerstone of Google's ability to generate advertising revenue. Facebook also monetises information generated from the users of its online platforms to garner advertising across industries. A major source of the revenue generated by Google and Facebook is advertising revenue. In 2016, Facebook generated 97 per cent of its revenue from advertising[10] while Google earned about 79.38 billion US dollars in 2016 from advertising.[11] While online companies use purchase and search history to place targeted advertisements, this is just a very small part of the value derived from our data. There is far more at play; this is how change and risk is being wrought by the 4IR.

In the digital world, valuations sky-rocket, responsibility nosedives

The new world driven by these technological changes is seeing a proliferation of startups which are questioning the status quo and disrupting industries. The sectors that are being disrupted are many. 3D printing is disrupting manufacturing, transportation is seeing cab aggregators shake up the industry, and the energy sector is seeing a radical shift with renewables and battery solutions. The list of industries that will change or are changing is rapidly increasing. The ones that are facing the brunt of these changes were based on past business models and are therefore faced with significant challenges of scale and people when it comes to being more agile. New companies armed with newer technologies, a radical new way of looking at things and agile low-cost business structures are threatening their very existence. Most startups don't particularly care about sustainability or social responsibility because their primary focus is gaining more customers, which in turn drives venture capital funding. This primacy of quantity over quality in the startup world is creating business models where sustainability is an afterthought, to be considered once the venture starts making profit. E-commerce companies routinely send products wrapped in several layers of packaging. While it is designed to protect the end-product, it leads to an excessive amount of waste. For instance, a brand new phone cable and battery comes in a foot-long cardboard box, besides being encased in two smaller separate boxes. Each of the smaller boxes have the products wrapped securely in layers of plastic. Online apparel companies are not far behind either in terms of generating waste.

While the old economy companies are embracing the responsible way of doing business, the start-up ecosystem, however, doesn't pay adequate attention. Many reasons are ascribed for their not being responsible. One is that they lack the resources to implement systems and processes for sustainability and CSR. Another argument is that they have little time or mind space during the early establishment phases and the early-growth phase to focus on social responsibility related issues. The CEO of an early internet multimedia company, was recently accused of sexual harassment and it came to light that the company had no mechanisms to deal with such issues.[12] The explanation was a combination of the lack of resources and mind space to deal with such matters. However, there is no tomorrow for imbibing social responsibility. It has to be here and now—a part of the DNA of the business.

Responsibility challenges in the digital world are many. The primary ones centre around privacy, unauthorised access and the problems that may arise when algorithms will drive decision-making in the near future.

Privacy concerns mount

The game is on! It's been on for a while now, and we've all been playing: you, me, social platform owners, brand managers, political parties and many others. While our motivations to play the game of social media may have differed, we have all grown to love the game. We have shared photos, likes, dislikes, views and more on Twitter, Facebook, Instagram and anything else that became the latest place to hang out.

For companies wanting to engage existing and potential customers, voters, donors and volunteers it was a field ready for picking. Instead of relying on the age-old marketing methods of post facto research, here was live data about what people believed in, expected, desired and bought. The information was gathered, analysed and then used to make focused campaign messages, videos, photos and sometimes, even news that resonated with the targeted customers. This in turn helped achieve the marketers' objective, i.e., product purchases, votes, donations and anything else that the campaign funder desired. The game became a self-feeding cycle wherein we shared a slice of our lives and marketers adapted the insight to give us new products and services. A win-win for all. We got appreciation, a chance to say our bit, sometimes huge visibility when a message, photo or video went viral and many times, a warm fuzzy feeling of well-being and togetherness. Marketers got a new sales channel with instant feedback loops of ready and willing customers. Social platforms backed by venture capitalists raised even more capital based on the rising numbers of advertisers and users. All was well with the world!

Who cared that the data was surreptitiously being aggregated, the communication was at times fake, and that digital surveillance was raising its ugly head? Privacy was dead after all. The Google CEO had announced it in 2008.[13]

Then came fake news, Cambridge Analytica and the deep inroads into Facebook data that seemingly swung the US elections. If true, it was a strike of unimaginable proportions. It shook the world in the same way that the atomic strikes had in 1945. There were no charred bodies this time around, but the smell of something rotten was so strong that it was impossible to breathe. But why did it raise such a stink this time round, given that it was marketing after all? The candidate was just a product, data had been available anyway and the campaigns had been based on what voters wanted to hear anyway! Analytics had simply generated remarkably accurate insights and remember, since privacy had been dead anyway, so really, what was the big deal?

This time though, it was different! The stakes were the biggest they could have ever been. The takeover of the highest office of a nation! Smart marketing driven by lax laws, and a receptive audience had converted the biggest show of democracy into a spectacle which would almost be comic, if it wasn't so tragic.

A vast amount of our personal data now lies with private companies and governments. Knowledge is power. And the more data we share, the more power we give to someone else. Can this be used against us? Can it influence our decision-making and limit our choices?

How secure is the data? Most of the data resides in the cloud. The cloud is a set of servers where data is managed and maintained. The cloud is seldom owned and operated by the company that you may be sharing the data with. In addition, data hacks and breaches are proliferating. Your banking information, emails and photographs are therefore all vulnerable.

Information access drives violence and crime

Digital platforms show some worrying trends too. The 2015 UN report, 'Cyber Violence Against Women and Girls',[14] reveals that almost three-quarters of women online have been exposed to some form of cyber violence. Threats of rape, death and stalking are common and cut across national boundaries. Open any online platform such as Twitter and one can see a surfeit of threats directed at women. Schoolgirls often complain of bullying from friends and peers on social platforms. Using technology to gain access to someone's computer and releasing their photographs is a common problem that women face. Some women have also found, and much to their horror, that they are being impersonated online and objectionable messages are being sent to friends and family on their behalf. Sex traffickers are also frequenting chat rooms, posting advertisements to recruit women that can get them into dangerous situations. Cyber violence has steadily increased with new terms such as 'revenge porn' and 'sexting' emerging. Some situations have also gone out of hand with many women committing suicide, where an ex-boyfriend or husband has uploaded the woman's intimate photographs and videos on social media.

Children are also increasingly at risk. They have easy access to social media through their parents' devices or their own phones and are inadvertently releasing information about themselves and their families. This lays them open to serious threats such as kidnapping, porn and a range of cybercrimes. In 2014, a virtual market was uncovered involving four websites, online forums and some thirty groups on a popular Chinese messaging platform, connecting traffickers with potential buyers.[15] Some 200,000 boys and girls are kidnapped in China every year and sold online.[16] Internet platforms profess to have stringent business policies to prevent abuse. However, it is getting increasingly difficult to believe social media companies when they say that they are investigating a matter. Most often, a complainant has to wait patiently even as an erring party take inordinately long in deleting objectionable images or blocking people who make threats. While specialist forums have been established by various countries to tackle cyber violence against women, there is very little tracking by company regulators.

With so much data about ourselves being available privacy and security will be a serious challenge:

- Your electric car managed largely by computers will know where you go and whom you meet.
- Your online searches and consumption of news will tell data miners about your likes and dislikes, and political leanings.
- Personal digital assistants such as smart TVs, smart refrigerators and personal robots who work on voice-activated commands will be able to listen in to your private conversations.

- Your privacy could be seriously compromised with your data being available to businesses and governments. A worrying trend, as this can be used to keep societies under undue surveillance.
- CCTV cameras are increasingly being used to record activities in public spaces; drone-based cameras will certainly pick up speed too. While these are now being used to help people during emergencies, natural disasters, and to keep people safe during terrorist threats, misuse is not far away. Technology such as this can easily be used to snoop around and monitor people.
- Digital responsibility and data ethics will take centre stage.

These are only some examples. The key point being that privacy protections and societal oversight must ensure a balance between undue surveillance and statutory requirements of a government or business needs.

CHALLENGE 2
Algorithms could heighten biases and reduce jobs

An algorithm is nothing but a set of rules followed in a calculation or for problem-solving. So, if you want to divide a sum of money among five people, you follow a set of rules and arrive at the money each person gets. The role of algorithms was further expanded with the advent of computers. The best-known example of the use of algorithms was in sorting, when the bubble sort algorithm was developed. Later, this was succeeded by the more efficient merge sort algorithm. Since then, algorithms have taken over our lives. When it started, Google employed the page rank algorithm to present the search results that were more important or valuable upfront. Today, one sees algorithms in a large number of applications—the sequence in which planes take off from an airport is decided by an algorithm, the route that a truck needs to take to serve a number of warehouses is determined by an algorithm, how Netflix shows the movies that you are most likely to watch is also determined by an algorithm and the computer programme that beats chess champions is also based on algorithms. Algorithms pervade almost all aspects of our lives.

Information has always been the lifeblood of companies and markets. At a very basic level, markets use information about the quality and availability of goods to determine price and reach out to customers, and companies have always used information to skilfully organise, coordinate and increase efficiencies. Information coupled with a company's ability to deploy machines to make goods faster and better has driven competitive advantage and higher value capture. However, decision-making has always been the domain of humans.

The proliferation of data has made it increasingly difficult to manage. As companies grew, they tried to manage information flows through corporate hierarchies, Standard Operating Procedures and techniques such as Six Sigma. But the sheer volume of information that is now available has meant that human beings are now beginning to rely more and more on machines for better decision-making.

Today's corporations that are often accused of being soulless, process-driven monoliths that transcend borders, will very soon have algorithms at the helm of decision-making. This can have some worrying implications.

Heightened biases: Take the case of heightened biases. This is a very real possibility because algorithms increasingly learn on their own. The biases of the individual get reflected into the choices that the algorithm may make. Take the fashion industry of the twentieth century, which in large part, perpetuated the myth of the perfect body type and led to body image issues for millions of young women, or the worrying tendency that Asians have, of wanting fair skin. Biases in books over the years have also had significant impact. Now, however, if the same biases were to get extended into algorithms they can wreak havoc in people's lives. We are all going to be dealing with agents and not humans. In the near-future where digital agents will help us through many things, imagine a digital security agent who is biased against Asians or a toy that thinks all girls want is to grow up and be fair princesses of a certain shape.

Jobs and inequality: While technology-based disruption is nothing new, what is worrying is the number of jobs that are likely to be lost and the significant role that technology will exercise in our lives. AI will automate many of the tasks of today. While the long run may create more jobs, the short term may see huge disruptions. 4IR will be a force of disruption, excluding people with less education and fewer skills. People will constantly have to learn new skills to stay relevant and those who won't, will find themselves lost in the new age. Governments and businesses will need to up the ante on jobs and reskilling. Talent development, lifelong learning, and career reinvention are going to be critical to the future workforce. Activities most likely to be automated include, physical ones in predictable environments—operating machines or preparing fast food. Data collection and data processing can possibly be done better and faster by machines than humans. This could impact jobs in many areas like paralegal, accounting, mortgage origination and back office transaction processing.[17] Automation is less likely to impact jobs that involve managing people, applying some kind of expertise, and social interactions.[18]

The algorithms that will rule our world will also lead to significant income disparities as they exercise disproportionate control over our lives. As we are already witnessing today, the economic benefits of technology and its wealth creation ability can serve the interests of small, powerful groups above the rest. The owners of the AI algorithms would gain disproportionately in such a society. According to the *World Economic Forum Global Risks Report 2017*, 'the Fourth Industrial Revolution has the potential to raise income levels and improve the quality of life for all people. But today, the economic benefits of the Fourth Industrial Revolution are becoming more concentrated among a small group. This increasing inequality can lead to political polarisation, social fragmentation, and lack of trust in institutions. To address these challenges, leaders in the public and private sectors need to have a deeper commitment to more inclusive development and equitable growth that lifts up all people.'[19]

The issue of social responsibility stemming because of automation and Artificial Intelligence is becoming increasingly relevant today. It is perhaps time to rethink what responsibility means in the new world.

AI will upend existing corporate and social structures

- Machines will take over most mundane, repetitive jobs. Companies will need to innovate around design and solutions to stay competitive
- Job losses will happen in the short run as industries struggle to evolve business models
- Social structures may be increasingly under stress. Governments and corporations will need to account for social responsibility in new ways, such as universal basic income, universal healthcare, skilling and measures that check the reign of technology
- Transparency and trust will become integral to algorithm design and become a part of business responsibility

CHALLENGE 3
Clean Energy will transform, but lead to stranded assets and new disruptions

The world has progressed in leaps and bounds because of our ability to harness energy. Most of the energy across the world has been generated through burning of various types of fuels such as, coal in large power plants and factories, and petrol in our vehicles. Coal and petroleum are highly polluting, leading to significant carbon emissions and climate change. It has now become more or less an accepted fact that the shift to renewable energy is not just desirable but urgently required to continue the quality of life we need to survive.

India, one of the world's fastest growing carbon emitters, may soon have the distinction of never needing another coal plant, according to The Energy and Resources Institute (TERI).[20] India has enough coal plants running or under construction, to meet its demands up to

2026, after which it is believed that renewables will only become cost competitive but a viable option to cater to India's energy needs. The last coal power stations are expected to be closed by 2050. However, the biggest impact around emissions can only happen if Indian corporations shift to renewables.

Reports indicate that the expansion of wind and solar power will enable India to exceed the targets set in the Paris Agreement (the target was 40 per cent by 2030) by almost half and entirely remove the need for new coal fired power stations. India will be able to cater to 57 per cent of its electricity capacity from renewable energy by 2027.[21] The government push as well as consumer adoption is fuelling the demand for solar energy. India unveiled the world's biggest solar farm this year and many such large installations are planned to increase solar capacity. NITI Aayog's India's Renewable Electricity Roadmap 2030,[22] says that India's major advantage today and going forward, is that its renewable energy potential is vast and largely untapped. India's large and untapped energy potential is not only a major advantage for India today, but also in the future. Recent estimates indicate that India's solar potential is greater than 10,000 GW and its wind potential could be higher than 2,000 GW.[23] Solar is expected to contribute about 50 per cent of the renewable energy targets by 2022.[24] India is expected to be the third largest market in solar energy after US and China. At the end of the first quarter of 2017, installations had reached around 12.8 GW, a combination of utility scale projects and rooftop installations.[25] The forecast of 10 GW increase in solar this year would mean a 130 per cent increase year-on-year compared to the 4.3 GW installed last year.[26] Six Indian states now have an installed capacity of over 1 GW.[27] Solar tariffs have declined by 75 per cent since 2010.[28]

Storage takes shape

With the increase in renewable energy, storage of renewable power is gaining importance. The Solar Energy Corporation of India (SECI), the government-owned company tasked with development of the solar energy sector in the country, is now issuing tenders for setting up solar plants with MW capacity storage units. India's biggest utility, National Thermal Power Corporation (NTPC) is seeking bidders to add a 6MW/24MWh battery energy storage system (BESS) to a 17MW PV plant in Manglutan, South Andaman.[29] These requirements have been largely brought on by the fact that renewable power generation is not always stable. For example, solar energy can be generated only in the day while wind power generation varies with wind speeds. Excess renewable energy, as of now, is simply wasted if not consumed. With India's increasing thrust on renewable power, it is becoming imperative that electricity storage should take centre stage in establishing reliable and stable sources of power. However, till recently, storage of large quantities of electricity was quite a challenge. With new technologies coming in, large quantities of electricity can be stored electrochemically in battery packs that can be the size of a television set or can even be scaled up to the size of shipping containers. Lithium-ion batteries, the kind used in cellphones, have emerged as a popular choice for electricity storage. However newer technologies such as 'flow batteries' are also entering the market.

The India Energy Storage Alliance estimates that the storage market is expected to grow to 70 GW by 2022.[30] Batteries will be used for electric vehicles, for roof top solar installations in homes and grid connected batteries will be used by power plants to balance electricity supply and demand as the installation of renewable energy ramps up. A report by Delhi-based Council on Energy, Environment and Water (CEEW) states that the energy storage market for off-grid renewable energy in India will be worth Rs 16,500 crores by 2022.[31] Rooftop solar alone will make up 80 per cent of this, touching Rs 13,000 crore. The Ministry of New and Renewable Energy's target to install 10,000 micro-grid/500 MW of micro and mini-grids will offer an additional opportunity to the tune of Rs 3,300 crore for battery manufacturers.[32]

Transportation goes electric

New advances in electrification of all modes of transport such as automobiles, trains, aircraft and ships are increasingly being announced. The International Energy Agency (IEA) is expected to reach the United Nations Framework Convention on Climate Change (UNFCCC) Paris Agreement targets of deploying 100 million electric cars by 2030.[33] According to the NITI Aayog, India can cut its energy demand by 64 per cent by making its transportation industry electric.[34] This has significant implications for India's electricity sector and economy, and supports India's ambitious renewable energy goals while saving money, providing jobs, and strengthening industry.

The Indian government under the 2020 plan of the National Electric Mobility Mission[35] plans to create a potential demand for 5–7 million electric vehicles (EV), including buses, light commercial vehicles, two-wheelers and three-wheelers, as well as electric cars.[36] In the same year, the government plans to invest up to Rs 23,500 crore ($4.3 billion) to promote demand, and create a sustainable infrastructure for the electric automotive industry.[37] The government has also launched a scheme called FAME (Faster Adoption and Manufacturing of Hybrid & Electric Vehicles, 2015) for promoting electric vehicles.[38] Most automobile companies have announced plans for EVs and even the cab sharing company, Ola has started a pilot on electric vehicles in India.

Keeping in mind the push towards electric vehicles, there is considerable excitement over the need for electric charging stations which will power these vehicles. There is much to be done, since at present, EV-charging stations in India stand at just a couple of hundred. This space is likely to see considerable action in the coming years as the EV infrastructure will need charging sites for various uses. Offices, multiplexes, residential complexes are the likely places where these are expected to come up soon. This will change the current fuelling paradigm where fuelling can only be done at petrol pumps. There will broadly be two kinds of charging: trip continuation charging and destination charging. Destination charging will be at the end of a journey and either at a home or office and will utilise lower voltage AC charging to deliver energy into the vehicle. Trip continuation charging will be done at a service station and will involve fast charging.

Recent announcements from automotive companies like Mahindra, utility companies like NTPC and Tata Power as well as solar energy companies have focused on their plans to set up EV charging stations. Ola has also announced plans to set up charging stations in the cities that they operate in.[39]

There are several implications for the grid with several thousand EV charging stations coming up. The foremost being the increase in electricity demand with a complete new sector moving towards electrification. This could also put a strain on residential and commercial transformers. In order to mitigate these risks, multiple technological solutions are being evolved so that grid reliability and stability can be maintained.

Utilities are under pressure to transform

India is one of the top five electricity consumers in the world. Keeping in mind India's growth ambitions and rapid urbanisation, electricity consumption is likely to increase further. India's energy infrastructure is not only centralised with utilities, it is also designed to handle only traditional power sources. However, utilities worldwide are transforming and older infrastructure is being changed to create smarter grids, which in turn are able to work with distributed sources of energy such as homes and offices with solar rooftops, wind farms and traditional power from utilities to provide high quality, reliable electricity supply, efficient billing and more customer services.

While the push towards renewables is good for the world at large, it is also causing significant disruption. It is not just the energy producers who are having to move out of fossil-based fuel production. Companies downstream, who use fossil fuel for their products are getting impacted too; some will shut down, others will innovate, and many will move towards making investments in renewable energy. Distribution companies will have to think of charging points rather than traditional distribution of petrol, gas or electricity. Houses will have to be rejigged to put up solar panels and storage batteries. Transportation going electric will imply that automobile companies must produce electric vehicles—not just cars, but buses and trucks too. Industries that consume large amounts of energy will move towards renewables too and that will necessitate changes to how they look at energy. This disruption will be a major one impacting each and every facet of business and life. Several utilities have made investments in coal. With declining costs of renewable energy, consumers are likely to shift to the lower cost renewable energy. Secondly, concerns about pollution are forcing companies to shut down power plants. These assets are called 'stranded assets'.

Simply put, stranded assets are those that have suffered from anticipated or premature write-downs, and arise due to regulatory changes, changes in market forces and socio-political forces. Stranded assets have manifold implications. People lose jobs as the plants are not operational; banks face non-performing assets as the planned future cash flows from these assets dry up. The land on which the plant is set up becomes locked and is unavailable for other economic activities. Customers who previously relied on the power company will now have to look at other sources. There would be implications for downstream activities too. Thus, the coal producer would also face stranded assets and employment opportunity in that sector could also dry up. There will be an impact upstream too. Power distribution companies will have power lines that may become stranded. Just as the disruption caused by automobiles made horse carriages stranded assets, renewable energy is causing power plants to become stranded assets.

In India, as the share of renewable energy increases, new technology-based solutions will need to be introduced to help create smart grids that can manage transactions in a transparent way with several thousand electricity buyers and sellers. A new initiative called the National Smart Grid Mission (NSGM) has been started under the aegis of the Power ministry which is pioneering the smart grid programme and has around fourteen smart grid projects under implementation. While changing India's complete energy infrastructure will take time, an increased focus on smart grid and smart city infrastructure is likely to be seen in the near future for increasing efficiency and reliability.

Clean energy will disrupt the status quo and impact utilities, transportation, manufacturing and almost everything that runs on electricity

- Companies' transition to renewable energy will involve significant investments.
- The electricity and electricals sector will be almost completely overhauled—smart meters, IOT-based electrical systems, smart homes and apps that manage energy usage will become prominent.
- Electrical utilities will transform from government-owned monopolies into consumer-facing services companies.
- The energy transition will lead to new investments by manufacturing plants and utilities and the shutting down of polluting units leading to financial stress and sometimes increase in costs.
- For sectors and companies undergoing massive shifts, value creation and profitability will need new models of sustainable growth and business responsibility.

CHALLENGE 4
Manufacturing will become decentralised and digital

Manufacturing in the 4IR is expected to go through a radical shift. This is brought on by the emergence of 3D printing, new emerging materials and trust-based systems such as blockchain.

3D printing could transform manufacturing and healthcare

3D printing is a process of additive manufacturing using a digital file and a specialised printer. It allows for the creation of complex shapes and, for the longest time was used to make prototypes. 3D printing will enable manufacturing of goods using various kinds of materials and a printer. While it may not replace the big factory, it will certainly democratise manufacturing, allowing multiple smaller and more local manufacturing hubs to emerge. This has actually been the dream of environmentalists and activists, who have long blamed centralised manufacturing and distribution as a key detriment to the creation of a circular economy. This method of manufacturing actually revolutionises the entire concept of supply chain and cuts down transportation and logistics.

3D printing is also expected to transform sources of value. The current system of manufacturing is geared towards creating profit through the replication of a design in a large manufacturing facility and its subsequent distribution and sale. 3D manufacturing is expected to change this as the value is now expected to be gained from the new design. The customers of the future will simply buy a new dress design instead of a dress. They would then download the digital file, print it on their own or shared 3D printer and use it. It also throws up interesting possibilities. For instance in the textile industry, a dress could be made out of recyclable material. Once consumers have worn the dress long enough, they could simply insert it back into the printer and convert it into something else. This could potentially transform retail as this may enable both production and design at the point of sale. Customer experience takes centre stage in this type of manufacturing. This can allow endless customisation, quick and easy repairs, recycling and easy upgrades.

The most unexpected use of 3D printing to date has been in healthcare. Bio-printing is now enabling customised printing of bones to fit the exact shape and size needed to replace a missing or damaged bone. In the future, stem cells from the patient could be used to print a host of other body parts. This is expected to be revolutionary, as the current practice of transplants is fraught with the potential risk of rejection by a patient's body.

The risks of 3D printing are also immense. Scientists fear that this technology could be used to enhance and develop human capacity beyond current capabilities. For example, should we consider creating and transplanting new lungs that oxygenate blood more efficiently, even in a more polluted environment? Should we make bones that are flexible and more resilient? Hearts that can pump faster and better? Who will control quality? Would this be a disincentive for living healthier lives?

Knowing the chain

The biggest problem with many of the products we use currently is the verification of source. For example, how does the consumer know if a certified product is organic? How do we really know if the diamonds are ethically sourced? Many of these new ways of providing transparency and accountability are being facilitated by a new technology called blockchain. The blockchain (or distributed ledger) is the technology that powers the digital currency, bitcoin. It is an open, distributed ledger that can record transactions between two parties in an efficient and verifiable manner. One can imagine blockchain as a giant spreadsheet that runs on millions of computers. The blockchain is distributed, open source and everyone can see what is going on. In the blockchain world, contracts are embedded in the digital code. This code is stored in transparent, shared databases where it is protected from deletion, revision, and tampering. In this world, every agreement, every process and every transaction has a digital record and signature that can be identified, validated, stored, and shared. Futurists anticipate that the need for intermediaries like lawyers and bankers is likely to disappear. Transactions are likely to become frictionless.

There are many new uses for blockchain that are emerging almost every day. This new way of transacting is supporting business responsibility in many ways by supporting green supply chains, measuring water use, emissions management and supporting the sharing economy. (See *TN 4: Blockchains and Responsible Business* for a detailed understanding of blockchains.)

Food companies are evaluating blockchain for extending the traceability of their products. If a farm field is certified as organic, this certification enters the blockchain as a contract. When the produce is moved to another intermediary, the contract containing details of the produce is passed on to the intermediary. This link continues till the food item or a product manufactured out of it reaches the customer. The customer can have a complete record of all the ingredients in the product providing assurance that the product contains what it is supposed to. This can serve a dual purpose by enhancing food safety and letting the customer know exactly where the produce came from.

The same process can be used for certifying gemstones or other rare materials. The mining sector in India (taking into account atomic, major and minor minerals and fuel) made up 2.4 per cent of the GDP in 2014–2015.[40] India produces eighty-eight minerals including four fuel minerals, three atomic minerals, twenty-six metallic and non-metallic minerals and fifty-five minor minerals (including building and other materials). Traditionally, the mining industry worked on the linear economy model, where resources were harvested in order to manufacture products, and then disposed of as waste at the end of their lives. There is a paradigm shift today, as mining companies are moving towards becoming a part of the circular economy, which works on the principle that mineral resources will be used in a 'responsible' manner to manufacture products that in turn, can become renewable mineral resources. Going forward, blockchain could take centre stage as the driver for innovation in the whole mining supply chain. Real time data and on-site information will mean that the general public and consumers will have access to data and social media platforms and can voice their opinion on a product generated in a specific mine. In addition to this, reuse and recycling of materials could impact the quantum of materials needed.

As the degree of a country's industrialisation continues to improve, the amount of metal consumption rapidly increases and, so too, the recyclable metal scrap. Developing the technology and market for the secondary use of metal is conducive to relieving the pressure on mineral resources supply, energy consumption and indeed, the environment itself. For instance, recovering aluminum from beverage cans, manganese, zinc and hydrargyrum from discarded batteries; transforming waste plastic into petrol and diesel, etc., could be thought of in large-scale terms. It is possible to reuse aluminum scrap collected in the society recovery network by mixing it with primary aluminum, consequently forming a closed loop and, thereby, developing a secondary aluminum industry. Utilising aluminum scrap not only decreases the development of primary aluminum and aluminum product waste, but also saves large amounts of electricity. It is estimated that recycling a kilogram of aluminum scrap can save about 46 kWh of electric energy.

Blockchain is also expected to improve water usage. Companies draw water from local sources for their operations. Water withdrawal can be recorded on distributed ledgers. Water additions and withdrawals can then be tracked at different places within the factory premises using smart meters. This recording could enable companies to track their water usage efficiently and effectively. A US-based research group has also created a new use for blockchain in purification of fracking water that is generated when oil is produced. (It takes up to ten barrels of water to produce one barrel of oil; this water cannot be reused as it is highly toxic.) The WaterToken.io represents the process that relies on three patented, licensed purification methods: ultrafiltration, coagulation, and ozone (O3) generation.[41] With this the water can be reused over and over again.

New Manufacturing will lead to new sources of value and experiences

- Manufacturing will become circular by becoming more decentralised, use fewer resources and enable repair, reuse and recycling. Enabling technologies such as 3D printing and blockchain will play an increasing role in making this a reality.
- These gains, though, may not cut across all industries. Easy manufacturing driven by 3D printing could also lead to some industries increasing the burden on natural resources and generation of waste if not managed properly.
- 3D printing will change sources of value. Intellectual property will take primacy.

- 3D printing in healthcare driven by printing of organs will raise many ethical and moral issues. New types of healthcare companies and new forms of business responsibility challenges will emerge.
- Trust based systems such as blockchain will replace third party institutions. The role of the middleman will increasingly be under threat.
- New manufacturing will disrupt retail. Customer experiences will go through a radical shift. Retailers will have to ensure that data, design and intellectual property are protected.

CHALLENGE 5
Finance gets digital, sustainable and social

Responsibility has now entered the hallowed halls of the financial world. The business world has for long been focussed on creating strategies for long-term value creation and financial performance. The understanding of how business organisations impact society has been limited. The push to create greater impact came from the financial world when in the beginning of 2018, Larry Fink, Chairman and Chief Executive Officer of BlackRock, Inc. wrote an open letter to the chief them of some of the world's largest companies.[42] He asked companies to contribute to society if they wanted the support of BlackRock. Coming from the firm that manages over six trillion US dollars trillion in assets, this is a very big deal. The letter says, 'We also see many governments failing to prepare for the future, on issues ranging from retirement and infrastructure to automation and worker retraining. As a result, society is increasingly turning to the private sector and asking that companies respond to broader societal challenges. Indeed, the public expectations of your company have never been greater. Society is demanding that companies, both public and private, serve a social purpose. To prosper over time, every company must not only deliver financial performance, but also show how it makes a positive contribution to society. Companies must benefit all of their stakeholders, including shareholders, employees, customers, and the communities in which they operate.'

DIGITAL

The financial world is changing. A major development has been the rise of cryptocurrencies like bitcoin. The development of blockchain (See *TN 4: Blockchains and Responsible Business* for a detailed understanding of blockchains) has brought into question the role of central banks. Though not a legal tender in most countries (Japan being a rare exception), the idea has got bankers thinking and some countries are even thinking about setting up their own cryptocurrencies. Although originally used for bitcoins, blockchains can be extensively used for property transfers, payments and investments.

This financial revolution is better known as fintech. Global investments in fintech ventures have grown by 75 per cent between 2010 and 2015 to reach $2.3billion in 2015.[43] The stakeholders have gained immensely by cutting down contracting costs, communication costs and intermediation costs. They have served as a means of increased financial inclusion, which is demonstrated by the fact that in a poor country like Kenya, M-Pesa has reached 89 per cent of households within four years.[44] The activities of fintech can be broadly categorised as:[45]

- Payment services and market infrastructure
    - » E-money and mobile money products
    - » Overlay of services on existing products
    - » Use of blockchain technology
- Leveraging transactions data and other sources of data for credit appraisal
    - » Transforming data from e-commerce and payments platforms (Flipkart and PayTm)
    - » Mobile phone usage data
    - » Social network related data
- Deposits, Lending and capital raising
    - » Crowdfunding
    - » Peer to Peer lending networks

- Investment management
  - » Automated processing and dissemination of investment advice

Banking is changing too, moving from physical to virtual locations. ATMs have already eliminated the need to visit a bank as cash is now available 24/7. The advent of internet banking have made visits to physical branches even less frequent. One can now undertake financial transactions at any time. The use of cheque leaves is becoming rare. Players like PayTm, PhonePe and the government sponsored BHIM have radically transformed the payments scenario even further in the country. Vegetable vendors, small shops, and small-scale enterprises have all benefitted immensely. The change has not happened just at the level of the individual. The bankers' tasks of record-keeping and reconciliations have become speedier and accurate with real-time accessibility enabling them to provide superior customer service.

Lending and borrowing has changed too. Earlier, the sources of funding were limited. One went to a money-lender, a bank or a financial institution to raise funds. These traditional channels have all gone digital allowing one to raise money much faster and more easily. The development of crowdfunding mechanisms for instance makes it easier to obtain funds as the information gap between the borrower and the lender decreases.

It is not just banking and payments systems that have been revolutionised. Non-banking activities have also undergone a rapid transformation. Take the case of insurance. Till a few years ago, if one wanted an insurance policy, one had to go around hunting for an insurance agent who would then help you make a decision on which policy to buy. In many cases, he would either hide or obfuscate inconvenient terms. Today, an insurance policy can be purchased online anytime and even compared with policies from several different providers. The premium can be paid anytime, claims lodged anytime and anywhere and even documents submitted online. One can pay the premium anytime, lodge claims anytime and anywhere and even submit documents online.

Investments have also undergone a rapid transformation. One can invest in shares and mutual funds from the convenience of one's home. Buy, sell, redeem—all can be done instantly. Investment advisory services are gradually moving to Artificial Intelligence and machine learning to make better investment decisions. With information availability becoming global and a level playing field being brought about by regulation, one can trade in multiple geographies concurrently.

Yet several concerns remain. Throughout history, money has been a man or woman's most intimate resource. We've always been scared of losing it, being swindled, or worrying about whether it is earning adequate returns. Fintech both alleviates and aggravates these problems. Security is the largest concern—will my money remain safe? Hacking, phishing, vishing, etc., dot the terminology that is at the heart of the security of one's money. Trust is at the heart of any financial transaction, which can easily be broken when financial institutions trade your private personal or financial information for gains. Accessibility is another critical aspect of money. For instance, if I lose my phone and hence cannot receive an OTP, I shall then be completely cut-off from the financial world. Thus, accessibility is another critical issue that faces fintech. Regulation is trying to keep pace with the rapid changes that the financial world is seeing. Yet, gaps remain that are often exploited by fraudulent intermediaries.

It becomes incumbent upon financial institutions to ensure that safety, security, trust and accessibility of a person's financial data is maintained.

SUSTAINABLE

The launch of the Equator Principles in June 2003 led to commercial banks taking the initiative to move towards developing a common set of environmental and social standards.[46] The Equator Principles provide a framework for banks to review, evaluate and mitigate, or avoid environmental and social impacts, as well as risks associated with projects that they finance. The principles are based on the

International Finance Corporation's (IFC) environmental and social safeguard policies. Almost 75 per cent of the project loan volumes worldwide follow the Equator Principles. Some of the other significant voluntary international sustainability mechanisms for the finance sector include:

IFC Performance Standards: The Sustainability Framework articulates IFC's strategic commitment to sustainable development and is an integral part of the approach to risk management.[47]

UNEP Finance Initiative: UNEP seeks to encourage the better implementation of sustainability principles at all levels of operations in financial institutions, namely through the incorporation of environmental, social and governance factors (ESG) in risk analyses.[48]

UN Principles for Responsible Investments: The United Nations-supported 'Principles for Responsible Investment' (PRI) is an international network of investors working together to put the six principles for responsible investment into practice. Its goal is to understand the implications of sustainability for investors and support signatories to incorporate these issues into their investment decision-making and ownership practices.[49]

UN Global Compact: The United Nations Global Compact is an initiative to encourage businesses worldwide to adopt sustainable and socially responsible policies, and to report on their implementation.

Carbon Disclosure Project: The CDP is an organisation based in the United Kingdom which works with shareholders and corporations to disclose the greenhouse gas emissions of major corporations.[50]

CERES Principles: These are a ten-point code of corporate environmental ideals to be publicly endorsed by companies as an environmental mission statement or ethic.[51]

For the significantly sustainability-sensitive industries, the relevant principles are:

Sector policies	*Policy document*
Mining	Equator Principles
Oil and gas	Equator Principles
Power generation	Equator Principles

And for the most critical policy issues:

Issue policies	*Policy document*
Biodiversity	Equator Principles/Global Compact
Climate change	Carbon Disclosure Project/Global Compact
Toxics	Global Compact

In 2002, a global coalition of non-governmental organisations (NGOs) including Friends of Earth, Rainforest Action Network, World Wildlife Fund (UK) and the Berne Declaration came together to promote sustainable finance in the commercial sector.[52] This informal network subsequently evolved into BankTrack, whose vision for a sustainable finance sector was expressed in the Collevecchio Declaration of January 2003.

The Collevecchio Declaration guides the financial industry (FI) to:[53]

- **Commit to sustainability:** FIs must expand their missions from ones that prioritise profit maximisation to a vision of social and environmental sustainability.
- **Commit to doing no harm:** FIs should commit to doing no harm by preventing and minimising the environmentally and/or socially detrimental impacts of their portfolios and their operations.
- **Commit to responsibility:** FIs should bear full responsibility for the environmental and social impacts of their transactions.
- **Commit to accountability:** FIs must be accountable to their stakeholders, particularly those that are affected by the activities and side effects of companies they finance.

- **Commit to transparency:** FIs must be transparent to stakeholders, not only through robust, regular and standardised disclosure, but also through being responsive to stakeholder needs for specialised information on FIs' policies, procedures and transactions.
- **Commit to sustainable markets and business practices:** FIs should ensure that markets are more capable of fostering sustainability by actively supporting public policy, regulatory and/or market mechanisms which facilitate sustainability and that foster the full cost accounting of social and environmental externalities.

Adherence to these principles is bringing about a change in the financial world. Banks are increasingly looking at sustainability-related metrics while evaluating projects. But what they also need to do is create blacklists that include industries with extensive negative externalities and should abstain from lending to these industries. Rather than a blanket ban, the banks could look at actions taken by firms to reduce the impact of negative externalities. Measured carefully, the mitigations can easily be incorporated into both the social return on investment and economic rate of return calculations. Approved projects must be carefully monitored on sustainability metrics post commissioning to ensure that mitigation of negative externalities is carried out and unsustainable projects don't slip through.

Another area that the banks can focus on is information sharing. There are times when a project rejected by one bank is accepted by another bank. Especially when the project has been rejected on sustainability grounds, the information sharing mechanism can enable banks to have a sharper analysis of the projects.

Banks and other lending institutions need to build strong capabilities to evaluate and measure the positive and negative externalities of a project. This requires investment in training and periodic scrutiny to ensure that adequate checks and balances are in place to monitor if appropriate evaluations are carried out. (See *TN 5:*

Understanding Climate Finance which details the various instruments that banks can use for managing climate related issues.)

SOCIAL

As they say, finance is the lifeline of any business. This is true even of the government. Over time, one sees that governments are generally short of funds. They face innumerable challenges. Across the world, two billion people do not have access to safe water, health care, or financial services. Over a billion people are still without access to electricity. Millions of children lack access to education or immunisation. Serious and large-scale problems need solutions. The private sector has surplus funds while the social/government sector is desperately in need of funds. Thus, it makes immense sense for the public sector to pitch in and help the social/government sector. Yet, the private sector is wary of investing in these black box projects. One way out of this situation is impact investing, which expands the role of the private sector in addressing the world's most serious problems.

Impact investing goes by various names like socially responsible investing, social investing, mission driven investing, etc. It is defined by the Global Impact Investing Network (GIIN) as: 'Investments made into companies, organisations, and funds with the intention to generate measurable social and environmental impact alongside a financial return.'[54] Although traditional investors have been foundations, development-related financial institutions and high net worth individuals have also contributed.

Impact investing has also created new financial instruments like Social Impact Bonds (SIB). These are contracts with the public sector in which a commitment is made to pay for improved social outcomes resulting in public sector savings.[55] In a SIB an organisation issuing the bonds raises funds from various sources. These sources include private-sector investors, charities or foundations. These funds are provided to service providers to cover their operating costs. Outcomes are decided in advance. If these outcomes are achieved, the government proceeds with payments to the bond-issuing organisation or to the investors.

The term 'bond' is really a misnomer; they represent future contracts on social outcomes. SIBs are also known by other names like Pay-for-Success bonds or Pay-for-Benefits bonds. An investor provides funding for an intervention. The investor is usually a private player. This money is then used as working capital for a service provider. The service provider is responsible for the social services delivery, and, the attainment of agreed outcomes. They are also required to make data available for these projects on need basis. The ultimate outcomes payer is the government or commissioner. It often determines the outcomes metrics and payments terms. An evaluator may be used for assessing the agreed outcomes and their impact. Finally, there are the beneficiaries who are the ultimate recipients of benefits from the project.

Social Impact Bonds (SIBs) can have different models and structures. These depend on the composition and the relationship among the actors involved, their functions, the process of structuring the deal and the accountability regarding the delivery of the expected outcomes.

Two models of SIBs have emerged—SIB funds and individual SIBs. SIB funds can issue multiple contracts dealing with the same, or similar social issues. On the other hand, individual SIBs operate one payment contract at a time.

In India, the growth of this sector was buoyed by the passage of Companies Act 2013 that mandated companies to spend 2 per cent of their profits on CSR. Sustainability programmes spend over and above this. The future growth in impact investing is likely to come from massive pent-up demand at the bottom of the pyramid, the push towards green models of growth and reconfiguration of social initiatives driven by public policy and private participation.

The Paris Agreement (COP21) has provided a significant push to green growth. With most countries around the world having pledged to reduce or cap their carbon emissions, a large opportunity has been created for producers and equipment manufacturers of renewables. With India at the forefront of renewables, this market is huge. Here, impact investing can play a significant role by providing funds to help reduce global warming effects.

Increasingly, private players are funding the provision of public goods. Much work has taken place on toll roads, bridges and airports. An increased push into other sectors that are critical for development, like healthcare, water supply, irrigation, etc., could usher in prosperity for the teeming millions. Impact investing is an ideal vehicle to proceed in these areas. Social impact bonds can be very useful in shifting the risks away from the government to the other stakeholders.

The LOHAS (Lifestyles Of Health And Sustainability) segment has become a darling of the impact investing community. It aims at consumers who, individually want their products to reflect their personal values and, collectively aspire to positively influence society with their purchases.[56] These consumers span the food, retail, real estate and transportation space. These consumers would pay a premium for an environmentally friendly product. This tends to be an attractive market for the impact investors and tends to have significant social impact.

Despite several impediments, impact investing is expected to grow and become part of the mainstream finance. (See *TN 6: Impact Investing* for details.)

4IR will transform finance while creating new models and unforeseen risks

- Rapid changes in business models
- The rise of fintech and slow disappearance of banks as we know them
- New ways of borrowing and lending
- New ways of managing investments
- Impact investing to grow rapidly.
- Sustainability standards and lending practices will incorporate these standards in decision making.

To address the challenges of the future new mechanisms and frameworks are required urgently.

CASE STUDY I

THE UTKRISHT IMPACT BOND

While India has seen a significant reduction in maternal and infant mortality rates over the past twenty-five years, the rates are still high by global standards. The statistics are startling—in Rajasthan the maternal mortality is at 244 per 100,000 per live births while infant mortality is at 47 per 1,000 live births. An estimated 80,000 children die every year in Rajasthan alone.

Over the past decade, there has been a significant shift from home births to hospital births, but efforts to improve the quality and consistency of care in hospitals have mainly concentrated on public providers.

Private facilities—used for over 25 per cent of all institutional deliveries in Rajasthan[57]—are filling the gaps in state maternal and new-born health provision and are utilised by women of all socio-economic backgrounds, but have not been a focus of improvement of quality of care. It is clear that if India is to further reduce its maternal and new-born mortality rate, improving standards and quality of care in private facilities must be prioritised.

The Social Impact bond – Utkrisht

Utkrisht Impact Bond was launched in 2017 and will run for three years. As stated previously, impact bonds are an innovative way to finance development. They are completely focused on outcomes and have the potential to leverage private investor capital to address some of the world's greatest challenges.

The bond aims to reduce the number of mother and baby deaths by improving the quality of maternal care in Rajasthan's health facilities. The Utkrisht (meaning excellent) Impact Bond is also the first to be launched that uses genuine private capital raised from private investors. Private capital from UBS Optimus Foundation will front the costs to improve the quality of health services in private health facilities in Rajasthan, and HLFPPT (Hindustan Latex Family Planning Promotion Trust) and

Population Services International (PSI) will use that capital to improve the quality of care in facilities by supporting up to 440 Small Healthcare Organisations (SHCOs) to improve services, meet new government quality standards and adhere to them over the long term. This will also help them become accredited. USAID and Merck for Mothers will pay back the investment only if certain targets are met.

With full adoption by the Indian government as the potential next step, this bond will provide an essential intermediate step as proof of concept for healthcare interventions and outcomes-based contracts throughout India.

How does Utkrisht work?

Utkrisht bond, along with the upfront funder, UBS Optimus Foundation, provides the initial working capital so that the service providers—PSI and HLFPPT—can begin work with the private facilities in Rajasthan. In a further innovation, all implementation partners are also co-investors, contributing between the three of them more than 20 per cent of the capital requirement. Under the scheme, all parties will be treated equally, fully aligning the risks and rewards. The outcome payers—USAID and MSD for Mothers—will pay back the investor the original amount invested, plus additional returns if predetermined targets are met. Progress will be assessed regularly by independent verifier Mathematica throughout the three-year programme. The impact bond was designed by Palladium, who will also act as the implementation manager throughout the term.

PSI has adapted its Engage, Launch and Support quality improvement framework and will be implementing this in fourteen districts of Rajasthan. HLFPPT will be working in nineteen districts to support and engage private medical facilities through capacity building, mentoring and ongoing support.

The outcomes

The success of the Utkrisht bond will be judged on whether healthcare facilities are able to achieve the new certification standard developed by the National Accreditation Board of Hospitals and Healthcare Providers, and the Federation of Obstetric and Gynaecological Societies of India. This means that, for the first time, quality maternal care will be certified and fully transparent in private health facilities.

The project will reach up to 600,000 pregnant women with improved care during delivery and save as many as 10,000 lives over a five-year period by improving the quality of private healthcare facilities that support a region of 75 million people. According to World Health Organisation (WHO) standards for cost effectiveness of saving a life, this is a highly cost- effective partnership.

CASE STUDY II

YES BANK – MAINSTREAMING SUSTAINABILITY IN GLOBAL FINANCE

In 2004, Rana Kapoor founded YES BANK which grew rapidly to become the fourth largest private sector bank in India. As a full-service bank, YES BANK operates in the areas of corporate, retail and SME banking, financial markets, investment banking, corporate finance, branch banking, business and transaction banking, and wealth management business lines across India.

Since its inception, the bank has felt that it had a proactive role to play as a sustainability catalyst to overcome India's developmental challenges and help it move towards a low carbon growth path. It views sustainability as 'ensuring long-term business success by contributing towards economic & social development, a healthy environment and a stable society.'

By approaching sustainability with a 360-degree view, YES BANK aims to be a leader in mainstreaming sustainability and CSR both within the global financial sector as well as across a broader stakeholder spectrum.

The ethos of 'Responsible Banking' has been a key differentiator of YES BANK and is one of its six strategic pillars, along with Growth, Trust, Human Capital and Technology. The mission of Responsible Banking was to use innovative business solutions to create stakeholder value and to ensure that sustainability principles were integrated with the core business strategy and processes at the bank. Towards this end, their focus lay in building innovative models to engage with external and internal stakeholders. The key facets of responsible banking include:

- Mainstreaming sustainability through policy advocacy and thought leadership, using a multi-stakeholder approach
- Supporting innovative financial solutions to address a gamut of development issues including sustainable livelihood, food security, climate change mitigation and adaptation, public health, education and financial literacy
- Adhering to the highest levels of transparency to communicate the bank's environmental, social and governance performance
- Creating shared value through positive impact CSR

The bank seeks to nurture these relationships to create innovative, scalable and financially viable approaches towards national development. The Responsible Banking vertical shapes the bank's sustainability strategy and approach. The sustainability and CSR strategy is driven by the board, including its Managing Director and CEO, Rana Kapoor, under whose guidance the unit has taken shape. The bank has dynamically adapted its CSR and sustainability focus areas to the Sustainable Development Goals and the Paris Agreement.

Headed by a Chief Sustainability Officer, the Responsible Banking team consists of sustainability practitioners with strong experience in climate change advisory, environmental management, research, CSR and triple bottom line accounting and reporting.

For the bank, financing for climate action is a strategic focus area, and they are striving to create new market opportunities to finance India's massive developmental needs. The year 2015 was a significant year for the bank, as it launched India's first green bond. The bank raised Rs. 1000 crores ($ 160 million), which was then used to fund clean energy in India.

Sustainable Finance at YES BANK

Given YES BANK's keen interest in promoting sustainability and its expertise in the financial sector, sustainable finance became an important area under its ethos of responsible banking.

The strategic initiatives in sustainable finance are underlined by:

- Intent to contribute: The bank on the occasion of Conference of Parties (COP21) climate summit in Paris, has targeted to mobilise $5 billion from 2015 to 2020 for climate action through lending, investing and raising capital towards mitigation, adaptation and resilience and will holistically impact and aid India's target of meeting its Nationally Determined Contributions (NDCs).
- Strict adherence to policies: The bank, in a structured way, puts in place relevant policies and processes that help achieve the aforementioned targets. YES BANK has in place a detailed set of internal guidelines for its green bonds to be Green Bond Principles compliant. The bank also instituted an Environmental

& Social policy to guide its lending decisions, while its resource management is upheld by an Environmental Management Policy.

- Collaborative leadership: Through its membership of various bodies including UNEP FI, National Capital Finance Alliance, United Nations Global Compact, Green Bond Principles the bank aims to not only adopt international best practices, but also strengthen the sustainable finance operations in the bank and act as a catalyst for the sector in the country.

Emphasis on few sectors: The bank focuses on certain areas for implementation of its sustainable finance programme. These include

- **Renewables:** In 2016, the bank signed an agreement with the Indian Renewable Energy Development Agency (IREDA) to foster renewable energy (RE) development in India. The MoU will boost green energy financing and strengthen the bank's efforts towards meeting its COP21 commitment.
- **Energy efficiency:** YES BANK signed a charter with the Bureau of Energy Efficiency (BEE) for empanelment of Participating Financial Institutions (PFIs) under Partial Risk Guarantee Fund for Energy Efficiency (PRGFEE), which is expected to get the ball rolling for other banks/ NBFCs to join this league and contribute in promoting energy efficiency in India.

Innovative financial structures: The bank promotes the use of innovative structures to promote responsible banking. The issue of green bonds by the bank are examples of such innovative methods:

- **February, 2015:** In a significant step, YES BANK issued India's first-ever Green Bonds (AA+ by CARE). The bank is one of the first amongst emerging economies to raise an amount of rupees ten billion, in accordance with Green Bond Principles.
- **August, 2015:** The bank's second issuance of a ten-year green bond raised Rs 3.15 billion on a private placement basis with IFC. It was the first ever investment by IFC in an emerging markets' green bond issue in the world
- **September, 2016:** YES BANK raised Rs 330 crores (3.30 billion) through an issue of a seven-year Green Infrastructure Bonds to

FMO, the Dutch Development Bank, on a private placement basis. This is FMO's first investment in a Green Bond issued by a bank in India.

The amount raised is being used by YES BANK to finance green infrastructure projects in renewable energy, solar power, wind power, biomass, and small hydel projects. These bonds were issued on the lines of green bond principles. The use of the revenue raised was to be verified through a third-party audit, and subject to external annual review.

In January this year, the bank became the sole arranger and subscriber to India's first social affordable housing bond issued by Indiabulls Housing Finance for Rs 1,000 crores. On the occasion of World Environment Day 2018, YES BANK launched India's first ever Green Retail Liability product—'Green Future Deposit', the proceeds of which would be earmarked towards SDG aligned projects.

Triple bottom line reporting

The bank has established a framework to recognise, evaluate, monitor and manage the environmental and social facets in the day-to-day decision-making process. It has become imperative for banks to consider the triple-bottom-line approach while making credit decisions.

In line with its Responsible Banking strategy and practices, YES BANK took a holistic risk management approach by considering the environmental and social impact of its lending activities. In 2006, YES BANK implemented an Environment and Social Policy through which the bank integrated environmental and social risks into its overall credit risk assessment framework. The bank has voluntarily adopted this policy which is based on international frameworks such as IFC guidelines.

YES BANK aims to continue its sustainable development journey through innovative financial and positive impact initiatives in line with national priorities. Its many industry-first initiatives hold it in good stead to be the benchmark institution for inclusivity and sustainability within the country.

CHAPTER 7

Data

The Newest Link in the Responsibility Chain

As data volumes have expanded over the years, data storage and analysis has become a new science. 'Big data' is a term for the collection and interpretation of large volumes of data. Search engines like Google, social media sites and e-commerce sites, along with the proliferation of devices have all lead to exponential growth in data. Almost 90 per cent of the data in the world today has been created in the past two years. In 2012, data was forecast to double every two years through the year 2020. In 2020, the amount of digital data produced will exceed 40 zettabytes, which is the equivalent of 5,200 gigabytes for every man, woman and child on planet earth.[1] Data is not just collected by search engines and social media companies, it is collected by marketers, advertising agencies and data broking companies and, in fact, anyone who can gather data has been doing so over the past few years.

When we began our research in 2013, there was little realisation that corporate responsibility and data were so closely linked. But, the proof, one could well say, is in the pudding. Technology was considered to be the clean green alternative to the big bad world of manufacturing. Technology companies seldom released sustainability reports and if they did they invariably spoke of green office campuses, energy savings and one-off charity projects. The last five years, though, have brought about a significant change in public consciousness about data, who owns it and what's being done with it. The discussions at the World Economic Forum of 2018 have been focused on setting the agenda for responsibility, driven by the twin challenges of climate change and the speedy convergence towards a data-dominated world. The Indian prime minister's speech, too, spoke of these challenges at the World Economic Forum.

It all began in 2014 when the European Court of Justice (ECJ) ruled that 'irrelevant' and outdated data should be erased on request.[2] This came to be known as 'the right to be forgotten'. Prior to this, anything and everything that went online stayed online. False posts, misleading information, private data, embarrassing content could not be removed. The 'right to be forgotten' changed that, as people started sending information to Google asking for specific content to be removed. The big technology companies fought back and this, in fact, led in part to the debate becoming centre stage, about how much information companies have on people and what is being done with it.

Recognising the fact that recent advances in computing power and the ability to store large volumes of data have led to collection and analysis capabilities which can create correlations and remarkable insights, the debate over privacy and data picked up steam. Concerned citizens, bureaucrats and judiciary pointed out that big data is so powerful that it can easily reveal information about people and open them up to manipulation and abuse by companies and governments.

The European Union, after much debate passed the General Data Protection Regulation (GDPR) which became law in May 2018.

In India, and the world over, there is increasing agreement that data management is very much a part of the responsibility of a company. How data is gathered, how it is used and what it is used for are all things that need deeper scrutiny. Almost everything is under review, data laws, privacy settings, news sources and feeds and above all the big question—how do we ensure a responsible corporate attitude towards data in a world driven by ever-changing technology?

Our digital identity

We define ourselves by our name, where we live and what we do. For companies though, we have always been consumers. Traditionally, marketing has been driven by finding the right customers for a company's products. Telecom companies wanted to know which customers will buy more data or voice, fashion companies wanted to know style preferences and automotive companies wanted to know how the latest features on their vehicles would be viewed by potential customers. Various market research tools were used to capture this information—calls, face to face interviews, focus group discussions and more. Basis this research, marketers created print and television advertising that highlighted product attributes focusing on customer needs.

The digital age transformed marketing forever. Marketers could now reach a much wider audience. An audience across the globe connected through search engines, social media platforms and websites. Companies could now see in real time what kind of content this audience liked, which campaigns were working and how they could be more persuasive. The audience in the digital world also functioned differently. When they used free online services they told service providers and advertisers what they liked and disliked. What they bought, who their friends were, where they went and what they did. Thereby creating a digital identity which was increasingly a surprisingly accurate version of each individual. Take a look at what Facebook knows about anyone of us:

- It can recognise your face with its facial recognition algorithm
- It knows every event you attended or signed up for
- Your contacts, friends and family and when you became friends with them
- Every topic you ever clicked on
- It has the list of the companies whose ads you may have clicked on
- It knows every time you logged in and your entire timeline ever since you first joined Facebook
- Every place you ever visited
- Messages to and from friends
- All the photographs that you uploaded or liked

Using such rich information, data scientists, who knew exactly where to look, were easily able to identify people in anonymous data sets. Marketing then became even more targeted. Data over time did not just stay personal it became a highly profitable, successful tool.

This is only the tip of the iceberg. Almost every social platform and how you use it can provide an imprint of your digital identity. Online services let users not only interact with each other, but also share data, likes and preferences, images, video clips and even location data with transaction companies such as payments banks, appointment booking systems, insurance companies and anyone who has a digital presence.

These customer profiles are very valuable to companies and have transformed the advertising and marketing industry creating new businesses that mine the digital identities of millions of consumers. Potential customers are then bombarded with advertising and communication to induce the purchase of products or services. For instance, companies know what kind of toothpaste you buy, where you stay, where your children go to school and how to persuade you through them to buy the new car that you wanted to buy but have been delaying. Ad tech (short form of advertising technology) stands for the software and tools that help agencies and brands target, deliver, and analyse their digital advertising efforts. Programmatic advertising buys target audiences instead of time slots: think about buying ad space that reaches a particular demographic wherever it is. Traditionally, brands purchased prime-time TV spots and hoped that the right people were watching. Omnichannel marketing reaches target consumers across all channels—mobile, video, desktop, and more—within the context of how they've interacted with a brand (those seeing an ad of the company for the first time could receive a different message from those who have engaged with that brand many times). Omnichannel and programmatic aren't the only two tools within ad tech, but they are most often used with newer interpretations emerging almost daily; sometimes to the detriment of the customer. Companies are now beginning to change their ad spends by adding more measures to track efficacy. Nevertheless Facebook and Google have seen their ad revenues grow.

Ad tech, however, conceals a dirty secret. It is increasingly personal and relies on tracking people. Retargeting has been used by marketers to follow customers around. Small bits of code that were downloaded onto your computers and mobile phones enable companies to track customers no matter which website they visit. This small code constantly aggregates data and serves up appropriate content, campaigns and banners to entice customers into buying whatever they are selling. If you visited a clothing website or clicked on a banner and were surprised that no matter where you go you get information about the same apparel company, you are being tracked! A constant reminder to finalise the purchase.

However, ad tech is also not the only culprit. Most online users have possibly never read the terms of use of any of the social platforms and are entirely unaware of how much companies know about them and how far information about them has already travelled. People are not really paying attention to their privacy. A massive legal document appears on the screen and customers just click 'accept' by default because the legal language is beyond their comprehension. People who want to know that the boundaries aren't being crossed don't even know what the boundaries are.

On the bright side, our digital identity can help solve a host of issues around health, travel, governance and much more. Personalised medicine and an improved quality of care can become possible with seamless transfer of data between people, doctors and medical establishments. Governments can ease the general bureaucratic tangles and delays around public services, improve tax collection and improve transparency and accountability for public spends. But in the hands of the wrong people data can create chaos. To some extent the recent scandals have helped turn a spotlight on what lax laws and unbridled access to data can actually do.

Data, a marketing tool gone rogue

In May 2017, Google's announcement to link in-store credit card transactions to the digital profiles of its users online profiles gathered through YouTube, Gmail, Google Maps and more made its advertisers very happy. Doing so would allow it to show hard evidence to advertisers that its online ads lead to in-store purchases. While Google was the first company to make this formal link, many technology companies have been rushing to create comprehensive user profiles so that their free services can be monetised. Google's new program is now the subject of a Federal Trade Commission complaint filed by the Electronic Privacy Information Center in late July of 2017.[3]

In January 2018 data from a hugely popular fitness app called Strava was hacked.[4] The app has a feature that depicted a heat map visualisation to show where its users were jogging, walking or travelling at any given time. The map covered almost some three trillion GPS data points. After the hack, many security analysts showed that because many American military service members were Strava users, the hack had inadvertently revealed the locations of military bases and the movements of their personnel. A seemingly innocuous service had opened up a national security challenge leading to a public outcry with many leading voices stating the apparent concerns about privacy and security. Clearly, in today's world, data and privacy are public goods like water and air. However, when left loose or unfettered, data can be weaponised leaving millions vulnerable.

Data can be used in many unforeseen ways. The data analytics firm Cambridge Analytica allegedly used personal information from more than 50 million Facebook profiles to target US voters with personalised political advertisements based on their psychological profiles. Employees of the company were also filmed boasting of using manufactured sex scandals, fake news and dirty tricks to swing elections around the world. Cambridge Analytica has since then also been accused of influencing the vote on Brexit and the Indian elections.

This alarming revelation implies that our digital identity and footprint is a source of power to companies and people we know little or nothing about, people and companies whom we have possibly never even interacted with. Machine learning algorithms obtain data from social media streams combined with other sources and reveal more than our favourite websites, preferred products, reading preferences and so on. They can also disclose sexual orientation, political affiliations, our use of addictive substances and many more things that we would rather not reveal publicly. The difference between the factories that cause environmental pollution and the digital world is that environmental pollution and damage is there for everyone to see and feel, the actions in the digital world, on the other hand remain largely hidden. What it really means for ordinary people is that we can be easily targeted, identified and therefore manipulated. AI, machine learning and deep learning are technologies that are increasingly being harnessed for competitive advantage by companies, countries and politicians.

Figure 7.1: Artificial Intelligence and its many uses

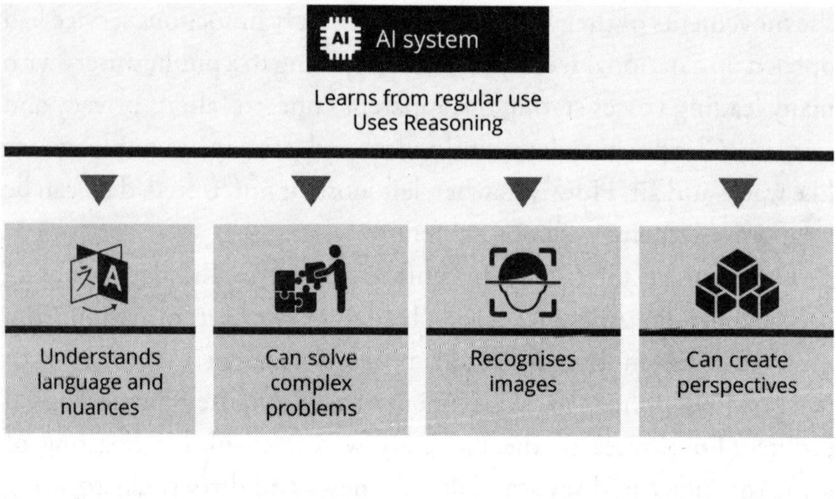

Recent events have shown that the promise of a technology driven world may not be all goodness and bright, happy, shining people but something far darker and disturbing.

In the early days, which were actually just about a decade ago, data collection was largely the domain of websites and mobile apps. Today, every sector is seeing the benefit of capturing data and using it for greater insight and increasing sales. Data personalisation is becoming central to the customer experience. Apple's virtual assistant Siri learns from increased usage and can fix appointments, answer emails and highlight important tasks. Google's Nest thermostat adjusts heating and cooling as it learns home owners' habits. This is not just because new technology is available, but because customers are changing the way they interact with brands. Today's customers want experiences that are personally relevant. A one-size-fits-all approach whether it be through advertising or through products is now changing. The rich landscape of digital experiences today is far beyond what we could ever have imagined.

Figure 7.2: Landscape of Digital Experiences

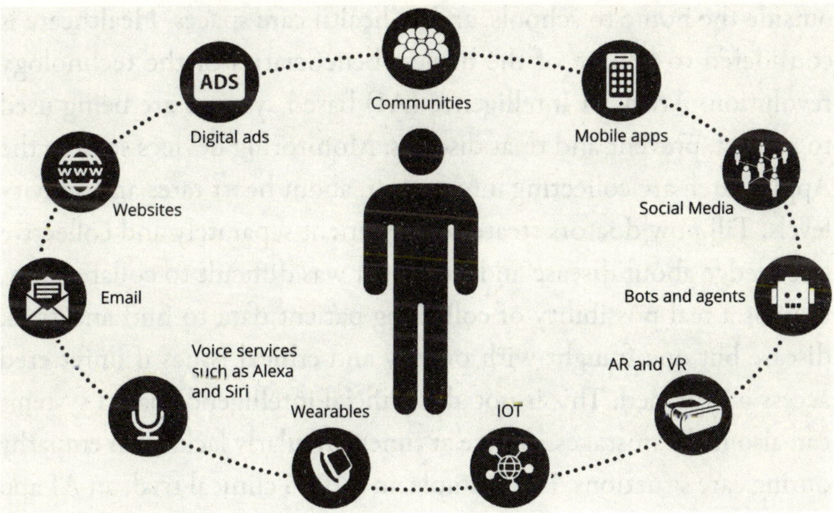

Technology is enabling smart devices to learn and personalise and this is only likely to grow with the proliferation of artificial intelligence, connected devices and high speed, readily available internet access. International Data Corporation (IDC) predicts that by 2019, 40 per cent of digital transformation initiatives will be supported by cognitive computing or AI efforts. Spotify (a music streaming service) uses AI to customise the listening experience according to user tastes. The entire business is based on data and AI. AI tracks trends, predicts customer preferences and creates custom lists for its users. Fashion and sports goods companies are using AI to make recommendations to customers not at the checkout counter but while buying. These predictions are based on body type, past purchases, weather, browsing history and more. There is also news that KFC is partnering with Chinese search engine Baidu to create a restaurant that uses AI facial recognition software to infer what a customer might want to order.[5] The program collects data like gender, facial expressions, and other visual features to provide menu recommendations to customers. It also saves previous orders, so returning customers can get recommendations based on what they've ordered before.

Technology is constantly moving ahead and has expanded outside the home to schools, and to health care spaces. Healthcare is considered to be one of the biggest beneficiaries of the technology revolution. Artificial Intelligence (AI) based systems are being used to predict, prevent and treat diseases. Monitoring devices such as the Apple watch are collecting information about heart rates and activity levels. Till now doctors treated each patient separately and collective knowledge about disease and treatment was difficult to collate. Now, there is a real possibility of collecting patient data to find and track disease but one fraught with privacy and ethical issues if unfettered access is provided. This is not all, artificial intelligence-based systems can also make mistakes and are at times singularly lacking in empathy during care situations. For example, in a 2015 clinical trial, an AI app was used to predict which patients were likely to develop complications following pneumonia, and therefore should be hospitalised.[6] This app erroneously instructed doctors to send home patients with asthma due to its inability to take contextual information into account. There are other threats too. Connected medical devices such as pacemakers have been shown to be vulnerable to hacking. A pacemaker is a small battery operated device which is surgically implanted into the chest of a patient. In 2017 the American Food and Drug Administration (FDA) recalled half a million pacemakers over hacking fears.[7] The security flaw could have enabled hackers to run down the battery and tamper with the patient's heart beat.

Banks have been using data tracking services to manage customer fraud for several years now. The rise of online and mobile banking has enabled banks and insurance companies to track customer usage patterns to identify at-risk customers. Insurance companies have started collaborating with health tracking apps and devices to surreptitiously increase premiums. Not far behind are banks who have started making profiles of potential defaulters. Banks can now, through sophisticated apps monitor, your spending pattern, who and what you spend on. Bank transaction data, credit behaviour and location data is readily available, this is then matched with advice and recommendations. The new set of fintech companies which consist of payment wallets, online lenders and more, rest their entire business models on knowing the customers' digital identity in great detail and customising services to their needs. Both old and new world financial companies and banks rely on security protocols to hold on to the hordes of data they collect. However, nothing is foolproof. In the middle of 2017, Equifax, one of the world's largest credit agencies, was hacked via a security flaw.[8] The hackers were able to steal the data of 143 million American citizens. The data consisted of addresses, names, social security numbers and credit profiles. But Equifax is not a bank, it is one of the many services providers used by banks and finance companies to render services. Your data therefore could be anywhere, with anyone.

Smart homes promise automated lighting, better water management and connected appliances. Lights that switch on and off, a coffee machine that makes coffee as soon as you wake up and room temperature that adjusts automatically. Significant time and resources could be saved if everyone were to live in a smart home. But at what cost? Smart homes collect and analyse a substantial amount of data. The systems learn from your usage patterns and adjust accordingly. This data then resides on servers. Also different companies sell different gadgets, e.g., the smart refrigerator and the smart light could come from different companies and capture data on different systems. The traditional home in this context sounds far more secure than a smart one where personal data and that of family members' could be open to scrutiny, hacks and misuse. Take the very real possibility of data being sold to insurance companies who could increase insurance premiums based on what you eat and how much exercise you do.

For most people, smart homes are a bit futuristic and some might even say these are first world problems. Let's then take a closer look at something closer home—the education ecosystem in India. Almost everyone would agree that India's transformation to a growing economy has come about due to improved education levels, made possible by public policy choices and parental awareness that schooling will ensure a better future. This push towards better education also spawned the concept of online testing, tuitions, hardware for digitally equipping classrooms and companies that provided these services. To this mix were also added school management software, curriculum automation and teacher training courses. A lot of the companies in this mix were and are startups and while some have succeeded, several have shut shop or been sold. The big question though, which no one is asking, is where has all the data gone? Data about all the children who attended these smart classes, tuitions and online tests. When children enroll into schools they give up all their social information but now because of technology someone knows what grades they achieved in every single class, what their strengths and weaknesses are, as well as their hobbies and interests.

One can argue that the influx of technology into education was the need of the hour and did the nation a huge service by scaling up learning in ways that were unimaginable. While that may be true, now that we are aware of the perils of data capture and misuse shouldn't we be asking the tough questions about us and our children's privacy? For many parents though, these questions are still far away.

Marketers, however, know an easy target when they see one. Children's toys are seeing a new kind of technology revolution with toys constantly connected to the internet and smart toys that capture information, learn and personalise content to the child's needs. In 2015, Hello Barbie started the smart toy revolution that allowed voice interaction between the child user and the doll.[9] With its microphone, voice recognition software and artificial intelligence the doll was considered a serious threat to child safety and privacy. The backlash and hacking concerns loomed so large that Hello Barbie got its own Twitter hashtag, #HellNoBarbie.[10] Baby products such as baby monitors and toys have been singled out over the past few years to be highly vulnerable. Baby monitors now have two-way audio, WiFi, motion sensors, integrated video (some with night vision), smartphone apps and 'ecosystems'. Some even talk of cloud storage, temperature monitoring and built-in lullabies. There are also watches that act as tracking devices allowing parents to know where their children are. While in itself technology is only acting as an enabler, the questions about who owns the data, where it is going and what is being captured remain. In countries such as India with lax laws around privacy and poor customer awareness, we seem to be sitting on a time bomb. This is likely to have significant consequences for the future of our children.

Increased connectivity increases not just the quantum of data but also the risk. Since everything we own is going digital we run the risk of allowing hackers into our homes through something as innocuous as a doll, a watch or even a lighting device. Apart from this, devices transmit location data so in effect we tell people where we work, stay, shop and pretty much everything else we do. Mobile cell towers can easily track signals to determine your location. In many cases this has been used for saving lives during natural calamities, discovering lost people and solving crimes. Location data, however, is not just stored in the servers of mobile phone companies. Many apps that you download switch on location tracking on phones whether they need it or not to provide the service you signed up for. While Uber certainly knows where you go, it is a real possibility that your bank, your newspaper, online grocery store and your insurance company do too.

This highlights questions around what you signed up for and what you didn't. The ethics of what is reasonable and what isn't. Not many of us read the terms of use and privacy policies. Companies use that to their advantage. Technology companies also deny access to a service if you don't sign up for the entirety of the data usage terms. This leaves users with little or no option—if they want to use the service, they have to agree to allow access to personal data. There is a desperate need for balance to be restored between technology companies, consumers and the data that drives the transactions between them.

The way forward

The internet is essential to the world we have now created. On it rests economic growth, our ability to trade, our ability to learn and our ability to interact. For companies to establish responsibility in the digital age a new set of norms is needed. The movement towards this has already begun. India has formed the Srikrishna committee to draft new privacy laws and define the dos and dont's for companies and modernise India's data privacy standards.[11] The Indian Supreme Court last year held that the right to privacy is a fundamental right and an integral part of the right to life and liberty. The United Kingdom is in the process of passing their own version of General Data Protection Regulation (GDPR), attempting to strengthen the idea that people own their personal data.

The GDPR gives consumers control over their data, allowing them to port data across service providers and knowing what this data is being used for. Consent will need to be freely given—specific, informed and unambiguous—and businesses will need to be able to prove they have it if they rely on it for processing data. A pre-ticked box will not be valid consent.[12] For businesses, GDPR introduces new obligations on security, privacy and ensuring they inform customers about data breaches.

In the US too, concerns over privacy are mounting. Other countries are likely to follow suit as the impact of the regulation is already impacting business as usual. There is a strong undercurrent of questioning data usage and a desire for transparency from companies. After GDPR, several complaints have been filed against firms by consumer rights organisations and privacy campaigners. On their part companies have updated their privacy policies and started reporting data breaches. GDPR increased maximum fines for malpractice to €20 million (£17.6m) or 4 per cent of a company's global turnover, whichever is higher, and companies are more likely to face higher fines if they delay reporting breaches.

Precisely why we need a new type of strategic responsibility framework for companies that are part of the fourth industrial revolution.

Privacy must become a part of responsibility. For companies, privacy is about protecting those who trust them. It's not just about collecting and securing data but also about not capturing it without knowledge. For customers it means awareness about what they are giving up and for governments, the importance of enacting public policy that balances out the needs of citizens, companies and governments.

Draw the boundaries: Privacy is not about keeping everything secret but the need for establishing rules about data capture, usage and storage. Thinking about privacy as a zero-sum game—either completely secret or completely public is neither realistic nor advisable. In a largely digital world we will share information with our hospitals, banks, mobile companies and cars. A laissez-faire approach to data is fraught with dangers. Big data is very powerful when aggregates are created. Hence, companies that aggregate data, third party service providers that have proliferated and apps that breach security protocols need to be reined in.

Big data analytics can predict, infer and enable many things. It's time we started thinking about what we will allow, and what we should not.

CASE STUDY

THE GENERAL DATA PROTECTION REGULATION (GDPR)

In January 2012, the European Commission set out plans for data protection reform across the European Union in order to make Europe fit for the digital age. Almost four years later, an agreement was reached on what that involved and how it will be enforced.

The General Data Protection Regulation (GDPR) is a regulation in EU law on data protection and privacy for all individuals within the European Union (EU) and the European Economic Area (EEA).[13] The law is a replacement for the 1995 Data Protection Directive, which has until now set the minimum standards for processing data in the EU.

At its core, GDPR is a new set of rules designed to give EU citizens more control over their personal data. It aims to simplify the regulatory environment for business so both citizens and businesses in the European Union can fully benefit from the digital economy. GDPR will significantly strengthen a number of rights. Individuals will find themselves with more power to demand that companies reveal or delete the personal data they hold. Regulators will be able to work in concert across the EU for the first time, rather than having to launch separate actions in each jurisdiction, and their enforcement actions will have real teeth, with the maximum fine now reaching the higher of €20m (Rs. 1595 million) or 4 per cent of the company's global turnover.

Key features of the regulation

Without a data subject's informed consent to data processing for one or more purposes, personal data may not be processed unless there is at least one legal basis to do so.

If informed consent is used as the lawful basis for processing, consent must have been explicit for data collected and for each purpose that the data is used for. Consent must be a specific, freely-given, plainly-worded, and unambiguous affirmation given by the data subject. An online form which has consent options structured as an opt-out selected by default is a violation of GDPR, as the consent is not unambiguously affirmed by the user. In addition, multiple types of processing may not be 'bundled' together into a single affirmation prompt, as this is not specific to each use of data, and individual permissions are not freely given.

A data controller may not refuse service to users who decline consent to processing that is not strictly necessary in order to use the service. Consent may be withdrawn at any time. Consent for children, defined in the regulation as being less than sixteen years old must be given by the child's parent or custodian, and verifiable.

If consent to processing was already provided under the Data Protection Directive, a data controller does not have to reobtain consent if the processing is documented and obtained in compliance with GDPR's requirements.

Who does GDPR apply to?

GDPR applies to any organisation operating within the EU, as well as any organisations outside of the EU which offer goods or services to customers or businesses in the EU. This means that almost every major corporation in the world will be subject to GDPR regulations. Even companies that are not subject to GDPR are implementing it since it gives them a strong public relations opportunity.

What is personal data?

Personal data includes name, address, and photos. GDPR extends the definition of personal data so that something like an IP address can be personal data. It also includes sensitive personal data such as genetic data, and biometric data which could be processed to uniquely identify an individual.

What does it mean for people?

Consumers are promised easier access to their own personal data in terms of how it is processed, with organisations told that they need to detail how they use customer information in a clear and understandable way. This paves the way for consumers to have greater control over who can access their data and how much.

One of the main changes GDPR will bring about is providing consumers with a right to know when their data has been hacked. Organisations will be required to notify the appropriate national bodies as soon as possible in order to ensure EU citizens can take appropriate measures to prevent their data from being abused.

GDPR is also set to bring a clarified 'right to be forgotten' process. This provides additional rights and freedoms to people who no longer want their personal data processed. They can move to have it deleted, provided there are no grounds for retaining it.

What does it mean for organisations?

There is a large amount of data that is hidden in unstructured content, and possibly within unsearchable documents stored as image formats, across an organisation. If this data includes sensitive information such as payment information, passport information, health information, or other personally identifiable information, it needs to be identified. This implies significant cost and effort for companies.

It is believed that by having a single supervisor authority for the entire EU, it will make it simpler and cheaper for businesses to operate within the region. The European Commission claims GDPR will save €2.3 billion (Rs 184 billion) per year across Europe.

Organisations are likely to proactively implement techniques like 'pseudonymisation' in order to benefit from collecting and analysing personal data, while the privacy of their customers is protected at the same time.

Organisations are also tasked with ensuring that the contracts contain provisions regarding the tasks and responsibilities of the third party data processor. This includes how and when data will be returned or deleted after processing, and the details of the processing, such as subject-matter, duration, nature, purpose, and type of data.

Is GDPR workable?

Companies are always working to get around regulations. However, with stiff penalties being imposed under GDPR, they will be a significant deterrent against its breach.

CHAPTER 8

Responsibility During the Fourth Industrial Revolution

Our dirty, polluted cities, the extreme poverty and the crazy traffic are just a few of the everyday challenges of urban living in India. They can't really be wished away, and neither can they be made to change purely by public policy and sporadic corporate action. Systemic change is required to solve many of the problems we see today, and, systems change when either collaborative action is taken, or the old system collapses due to a disruptive innovation.

The fourth industrial revolution will be a time of change. New technologies will emerge, new types of companies and business models will be formed and so will new type of lifestyles and a new ethos. While Chapter 6 spoke of new challenges, new solutions will emerge too, as sustainability, social responsibility and data challenges increasingly take mindshare.

The world of the future is likely to witness six megatrends that will have a significant impact on business responsibility as we know it today:

Six megatrends impacting business responsibility

1. **Increased inequalities:** As opportunities open up, people will find jobs in areas that were unheard of. People born in the late Sixties, for instance, had far fewer options than the youth of today. Now you can be a data scientist, a software engineer or a content manager with relative ease. Couple that with entrepreneurship and one can foresee a more egalitarian society as well as an

increase in income opportunities. However, in the future, increased opportunities will be increasingly limited to those who have digital access. People who have been left behind in the digital revolution, and there is a likelihood that this will be a substantial number, will lose out. Inequalities might therefore increase.

2. **Data and algorithms:** Increased availability of data to producers and marketers has made it possible for companies to understand and satisfy consumer needs far better. It also enables companies to target and market their products precisely. Not just companies, individuals and small businesses will gain too. Algorithms in the form of artificial intelligence and machine learning are likely to enable faster and superior decision making.

3. **Automation:** The advent of robots and drones are slowly but quietly transforming industrial landscapes. It is estimated that global spending on robotics is likely to reach $67 billion by 2025.[1] Of this, roughly 61 per cent is likely to be for commercial and industrial uses. Does this mean that humans will not have jobs? There are predictions which show that while automation is likely to take away mechanical jobs, newer kinds of jobs that require other types of skills are likely to emerge.

4. **New materials and technologies:** Developments in material sciences will lead to improved utilisation of exiting raw materials, which may replace unsustainable products and processes with better, healthier products and reduce harmful emissions in the process. Bioplastics are likely to replace plastics, hydroponics will enable creating of green areas, graphene will replace lithium iron in batteries, improved battery technology will enable storage of power, fossil fuel will be replaced by renewable energy for transportation, industries and home-use. Food is going organic and artisanal, fashion is going atelier, jewellery is becoming responsible, and clothes are being shared and recycled. In addition, developments like hyperloop and rocket technology will transform the way we commute and travel.

5. **Urban living:** Living in urban cities and towns is fast becoming impossible. The clogged roads, disappearing footpaths, dust, grime and pollution, poor garbage management, lack of physical security, unplanned housing layouts and so on have made urban life extremely trying. The public is now putting considerable pressure on local and central governments to shift their attention towards making living easier and smoother for the citizens. We see these pressures increasing and a gradual improvement in people's lives. While we speak of urban living, the same principles hold true for rural areas too.
6. **Climate change and the environment:** Countries and people are becoming more sensitive to climate change issues. The Paris Agreement has brought responsibility to the forefront. Companies are now starting to look at their entire value chains and trying to figure out how they can become more responsible and sustainable. Indian companies have started taking steps to improve this. The government is focusing on shifting from fossil fuel to renewable sources of energy and moving transportation from fossil fuel to

Figure 8.1: Responsibility megatrends

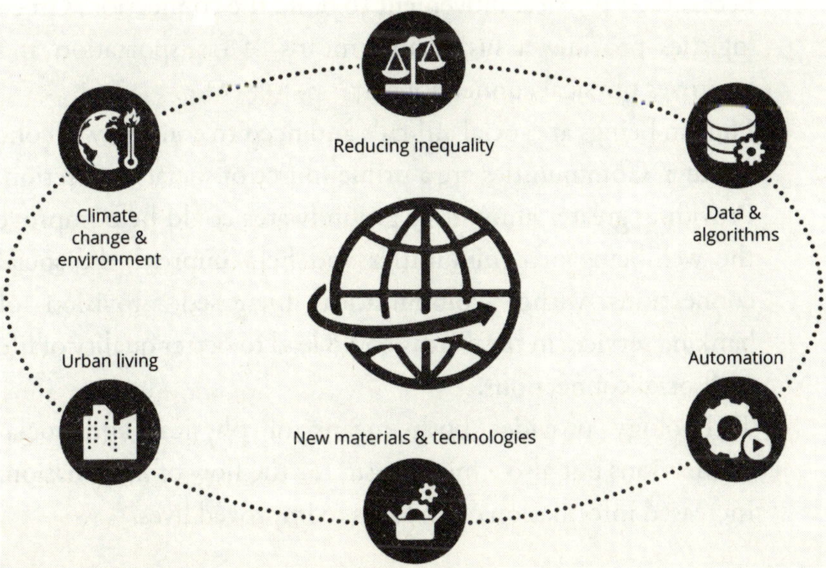

electric. Water is seen as a huge challenge that requires cleaning of rivers and lakes, adopting water management strategies like rainwater harvesting and planting more trees to attract rains. These trends are likely to see exponential growth.

One may wonder whether these trends apply to all people everywhere. The simple answer is that they do not. Issues like data and algorithms, automation and new technologies are likely to impact urban populations first. But as technologies develop, these are likely to have an impact on everybody over time. Some of these technologies may enable them to lead better lives while others may completely miss out as they may be out of the digital ecosystem.

Responsibility megatrends in a connected world

In a connected world business responsibility transcends borders. It impacts people, places and things and can have far reaching consequences. Connections in today's world manifest in various forms. We see them at three levels: physical, social and technology-led.

- Physical connections are in the form of transportation and movement. Goods need to move from place A to place B. This necessitates physical movement to build the connection. Green logistics provides a sustainable means of transportation and improves physical connections.
- Human beings are social animals and need to connect with one another. Communities are a prime source of social connection. Providing greater amount of groundwater could help improve the well-being of communities and help improve the social connections within communities. Increased provision of banking services in rural areas could lead to better quality of life and social connections.
- Technology provides both means of physical and social connections but also a mechanism for the flow of information. Increased information often leads to improved lives.

However, we do need to keep in mind that these connections (physical, social and technology) are very interdependent. We use internet technology to order physical goods. Social connections are the glue that enable physical and technology connections. Connections, therefore, are made through physical, social or technological means. These operate at different scales at different geographical levels—often blurring political boundaries.

Global: For firms operating on a global scale, learnings from one part of the world can be applied to another part of the world. For instance, the sustainable development goals (SDGs) aimed at ending poverty, protecting the planet, and ensuring prosperity for all is a global pact that operates across countries. Similarly, the Paris Agreement at COP21 is a global pact that has agreement across the world.

Cross-country: Issues and impacts are often cross-country in nature. For example, Lafarge Holcim (a large global cement producer) adopted the practices in water conservation and management undertaken at Ambuja Cement (its Indian subsidiary). Similarities between crop burning practices in Indonesia and India also point towards similar approaches.

Country: Countries have national policies and programmes. They are relatively homogenous in target and relatively large in scale. These are often implemented over disparate geographies and cultures but are connected in aim and impact. Thus UK's offshore wind farms development programme aims at substituting conventional fuel with renewable energy for UK. Another example is India's mid-day meal programme aimed at mitigating malnourishment among children as a part of SDGs.

Local: At local levels, programmes are fine tuned to local requirements. Where water supply is not plentiful, rooftop rainwater harvesting or building check dams and farm ponds becomes essential. Communities in similar neighbourhoods adopt similar practices to solve their water problems. Often a farmer who adopts drip irrigation is mimicked by a neighbour, creating connections and ripples of development.

So, what are some of the implications of a connected world?

- **Traceability:** The connected world means that we need to trace the source inputs to ensure that supply chains are traceable and the final product is sustainable.
- **Learning:** We need to look around and see if a similar problem has been solved elsewhere. This reduces the need to reinvent the wheel.
- **Big picture:** We often see problems in isolation like the six blind men and the elephant. We see either a trunk or a tail but can't see the elephant. Tools like systems thinking enable us to figure out the connections.

Figure 8.2: Megatrends in a connected world

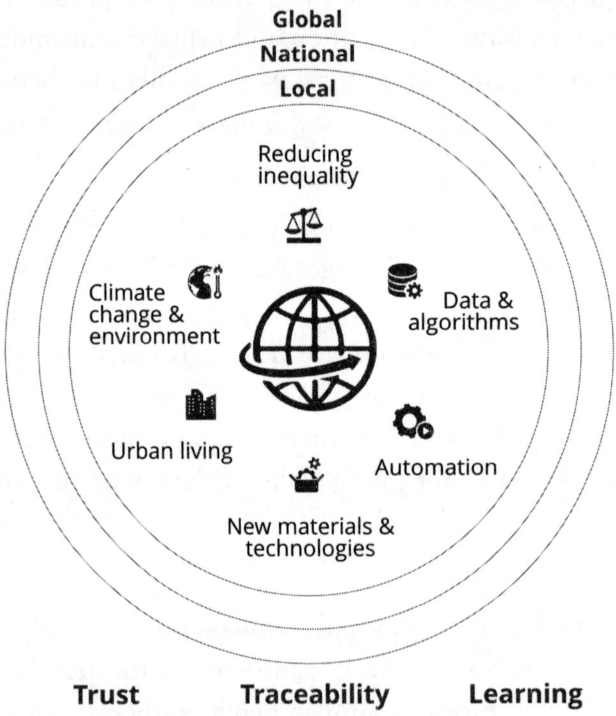

At the moment the current systems around us that we take for granted are in a state of flux driven by rapid technological advancement and sustainability challenges. Besides, sustainability and social responsibility have largely become compliance issues. While sustainability reports based on 'people, planet and profit' abound, the world is facing significant sustainability challenges. In a recent article John Elkington, the person who coined the phrase 'Triple Bottom Line', remarked, 'Fundamentally, we have a hard-wired cultural problem in business, finance and markets. Whereas CEOs, CFOs, and other corporate leaders move heaven and earth to ensure that they hit their profit targets, the same is very rarely true of their people and planet targets. Clearly, the Triple Bottom Line has failed to bury the single bottom line paradigm.'[2]

While most business leaders express serious concerns about business responsibility in interviews and discussions, most realise that systemic change is not easy. For instance, 85 per cent of India's top 200 companies are investing in creating sustainable products and services though just a handful are actually investing in systemic change or working collaboratively to ensure success.[3] Which is actually a pity, because as Churchill once said, 'one should never waste a good crisis.' Which is why the time has come to initiate a more holistic approach that defines progress and the responsibility of business.

A new paradigm of responsibility is needed

Most of the constructs of business responsibility mainly talk about environmental sustainability and contributing to society. These frameworks, models and measurement systems were designed for the industrial world and have played a significant role in helping companies tread the path towards better corporate responsibility. However, most of these constructs fail when applied to the world's largest technology companies in three fundamental ways:

Relevance: Technology companies don't really manufacture anything other than software, knowledge and data. While one can point out that servers do generate huge amounts of greenhouse gases and e-waste is a growing problem, most companies outsource their servers and send off their waste to recyclers. This is possibly why most of them don't see the point in generating sustainability reports or think that carbon reduction is a waste of time and just a compliance issue.

Data and the materiality matrix: In Chapter 4 we saw how companies create business responsibility strategies based on the materiality matrix. As a first step companies define their internal and external stakeholders (executive leadership, directors, regional managers, employees) and external contacts (trade associations, key customers, NGOs). After this, stakeholder feedback is taken on a variety of issues through interviews, surveys and consultations. After this, responsibility indicators are often categorised in three ways and prioritised:

- Economic (e.g., revenue, profit, company turnover)
- Social (e.g., labour statistics, human rights, consumer issues, community impact)
- Environmental (e.g., water stewardship, greenhouse gas emissions, waste management)

While this analysis is relevant and impactful for manufacturing companies, technology and data-driven companies would actually struggle to find anything of value from a data context. This is because data capture, aggregation and use is largely unknown to consumers and even employees. These are often highly secretive activities driven by opaque software processes, strengthened by legalese. Stakeholders can therefore not comment on things they know nothing of.

Post facto: The responsibility frameworks of today also look at post facto interventions to define social and environmental responsibility. For instance, the real issue with the online violence against women is not that social platforms don't react; they do. However, in a fast-moving world, they react far too late. Responsibility in the twenty-first-century has to be about creating a better world today and not waiting for harm to happen and then correcting it. In today's world and increasingly in the future we are looking at real-time responses to everything. The capability for real-time responsibility is already becoming part of the ecosystem. Sensors on machines give real time information to companies to generate digital replicas so that they can capture breakdowns. Wearable devices such as smart watches capture health data and can predict a heart attack three hours before it occurs. Algorithms can take decisions in seconds and reach tremendous scale with big data. Since the world is changing fast we can't really have responsibility models that rest on mere compliance or remediation. We need better decisions now!

It's not just sustainability and CSR models that need better application, company strategies are also often fundamentally flawed.

The future is not more of the past: It's a time of change. In part, the change is brought upon by the problems of unsustainable and unbalanced growth, at another level, the change is brought upon by the tremendous advances in technology called the fourth industrial revolution (4IR). Many of these trends are an acceleration of the changes that have already started today and to be truly relevant, businesses need to ask, 'Where are we today and where will we be in ten, fifteen or twenty years from now? What will be our responsibility strategy in that context and what needs to be done?'

There are very few companies that actually do a scenario analysis. The global oil and gas company Shell has been developing possible visions of the future since the early 1970s, helping generations of Shell leaders, academics, governments and businesses to explore ways forward and make better decisions.[4] Shell scenarios ask 'what if?' questions, encouraging leaders to consider events that may only be remote possibilities and stretch their thinking.

While everyone can't do such an extensive exercise, it's becoming imperative that the idea of sustainability and social responsibility in the modern world needs to be in keeping with corporate ambition, much greater than the sum of its parts.

Broken circles of trust: In the desire to innovate and be quick to change, companies are creating disruptive models. While speed and efficiency are gaining priority, customer trust is at an all-time low. Some of the disruption is caused because a new technology comes in and the company stops supporting the previous one. Customers are forced to either invest in the new product or live with an unsupported product. Other times it may be employees who face an uncertain future, having been rendered jobless and lacking in relevant skills. With important stakeholders such as employees and customers increasingly doubtful of company promises, it is no surprise that trust in companies is now at an all-time low. Therefore, no matter what the company may do in terms of path-breaking sustainability strategy, it may not achieve the intended goals of better reputation management, risk management and better brand positioning.

The connected world magnifies the smallest risk: While the cross-cutting nature of connections provide huge benefits they are also incredibly difficult to implement because of the sheer complexity and scale of the task. The system therefore needs to be changed from the inside; from parts of the business that drive value and not just the areas that contribute to risk.

Business responsibility therefore needs a modern context. It needs to bring in the many connections and technology interchanges that really define the twenty-first century, as well as build frameworks that reflect the changing realities. If done right, responsibility for the modern world can define the boundaries of the corporation—and its very soul!

A framework of decision making for responsible choices: Given the scenario that we face, we need new ways of looking at things. One such lens is the concept of trusteeship.

Figure 8.3: Implications for Responsible business

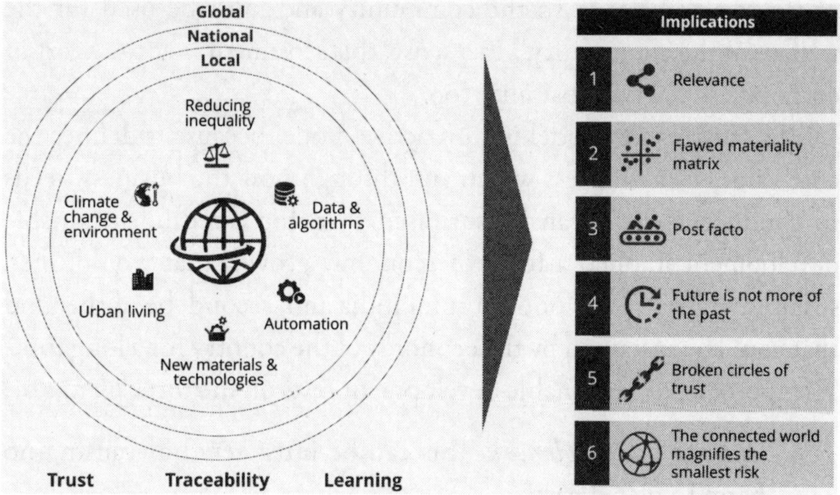

Revisiting Trusteeship

The Gandhian Model of Trusteeship is one such approach that, while being uniquely Indian, provides a means of transforming the present unequal order of society into an egalitarian one. It specifies that everything we do must be economically viable as well as ethical—at the same time making sure we build sustainable livelihoods for all. This model was debated in the 1940s and '50s and has had no real takers for most of the twentieth century. However, the challenges thrown up by the twenty-first century such as economic collapse, the absence of values and challenges of sustainable growth necessitate another look at trusteeship.

Trusteeship is a socio-economic philosophy that was propounded by Mahatma Gandhi. It provides a means by which the wealthy would be the trustees of trusts that looked after the welfare of the people in general. Gandhi was convinced that the wealthy could be persuaded to part with their wealth to help the poor. In his words, 'Supposing I have come by a fair amount of wealth—either by way of legacy, or by means of trade and industry—I must know that all that wealth does not belong to me; what belongs to me is the right to an honourable livelihood, no better than that enjoyed by millions of others. The rest of my wealth belongs to the community and must be used for the welfare of the community.'[5] In a sense, this sentiment is at the heart of corporate social responsibility too.

The trusteeship model is a proactive model because it defines the core values of a business which run through how the business needs to conduct itself. It can be surmised that, for Gandhi, sustainable development implied a form of economic growth that would, first, sustain the lives of the poor in rural India and, second, be of the kind that could be sustained by the economy of the country for a long time. His approach to sustainable development rests on the three planks of:

- *Ahimsa (non-violence):* This can be interpreted as causing no harm to planet earth.
- *Swaraj (self-control):* This can be interpreted as better decision-making.
- *Sarvodaya (benefit to all):* This can be interpreted as welfare for all while tackling areas of human rights, labour exploitation, etc.

The trusteeship model ties in with the recently created shared value framework as well as Thomas Piketty's book, *Capital in the Twenty-first Century*, which looks at global inequality.[6]

Thomas Piketty's book draws on more than a decade of research by Piketty and a handful of other economists, detailing historical changes in the concentration of income and wealth. Piketty's thesis is that the rate of capital return in developed countries is persistently higher than economic growth, and that this will lead to increasing income inequality. While Piketty favours wealth redistribution through a global tax on wealth, Gandhi argues for pure moral suasion. Both inequitable distribution of wealth and businesses' linkages with society were dear to Gandhi's heart and these recent thoughts on social responsibility carry forward the trusteeship model.

The key implications of trusteeship when applied to today's world could be:

- Surplus Wealth (**knowledge**) needs to be kept in trusts for the common good and the welfare of others.
- A non-violent approach needs to be adopted. (**Equity**)
- Everything that we do must be economically viable as well as ethical, while at the same time making sure that we build sustainable livelihoods for all. (**Balance**)
- Economic equality through trusteeship will thus ensure an equitable distribution of wealth amongst all. (**Equity**)

Absolute trusteeship is unattainable—but if people behave as trustees then we can develop institutions that are economically viable yet benign. The world in 2030 will see the proliferation of artificial intelligence and connected devices. Businesses will automate complicated tasks, reduce production costs and reach new markets. Continued growth in internet access will further accelerate change. What will responsible leadership mean in this context?

Responsibility 4.0

Leadership today has come to mean saying the right things. Instead it should be about doing the right thing. Trusteeship is not just a few well-meaning words. It's about guardianship/stewardship and basic decency, it's about creating a better world for the future. While twentieth century responsibility talked of doing no harm, circular systems and remediation for damage, 'responsibility' in 4IR or 'Responsibility 4.0' which rests on trusteeship can then embody the ideals of the society of the digital age. There are three basic tenets under which Responsibility 4.0 needs to be managed. These are Trust, Public Good and Equity.

Trust

The discussion around data privacy and security has mostly been thought of as something that impacted human rights. However, this is a corporate responsibility issue. The flow of information between the company and its customers and the company's ability to use it implies a deeper more fundamental relationship at work: the one of trust. What should then define 'materiality' for a digital company? Is it even a relevant concept? While materiality in its truest sense refers to relevance, it is rooted in the old word meaning 'materials' or hard goods.

In a data-driven world, if trust holds the key to everything, what does it really mean to see that you 'trust' the company with your data? At the simplest level, trust is a contract of faith between two parties. The individual shares information with a company that then provides access to information and services. At one level, there is a barter between the company and the individual where both parties trade in information. The individual knowingly or unknowingly gives the company access to data about him/her and trusts that the information shared will not be used to harm the owner of the information. The software platform or company gives access to information or a platform with the belief that it will be used well. The more a person uses the software or platform, the more information they end up sharing and then the relationship becomes an unequal one after a point where the company knows more and more about how the person operates and how he/she can be influenced.

The billions of connected users who are part of the data ecosystem give away data, sometimes willingly and many times unknowingly. Most times, they have no knowledge about how their data is being used. While companies say that this data has been aggregated with valid consent, most customers who clicked on the long legal document that defines the privacy policy of a company would disagree. For instance, most of us today use cloud services to store our documents and personal information such as videos and photos. The legal agreement promises safe storage, but it doesn't actually say that the storage company won't take a peek into the files. There could also be instances where they don't look into them but allow government agencies to look into them. Also, many of the companies that inhabit the digital world are transnationals and one doesn't know which country's rules they actually follow.

As users of social media, we share the most precious moments of our lives with friends, family and peers and also with the large technology companies that own Facebook, Google and Twitter among others. Important events, friendships, likes, dislikes and moments that define our identity are now part of the digital world. We are giving away so much data that there are 52,000 unique attributes that Facebook has used to classify users.[7] What are the boundaries that define how companies should be able to use this data?

The issues outlined so far are just the tip of the iceberg. In summary:

- In a digital world customer data is highly valued.
- The world of 2030 will be one where all companies are digital.
- The increasing number of digital transactions mean that digital companies know almost everything about us.
- Digital platforms can potentially control what we see, hear, buy and even vote for.

Viviane Reding, EU Justice Commissioner, said, 'Personal data is the currency of today's digital market. And like any currency it needs stability and trust. Only if consumers can "trust" that their data is well-protected, will they continue to entrust businesses and authorities with it, buy online, and accept new services—the new services, you in this audience, invent and develop. Reliable, consistently applied rules make data processing safer, cheaper and inspire users' confidence.'[8]

It is therefore not okay for companies to:

- record customer location after location is switched off on apps
- use apps to snoop into customer call records to see if they are calling up or receiving calls from competitors
- sell data of low value customers to data exchanges
- outsource data management to companies in countries with no data protection or privacy laws.

Acting as trustees to the data of customers implies that transparency of usage is critical. There may be reports on usage, perhaps a board with oversight on usage and also the underlying algorithms.

Building Trust, therefore, is the first principle of Responsibility 4.0.

Public Good

Defining the responsibility of a digital company can be done by first defining their exact role in our society. Digital companies like Facebook and Twitter are places for social interaction, companies like Microsoft and SAP provide software that allows us to do certain tasks, platforms like Paytm (Indian digital payments platform), Aadhaar, Uber and Airbnb provide services based on technology. Digital companies manage resources and infrastructure, impact the flow of data and information and function as 'information gatekeepers'. Since information is the cornerstone of today's society, it gives the provider a moral responsibility to function as a trustee for public good. Twitter's social responsibility initiative 'Twitter for Good' states its commitment to safety, equality, and free expression and supports initiatives such as internet safety and education, freedom of expression and civil liberties. Microsoft, as part of its materiality assessment has identified human rights as one of the top issues. More than that, Microsoft talks about commitments to accessibility, global diversity and inclusion, and empowering communities as part of its policy framework, 'A cloud for Global Good'. Traditionally though, rights were the domain of governments. For instance, the Indian Constitution grants its citizens the Right to Equality, Freedom, Religion, Education, Culture and the Right against Exploitation. However, can private companies that have responsibilities to shareholders really be responsible for public good? How do we draw the line between issues that impact individual rights and corporate profits? Which one should be a priority?

The discussion around sustainability and CSR has repeatedly highlighted the need for balance. The list of things that are in excess and their consequences is a large one: excessive emissions have led to climate change, excessive consumption to waste, excessive water usage to droughts, excessive concretisation in cities has caused flooding and so on. It is therefore surprising that many business models of the twenty-first century, largely based around technology, are about disruption or creating an imbalance and profiting from it. The consequences of imbalance are mostly seen in the long term and if allowed to go unchecked, disruption caused by a business at one level may lead to huge imbalances in society.

Take the case of car aggregation services that say that car drivers are entrepreneurs. At one level, it's a great example of using technology to provide transparency of location to customers. At another level, the car aggregation service can eventually have disproportionate power because it will know where customers go, when, with whom, where they stay and work and much, much, more. The car company will then need to have rules not just about privacy and security and about drawing a balance between their desire for profit and customers rights and to a larger level public good. The car aggregators today frequently complain about the hassles of managing drivers, while at the same time calling them partners. If all the car aggregation services move to driverless cars, where will the drivers go? Companies will need to factor in long term thinking in their decision making. Decision making in Industry 4.0 is very much about taking responsibility for the consequences of your decisions. It is about drawing a balance between automation and job losses, a balance between profit and public good.

Keeping knowledge between the walls of the company is indeed a source of competitive advantage but data sharing can achieve miracles.

The Human Genome Project was a pioneer for encouraging open access to scientific research. In 1996, those involved agreed that all new information produced should be made freely available to all within twenty-four hours. Before the Human Genome Project, scientists had only ever shared their research findings in scientific journals. In April 2003, the Human Genome Project was completed, presenting the world with the human genetic blueprint. Sequencing the human genome and making the data rapidly and broadly available led to a paradigm shift in the way science is conducted. The project created a living resource that provides the foundation for entire fields of cutting edge research, and paid deep dividends in a myriad of ways. To date, the Human Genome Project has already generated $965 billion in economic output between

> 1988 and 2012, creating more than $293 billion in personal income through wages and benefits, and nearly four million jobs (directly and indirectly).

Reaping the quickest benefits from business decisions and maximising profits in the short run are great business strategies for companies that don't really want to play the long-term game. A related issue with today's companies is the divorce between owners and managers. As more companies are becoming manager-led rather than owner-led and significant effort goes into bonding the owner and managers' interests, governance has come under strained. Corporate boards need to imbibe the concept of trusteeship as a vehicle of their social responsibility.

The desire for growth and human ambition are a given. The growing footprint of the corporation means that ground rules too need a refresh or a new articulation. Data and infrastructure that extends beyond social and national boundaries cannot be left with a few. Data is the new oil is a capitalist's statement. Data for good is a social intent. The societal contract around data and very large companies must factor in intent, rapid change, the changing role of government and oversight.

Balance between profit and public good is the second principle.

Equity

Technology can reinforce the global divide. It can break the social fabric and twist it into inconceivable ways. Knowledge can be a great advantage. By this we also mean that people who don't have this knowledge or don't have the ability to access it can be at a significant disadvantage. In the future, the internet will be everywhere. We will always be connected with our devices and with permanent flows of information all around us. The digitally disadvantaged, either because of a disability, language issues or literacy may face huge, disproportionate challenges. There may be other challenges too. The challenge of partial information, fake news, search engines favouring certain types of results and so on. Wherever information access is partial, denied or incorrect it will give rise to inequality.

We need a plan to include the disadvantaged, the people who will be left out.

In India, several concerns have been highlighted against the implementation of Aadhaar, a system of digital identity. The Aadhaar system is at its core, a simple way of identifying citizens, at another level it is leading to considerable challenges in equity. The digital identity is linked to bank accounts where social benefit transfers, pensions are being transferred. It is helping in weeding out fake names and corruption in many government schemes; but for the illiterate, elderly and differently abled who cannot operate bank accounts, are unable to read documents and don't have mobile phones or internet access it is posing enormous challenges. Overall, Aadhaar needs to build societal confidence in its efficacy and safeguards. Additional services can be designed keeping in mind inputs from citizens and experts in an ongoing transparent way.

Technology will reinforce inequality by twisting information access and creating a parallel reality. Fake news is just that. Interested parties with terabytes of data can do micro targeting to achieve their purposes. In many parts of the world such as Latin America and Africa large parts have no access to broadband. And it's not just about access, in the UK alone over 12 million adults lack digital skills to manage the digital world. Access to technology is not the only answer to bringing equity, it is equally about education and empowerment.

In 2012, a study in a semi-urban area found that mobile phones were largely owned by men in small income homes. In most of these homes, both husbands and wives were daily wagers, doing a variety of jobs in the close-by industrial hub near Delhi. As part of a social experiment free mobile phones were given to the women. The women were trained to use the phones and the phone interface was converted into the local language, Hindi. Within two months another survey was conducted which found that almost 90 per cent of the phones had been taken away by the brothers, sons or the husbands. Even though the phones helped women get information about jobs and helped them stay connected, the men felt that giving them a phone was futile. In some cases, they even sold off their phones.

UNESCO Director General Irina Bokova said in 2016 at the World Economic Forum, 'Whether based on education, gender, jobs, health or resources, inequality is one of the gravest threats to our common future. In the face of polarisation, fragmentation and exclusion, we must respond with human-centred policies that empower all women and men, strengthen the capacity of governments and rally the multilateral system around shared narratives, solidarity and understanding to protect what is common to us all—our culture, our humanity, our planet.

'This begins with education and skills and calls for a special focus on narrowing the gender gap, especially in the growth sector constituted by professions requiring a background in science, technology, engineering and mathematics. This is our message in Davos—the 4th Industrial Revolution must be a development revolution.'

The Forum's annual Gender Gap Report finds that across health, education, economic opportunity and politics, this gap has closed by

Figure 8.4: Trusteeship as a solution approach

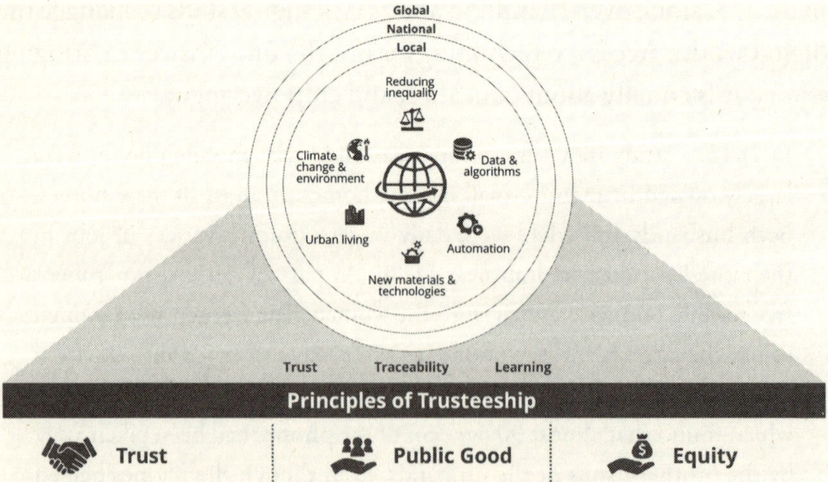

only 4 per cent in the past decade, suggesting it will take another 118 years to close the gap completely.

Equitable access to knowledge is the third principle.

Responsibility 4.0 – The Framework

While several sustainable development models have proliferated, the most commonly used one in corporate boardrooms is triple bottom line. This is a metaphor that uses the business language of the 'bottom line' to propose that corporations are not just accountable for the economic value they add to stakeholders, but also for the environmental and social value that they add, or destroy.[9] Also known as the 3P's: people, planet, and profit. The companies that will inhabit the world in 2030 will have a key element that will take precedence over everything else—data. Data is the key competitive advantage for the twenty-first century corporation. It is also a key input that drives the creation of new products and services which is not factored into the earlier models of responsible growth. How do you ascribe responsibility to the digital company? In the same way

Figure 8.5: Responsibility 4.0 Framework

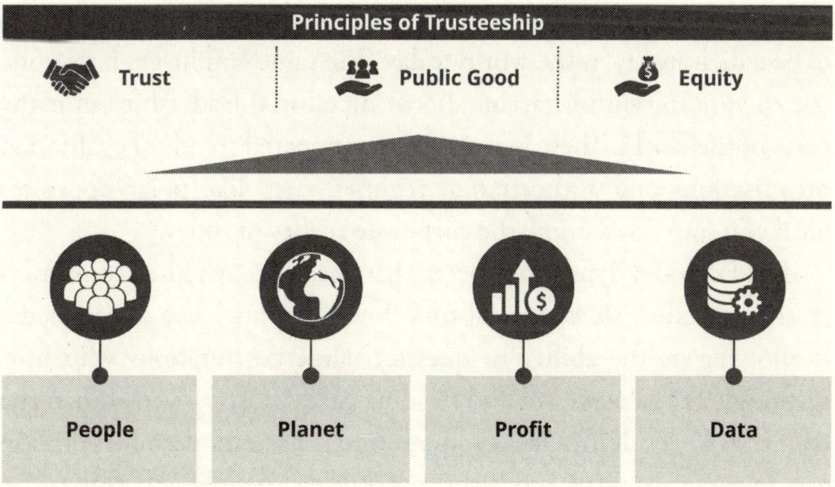

that we planted trees in the physical world, opened schools, generated livelihoods, what is our digital give back? When we encompass the circles that normally represent the 3P's framework with data we get a model that looks a bit like the one in figure 8.5.

Responsibility 4.0 thus keeps the people, planet and profit at its core but with the added element of data that gets generated by people and the environment, which is so valuable to companies. There can be an argument that data was always inherent in business and it needn't be a separate element. While another view, the one shared by the authors is that data will drive the twenty-first century and therefore needs to be a key element and not just a subset of people, planet and profit.

The Responsibility 4.0 framework defines the role of the board and the company as a trustee for the resources it uses and for the people it works with, changing the role of business from just an equitable user of resources to someone who cares for them.

Business theory in the recent past has talked of technology as a route to unlimited growth, the ability to voice one's thoughts on social media as egalitarianism and the twenty-first century as a world of equality. Matrix organisations, holacracy (a method of decentralised management and organisational governance) and open plan offices have been the new trends ruling the corporate world. Yet there seems to be a dichotomy in the world today. The same employees have gone out to vote for authoritarian, almost dictatorial leaderships in many parts of the world. These seemingly unconnected trends of egalitarian organisations and authoritarian regimes seem like polar opposites until you start to examine the corporate reality of today.

The Edelman Trust Barometer that measures whether consumers trust companies shows an all-time low. Is it just that social media is allowing us the ability to question large corporations who now seemingly are as powerful and in some cases more powerful than the countries we reside in? Or is it something else? The modern corporation is a vast monolith of processes, procedures, people and things. To this maze is getting added the digital interfaces and automation algorithms, destroying the soul of the organisation. Perhaps the time has come to re-examine what organisations really need to stand for, measure things that till now have been called the 'soft stuff' and bring some humanity into our world. In a manufacturing world one used resources and then thought about giving back and mitigating the damage. In a technology-driven fast paced world you do not have the luxury of time, of thinking post facto about the damage you may have caused.

> 'The Fourth Industrial Revolution can compromise humanity's traditional sources of meaning—work, community, family, and identity—or it can lift humanity into a new collective and moral consciousness based on a sense of shared destiny. The choice is ours.'
>
> —Klaus Schwab, *The Fourth Industrial Revolution*[10]

Technology is creating new winners but many business models are failing. For instance, the technology outsourcing model on the basis of which India transformed itself from a poor underdeveloped country into a developing one, is taking its last breath. The Indian automotive industry is looking at job losses up to 42 per cent of current employee strength due to the push for electric vehicles. In an earlier world we could have simply said, 'reskill employees'. However, when business models fail everything is up for question. Education too is in a state of flux. Universities are training people for jobs they may never have. According to data scientists, there will be no jobs for radiologists in the next five years. Imagine the state of a student who passes out of medical school after years of hard work and a hefty fee with a radiologist's degree, but with a one-year career prospect! Leadership in this world where responsibility blurs the line between companies and society will be driven by a deeper sense of right and wrong rather than a simple bottom-line focused approach. This is where Responsibility 4.0 comes in. A framework rooted in the philosophy of trusteeship which keeps equity, public good and trust at the very centre.

Responsibility 4.0 – key highlights

Trusteeship as a governance and decision making philosophy

Trust, Public good and Equity as basic principles

Data as a new element in addition to planet, people and profit

Real time not post facto

Responsibility by design

Such a fundamental change, though, has many implications. How should a responsibility strategy then be created? What are the things that will change for existing businesses and new businesses? How will business responsibility then be measured? How will the role of the sustainability and CSR managers change in the coming years?

CHAPTER 9

Finding Balance—the Prime Directive

In 2013, on visiting Ahmedabad after many years, our batch mates from the Indian Institute of Management, Ahmedabad (IIM-A) had remarked on how much development had taken place in the city. New roads, flyovers and buildings had transformed the sleepy little town that had played such an important role in our formative years. No one remarked on the trees that had been cut down and the slightly smoky quality to the air that was now part of every Indian city. After all, development came at a price! Last winter though, the batch reunion seemed a bit different. Taking off from grey Delhi into a slightly less grey Ahmedabad seemed to frustrate many of our friends who had come from abroad. 'Why can't you guys do something about this?' remarked more than one voice. 'Public apathy and government apathy' coughed an old soul who had been living in Delhi and had by now given up on any hope for change.

In June 2018 though, things seemed to be changing. Citizens across Delhi started a public campaign supported by radio, TV and social media to stop the felling of over 14000 trees in the heart of the city. The municipal corporation was clearing up land for new government homes and under immense public pressure had to put a stop to the plan.[1]

A few months back, the state of Maharashtra banned plastic,[2] and shortly thereafter complaints piled up from many sectors that the ban be reversed. While the government has backtracked in some areas, most realise that this is only a temporary reprieve and alternatives to plastic must be found.

The response to the Indian government-appointed Srikrishna committee on data protection had been muted till the Cambridge Analytica scandal hit the world's newspapers.[3] Public apathy over privacy and data suddenly gave way to consciousness about the need to protect information about us. The proposed ambitious legislation would regulate and monitor issues on data transfer and accumulation, informed consent, data portability, as well as appointment of a data authority. People suddenly started reading the terms of use of the multiple digital services they had subscribed to.

Slowly, a consciousness and a belief is emerging, that we really do need to change. Our lifestyle and growth cannot be at all costs. A balance is necessary.

Moreover, this is not an isolated thought.

The tussle between private profit and public good is emerging everywhere. The tentacles of corporate power strengthened by technology need to be reined in for society to flourish. In the *Star Trek* television and movie franchise, the 'Prime Directive' was a crucial element that bound the behaviour of its personnel. It stated, 'No identification of self or mission; no interference with the social development of said planet; no references to space, other worlds, or advanced civilisations.'

The planet needs a Prime Directive too. One that serves as a moral compass and yet doesn't derail growth. A twenty-first century ideal that binds us as people who only have one planet to live on and each other to support. We are no longer citizens of just countries, we are defined by the companies we work with and the brands we buy into. Our movements, thoughts and secrets are known to many people, companies and governments. They know our friends and families, they know not just what we buy but how we think.

Unless there is a moral compass, strengthening legislation, public policy and public consciousness, we will soon be a lost civilisation; drowning in plastic and mortgaged to technology. We are better than that. If we are smart enough to create the stuff and the technology, surely we can be smarter than letting it rule us.

Gandhi led India's freedom movement based on the core tenets of non-violence and equity. And it changed the world. He proved that freedom could be one based on non-violence. We need a modern day ethos of defining life on earth and maintaining the balance that will allow us to progress—the Prime Directive for the twenty-first century. Could Trusteeship be that philosophy? Could leaders become Trustees who focus on business growth as well as public good?

Trusteeship—a moral compass

Leadership for the fourth industrial revolution has to be about mindfulness. It has to be about people. Technology is based on zeroes and ones and has somehow reduced corporate thinking into binaries too. How can companies balance the need for responsibility and profit, public causes and customer needs? A new kind of leadership is needed that builds trust, is driven by values and is open to change.

The leader has to be a trustee to all the stakeholders, rising above the stereotypes to decide what she will and will not do. As a trustee to the organisation, there is no exit strategy. The leader is responsible for the impact of her decisions. This could be food for thought for venture funded companies that are currently destroying business models without taking responsibility for the damages caused. Their current philosophy is: if we don't do it someone else will. Perhaps it could change to, 'If it can be done, let's do it right and take people along.'

In the recent past, social network CEOs expressed public remorse over wrongdoing. This is no longer good enough. By the time the regulators and general public reacted, the social network that sought to target children in the first instance, but ought to have known better, had all the data on children that it needed. In another instance, the election had already been won or lost depending on whose side you took. Sneaking up on unsuspecting people for data aggregation or selling them something whether it is a product, or a president, is not a good thing. It's certainly not innovative and neither is it trustworthy. In the world of large transaction data, ethics and responsibility have now merged. We can't any longer say, 'Hey, this is a new innovative product that will be loved by millions but there will be a few downstream issues. But we needn't look at them now, let's cross that bridge when we get to it.' Companies, reputations and lives will get destroyed with such short-term thinking. Trusteeship is about taking the higher ground, about getting the design right in the first place. Proactive is the default norm. The post facto CEO would make the faulty product, maximise short term profit, hire a PR firm and say, 'I am setting up a committee to look into this. So sorry, won't happen again.'

New ways of thinking and acting are required from all stakeholders, including individuals, business executives, social influencers and policy-makers. There are no outsiders anymore. Deep, meaningful conversations and not just excel sheets hold the key to responsibility. This means thinking not just about what new perspectives might be needed, but finding entirely new ways to create and update our thinking over time in collaboration with other people in the industry, policy makers and customers themselves. The corporate brand needs to move from product attributes, smart logos and great TV advertisements into being more human, responsive and above all trustworthy.

Collaborate to build a better world

Throughout human history, the human spirit has risen above our instinctive greed. There have been many instances where the world has come together for a higher cause. The space station is an excellent example in this regard. The space station, emerging at the demise of the Cold War, was a place set up in space over the earth to monitor the activities of the planet and its outer scape. Russians, Americans, Chinese, Indians and even Iranians have visited it on an ongoing basis, benefited from it and added technology and resources to it. The space station is a place for common good, looked after by everyone and benefiting everyone. Ironically, the space station is surrounded by private and country satellites whose primary job is surveillance.

If two formerly warring countries emerging into a new world at the end of their Cold War could put aside their differences and collaborate for well over twenty-five years, the corporate world can easily come together to determine what public data is going to be all about. This is the critical conversation that needs to happen. Climate change got people together and the Paris Agreement was signed. SDGs emerged out of deep deliberation with companies and countries. Now, as far as data and algorithms are concerned, new leadership needs to emerge from companies that takes into account that trusteeship for public goodwill either transform us or its absence will divide societies and create instability around the world.

Responsibility 4.0 is about managing an accelerating world in a better way, by working as trustees for the common good. We no longer have the luxury of learning from our mistakes.

Collaborating to create shared value can further add impetus to achieving greater development impacts. Health, water and energy are common themes in many corporate board rooms. Collaborative efforts in these areas could improve the living conditions of millions, while at the same time contributing to corporate brand value.

Bringing intent and action together

Business responsibility is not a new phrase. Everything that needed to be said about it has possibly already been said in many forums, several times over. Still, there is a gap between intent and action. CEOs say the right things all the time, yet companies continue to bypass every single responsibility paradigm. Why? What stops them from doing the right thing?

Responsibility is an abstract term. So are sustainability, ethics, CSR and values. The purpose of this book is to highlight how business responsibility is integral to every aspect of decision making. Embracing responsibility means bringing change in the organisation. And change is never easy. It brings pain. It brings resistance. Change is also not a single event. It is a series of events, involving several things and the biggest of them involves emotions and the inherent human resistance to change. What will bridge this gap between intent and action? Do corporate incentives need to change? Do processes need to change? Do we need more transparency?

The fashion business has routinely focused on creating products from fabrics, shoes and accessories based on petroleum. Sustainable, eco-friendly and handmade fabrics have become more expensive. Is there a case for fashion brands to take a fresh look at the total environmental cost rather than race to the bottom to produce even cheaper products? The same is the case with electric vehicles. While they can solve the urban pollution problem, could they lead to certain other consequences? What could be the end of life process for an electric vehicle? What about the batteries that would be used? How would they be disposed of?

The big questions companies should be asking are: Will the product/service add to the current social and sustainability challenges? Will it create certain unintended consequences? For instance, microbeads, or micro-millimetre sized plastic beads inserted into toothpaste and beauty products ended up adding to water pollution. They also got consumed by fish and entered the human food chain. Is something akin to this a likelihood for the products/services that are proposed to be introduced by the company in question?

Another question is, could a product/service create a need or dependence? Certain software and social media products are getting a large number of hits but are also getting people addicted to them and in some instances also creating mental health issues. It is therefore crucial to think of remediation measures and limiting adverse impacts. What plans are in place to ensure this can be done quickly with minimal impact? What would be the possible costs of withdrawal, remediation or containment of adverse effects?

How can we ensure that AI-based systems are forces for good and continue to be so? Many products and services have little to no adverse impacts in the short run. It is in the long term when one begins to see a different side. For example, many chemicals that are banned today were considered revolutionary in their time. In the case of AI, we need to ask, can the product/service or application destabilise or take away livelihoods? What will happen to the people who are rendered jobless? What is the human cost of the actions taken today, in the short, medium and long term?

The emerging role of the Chief Responsibility Officer

The other critical issue is that current models of responsibility are mostly reactive. They seek to rectify damage to the environment and social systems. In a data-driven world, there is the potential to cause massive damage with far-reaching consequences. In the next few years, existing systems and value chains will need a reboot not just in terms of finding newer markets and growth avenues, they will come under increasing regulatory and public pressure for transparency, trustworthiness and public good. The role of the Chief Responsibility Officer, will therefore, become central to change management in the coming years.

In several organisations, CSR, sustainability, ethics and human rights reside under different departments. In the digital age, most of these issues have blurred boundaries. Take the case of consumer durable companies that are giving away medical equipment to government clinics in rural India. Most modern medical equipment is connected and capable of saving and transmitting data. Hence, while the CSR department is giving these donations, the marketing wing is busy aggregating patient data from this equipment. What are the ethics of this practice? Is this a CSR issue, a marketing one or one that might fall under Responsibility 4.0? When viewed through the lens of trusteeship the company might choose to define processes and systems that take customers, medical practitioners and government on board and contribute to society not just through equipment but design a way of data capture benefitting all to create shared value—a digital give-back to the collaborators.

These decisions, possibly overseen by the Chief Responsibility Officer, could become commonplace very soon. However, the system therefore needs to create the space for a Chief Responsibility Officer and responsibility needs to be inbuilt into organisational structures.

In such a situation, the Chief Responsibility Officer needs to work as a designer and not just function as a manager. Her imagination has to be used to design better frameworks, better products, better roads, better homes and better cities. Post facto responsibility can't function in a real time world. Hence, responsibility needs to permeate every job function and must be the prime directive. Responsibility check and balances are required as part of the ordinary course of business and not as risk management afterthoughts.

Conclusion

Today's seven year olds will be the first digital natives. The kids who grew up with an iPad are mostly urban and will have a significant influence on the shape of things to come. But they are also a generation under threat. Apart from environmental constraints, technology is making several jobs obsolete. It is not just low paying jobs that are giving way to automation but high end jobs too. Medical and legal responsibilities are getting automated as are other professions. Rapid changes driven by technology and globalisation are leading to economic insecurity; at the same time, the global system is marred with distrust. We no longer trust the news that is served to us, employees don't trust the companies they work for, consumers don't trust the brands they buy and citizens don't trust governments. This is the result of an ecosystem that maximised short term return for personal gain.

Natural ecosystems create balance through checks and measures, most times ensuring that no one species gets out of control. The same needs to be done to companies. They need to be counter-balanced by another paradigm—ecosystems of trust, equity and public good.

News companies know the damage fake news has done to their business model. Brands realise the deep cuts that environmental short-termism can cause and social media platforms have seen that not taking responsibility can lead to public outrage and government push back that can be far reaching in its consequences. Slowly but surely, the need for balance is permeating our world again.

To create balance though, we need to develop a language of balance, away from the language of war that permeates business corridors today. For the language of war already assumes that everything else has failed and that destruction is the only road to success. The language of balance will create a world that defines the fourth industrial revolution before it defines us. Can we use this to redesign better systems? Design for responsibility? And responsibility by design? Not as an afterthought, but through genuine impact by being trustees of the world that has given and continues to give us so much.

TECHNICAL NOTES

TN 1: EXTERNALITIES AND THEIR IMPLICATIONS

Externality refers to the consequence of an industrial or commercial activity which affects other parties without this being reflected in market prices, such as the pollination of surrounding crops by bees kept for honey.

Externalities are of two types:

A negative externality (also called 'external cost' or 'external diseconomy') is an economic activity that imposes a negative effect on an unrelated third party.

A positive externality (also called 'external benefit' or 'external economy' or 'beneficial externality') is the positive effect an activity imposes on an unrelated third party.

Let us, now, look at the impact of externalities.[1] Consider the case of negative externalities. For example, a company's production process causes pollution in a river nearby. The production process may also require a large amount of water. Reduction in water availability causes distress to people living in surrounding areas. It is not necessary for the affected people to be consuming the company's products. In both the situations the producer's private costs do not match the social costs as the social costs include private costs as well as external costs to third parties. The presence of negative externalities prevents markets from achieving maximum welfare.

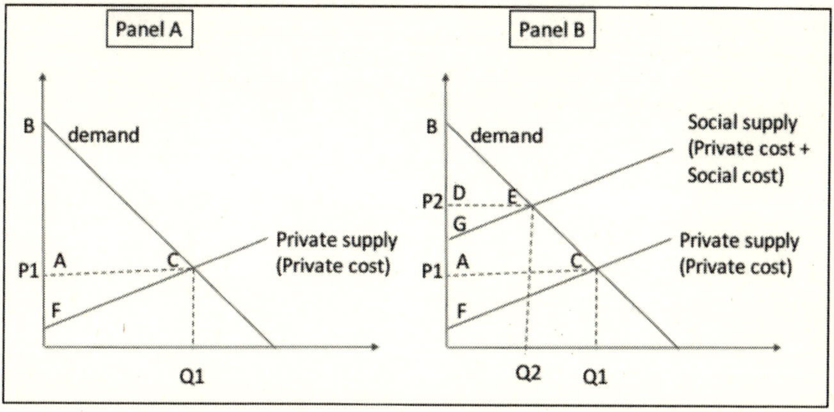

Adapted from Externality, Wikipedia, https://en.m.wikipedia.org/wiki/Externality

[1] This section is based on Externality, Wikipedia, https://en.m.wikipedia.org/wiki/Externality and Debaere, Peter and Jay Shimshack, *The Economics of Corporate Social Responsibility*, Darden Business Publishing, Case UV7168..

We continue with the case of negative externalities. The diagram above illustrates this impact.

Panel A depicts the situation without externalities. A regular private market will be in equilibrium at price P1 and quantity Q1. At this price-quantity, both the producer as well consumer welfare is maximised. The consumer surplus is depicted by ABC and the producer's surplus by ACF. Now an externality (say, pollution) is introduced. Panel B depicts the impact of this externality. The higher supply cost now changes the market equilibrium and price-quantity shifts to price P2 and quantity Q2. At this level, the consumer surplus gets reduced to ADE. The producer's surplus is also reduced to DEG.

Companies attempt to reduce the social costs by undertaking activities that reduce the cost of the externalities and consequently shift the supply curve downwards. The reduction in the cost of externalities comes about as companies invest in profitable sustainable projects. Investment in sustainable projects will be positive when the present value of reduced externalities is more than the present value of the costs of implementing the project – a positive NPV project. Any project that is not positive NPV will not be accepted.

TN 2: SOCIAL RETURN ON INVESTMENT

The concept of Social Return on Investment (SROI) emerged from the work done by the Roberts Enterprise Development Foundation (REDF). Originally intended for large social enterprises, over time it has been fine-tuned to meet the requirements of various types of organisations. SROI is an outcomes-based measurement tool that helps organisations to understand and quantify the social, environmental and economic value they are creating. In effect, SROI captures the triple bottom-line of people, profits and planet.

In practice, there are two ways of calculating SROI depending on the level of measurement. When the measurement is undertaken at the company's level, it is based on both social and economic benefits and considers economic as well as social investments. On the other hand, when the measurement is undertaken at project level it is simpler to look at only social costs and benefits and relate them to social investments.

Thus, the company level measurement is defined as:

$$\text{SROI} = \frac{\text{Economic profit} + \text{Social profit}}{\text{Economic investment} + \text{Social investment}}$$

where social profit is social benefits less social costs.

And, the project level measurement is defined as:

$$\text{SROI} = \frac{\text{Social profit}}{\text{Social investment}}$$

The Principles of SROI

There are seven principles of SROI that support the application of SROI. These are:

Involve stakeholders: Stakeholders are the ones who are most impacted by the change being brought about. They should be informed and identified and involved during the entire process.

Understand what changes: There are two types of outcomes of any change process—intended outcomes and unintended outcomes. It is necessary to have sufficient proof of the changes that have been brought about.

Value the things that matter: Value all things that matter. Where direct measures are unavailable, suitable proxies should be used.

Only include what is material: Materiality requires an assessment of the criticality of that piece of information to the decision at hand. If this information is excluded would the decision-maker make a different decision?

Do not over-claim: Only that portion of benefits should be claimed that the organisation is responsible for creating.

Be transparent: All inputs and outcomes must be documented and made available to the stakeholders.

Verify the result: The results of SROI should be vetted by an independent assurance agency for it to be credible.

The SROI Measurement Process

Unless one follows a systematic process to arrive at SROI, the outcome is unlikely to be credible and reliable. The following steps are recommended for arriving at a credible and reliable SROI.

Step 1 – Map the stakeholders: It is important to establish the boundaries of the SROI measurement. First, one needs to figure out outcomes of the social intervention. Second, figure out who the stakeholders of the social project are. It may be worthwhile to list the stakeholders. Finally, one needs to understand how to involve the stakeholders in the project.

Step 2 – Map the outcomes: Once the project has gone mainstream the outcome of the project must be measured. This is typically done through an impact map. The creation of an impact map involves (a) starting on the Impact Map; (b) identifying inputs; (c) valuing inputs; (d) clarifying outputs; and (e) describing outcomes.[2]

Step 3 – Evidencing the outcomes and giving them a value: Step 2 provided a qualitative measure of the outcome of the social project. However, it is also important to put a monetary value to the outcome. This involves (i) developing outcome indicators; (ii) collecting outcomes

[2] SROI Network, 'A Guide to Social Return on Investment', London: Cabinet Office, 2012

data; (iii) establishing how long outcomes last; and (iv) putting a value on the outcome.[3]

Step 4: – Establishing the impact: The outcomes that we measure should be auditable. Hence it is essential that outcomes are not over claimed. Also, we need to figure out how much of the impact is because of one's own activity and how much of it would have taken place anyway or how much of the outcome would have occurred without our intervention and how long will the benefits last. This requires measurement of three key metrics:

Deadweight is a measure of the amount of outcome that would have happened even if the activity had not taken place. It is calculated as a percentage.

Attribution is an assessment of how much of the outcome was caused by the contribution of other organisations or people.

Drop-off is used to account for how the outcomes, in future, are likely to be less than current measurements. It is only calculated for outcomes that last more than one year

Step 5 – Calculating the return: Now all the inputs and outputs have been measured, SROI can be calculated using formula listed in the section *Social Return on Investment.*

Step 6 – Conducting a sensitivity analysis: Relying on a single SROI number can be dangerous. Many assumptions are made while computing SROI. Hence it makes sense to test the robustness of SROI to these assumptions.

Advantages and Disadvantages of SROI

Like any measurement, SROI also has its advantages and disadvantages. All the advantages and disadvantages of economic ROI apply to SROI as well, and some more.

Advantages

1. It is simple and easy to calculate. Requires only two pieces of information—profits and investment—numbers that are already available in financial statements.
2. It measures profitability by scaling social profits to the investment made. Thus, companies are comparable on SROI.

[3] ibid.

Disadvantages

1. SROI measurement is impacted by the point of time when the measurement is undertaken.
2. Profit (the numerator) is impacted by accounting choices.
3. Measuring social costs and benefits often requires measuring shadow prices—making it complicated to apply in practice. For example, where water is conserved in a water scarce area, the value of water conservation depends upon the extent of water scarcity. The higher the water scarcity, higher would be the value of water.
4. Measurement of deadweight, attribution and drop off poses significant challenges as there are no direct measures. Estimates must be made based on prevailing local conditions. Such measurement errors could have a significant impact on SROI.

TN 3: THE INTEGRATED REPORTING FRAMEWORK

A company's performance is no longer limited to financial numbers. Companies also look to be seen as responsible citizens and like to report a host of factors such as sustainability, corporate governance. For the past couple of decades companies are generating sustainability reports alongside annual reports. In India, there is another format, Business Responsibility Report (BRR), a requirement mandated for the top 500 companies by the Securities and Exchange Board of India (SEBI) in 2015.

Current forms of business reporting have many nagging issues. Many companies still believe that reporting is merely a compliance issue. They tend to miss the focus on communication to key stakeholders. Different strands of reporting have also evolved separately, with new additions being constantly made to the reporting guidelines. The volume of information is therefore increasing at a rapid pace. Lengthy documents are being created that leads to obfuscation of critical information. Since all information is not available in one document, analysing the actions of a company becomes difficult and does not really give a complete picture to all stakeholders. For instance, critical linkages between strategy and risk, financial and non-financial performance are often not explained or remain unclear. Diverging disclosure practices in different countries also inhibits stakeholders from understanding and comparing the information they need for decision making.

All this, possibly, led to the conception of the Integrated Reporting format a few years back. Integrated Reporting aims to bring together material information about an organisation's strategy, governance, performance and prospects in a single document. It is designed to reflect the commercial, social and environmental context within which a company operates. An integrated report provides a clear and concise representation of how an organisation demonstrates stewardship and how it creates and sustains value. According to International Integrated Reporting Council (IIRC), 'All organisations depend on various forms of capital for their success. It is important that all such forms of capital are disclosed to stakeholders to enable informed investment decision making.' IIRC has categorised the forms of capital as: Financial capital, Manufactured capital, Intellectual capital, Human capital, Social and Relationship capital and Natural capital. IIRC establishes guidelines for the creation of a comprehensive report.

SEBI released a circular some time back that encourages the top 500 BSE listed companies to use Integrated Reporting framework to improve the quality and relevance of the information. The circular states that Integrated Reporting may be adopted on a voluntary basis from the financial year 2017-18 by Top 500 companies. These are also the companies that are required to prepare a BRR. It suggests that the information related to Integrated Reporting may be provided in the annual report separately or by incorporating into 'Management Discussion and Analysis' or by preparing a separate annual report as per IR framework.

This is a huge change not just in terms of reporting but also reflects on how companies need to think about responsible growth. With this circular, SEBI has initiated a process for companies to move out of their current reporting formats and integrate reporting with business decisions.

TN 4: BLOCKCHAINS AND RESPONSIBLE BUSINESS

Contracts, transactions and their record form the foundation of our economic, legal and political systems. They help protect assets and set the boundaries of an organisation. They are critical to establishing and verifying identities and recording events. Contracts govern interactions among organisations, communities, and individuals. They also guide managerial and social action. With large amounts of data sweeping through corporate systems it has become impossible to keep a good track of the contracts, transactions and their records. This is where blockchain comes in.

So, what is blockchain? A block chain is a mathematical structure to store data, that is nearly impossible to fake. Blockchain technology is also known as a distributed ledger technology. It is an open, distributed ledger that can record transactions between two parties in an efficient and verifiable manner. One can imagine blockchain as a giant spreadsheet that runs on millions of computers. The blockchain is distributed, open source and everyone can see what is going on.

These ledgers perform the following functions:

- **They confirm identity:** Just like Permanent Account Numbers (PAN) and Aadhaar numbers, companies and individuals can be identified and lined in a way that eliminates duplication, impersonation and forgery.
- **They confirm status:** Companies are identified by their Corporate Identification Number (CIN), the individual's residential status is identified by her passport number. These numbers form a part of the ledger and confirm an entity's or individual's status.
- **They confirm authority:** Ledgers identify who can validly sit in parliament, who can access what bank account, who can work with children, who can enter restricted areas.
- **They map social and economic relations:** They are indicative of relations and how they change. Thus, if an individual changes her status from resident to non-resident, ledgers track them. Thus, they are able to provide an accurate indicator of the current status of social and economic relations.

In the blockchain world contracts are embedded in the digital code. This code is stored in transparent, shared databases where they are protected from deletion, revision, and tampering. In this world, every agreement, every process and every transaction has a digital record and signature that can be identified, validated, stored, and shared.

The real thing happens when these digital ledger entries are being distributed among a deployment or infrastructure. These additional nodes and layers in the infrastructure serve the purpose of providing a consensus about the state of a transaction at any given second. They all have copies of the existing authenticated ledger distributed amongst them.

When a new transaction or an edit to an existing transaction comes in, generally a majority of the nodes within a blockchain implementation must execute some algorithms and essentially evaluate and verify the history of the individual blockchain block that is proposed, and come to a consensus that the history and signature is valid, then the new transaction is accepted into the ledger and a new block is added to the chain of transactions. If a majority of nodes do not concede to the addition or modification of the ledger entry, then it is denied and not added to the chain. This distributed consensus model is what allows blockchain to run as a distributed ledger without the need for some central, unifying authority saying what transactions are valid and (perhaps more importantly) which ones are not.

Futurists anticipate that the need for intermediaries like lawyers and bankers is likely to disappear. Transactions are likely to become frictionless.

There are many new uses for blockchain emerging almost every day. This new way of transacting could support business responsibility in many ways by supporting green supply chains, measuring water use, emissions management and supporting the sharing economy.

TN 5: UNDERSTANDING CLIMATE FINANCE

There is an urgent need to stabilise the global climate and this will be a priority in the coming decades. The phenomenon of global warming is upon us and affects all people and ecosystems. It will impact the poor disproportionately. Large scale investments are required to take to decarbonise the world and reduce greenhouse gas concentration. This is a costly exercise. The World Economic Forum[4] projects that by 2020, about $5.7 trillion will need to be invested annually in green infrastructure, much of which will be in today's developing world. Resources of developing countries are limited and undertaking massive investments poses challenges. This is where climate finance comes. A cursory look at the world map shows that more countries need money than countries that provide money.

Climate finance refers to financing channelled by national, regional and international entities for climate change mitigation and adaptation projects and programs. They include climate specific support mechanisms and financial aid for mitigation and adaptation activities to spur and enable the transition towards low-carbon, climate-resilient growth and development through capacity building, R&D and economic development.

What distinguishes Climate Finance?

There are differences between climate finance and conventional financing that companies source. The differences arise due to:

1. Risks — Difficulty in evaluating climate projects—higher and different kinds of risks entailed.
2. Sources of funding — Significant chunks of funding from governments and multilateral agencies.
3. Purpose: The use to which money is put to mitigate the impact of climate change.

[4] World Economic Forum, The Green Investment Report The ways and means to unlock private finance for green growth. 2013 https://www3.weforum.org/docs/WEF_GreenInvestment_Report_2013.pdf

Classification of Climate Finance

What is part of climate finance and what is not? Separating the two is problematic. This is more so when it comes to dealing with the impacts of climate change.

Several actions will make countries more resilient to climate change. These include better education and healthcare, access to safe drinking water, improved disaster relief and the availability of micro-finance. However, these are also basic development objectives. Therefore if the aim is climate-resilient development, there is no clear distinction between adaptation assistance and development aid.

The structure of Climate Finance

Finance is sourced from public, private and public-private sectors. It can be channelled through various intermediaries, notably Development Financial Institutions, Multilateral Financial Institutions, development cooperation agencies, the UNFCCC (various funds including those managed by the Global Environment Facility), non-governmental organisations and the private sector. The financial flows can flow from developed to developing countries (North-South), from developing to developing countries (South-South), from developed to developed countries (North-North) and domestic climate finance flows in developed and developing countries.

Instruments and Innovations in Climate Finance

Green bonds

A green bond is quite like a regular bond. The difference is that the issuer of a green bond publicly states that capital is being raised to fund 'green' projects. Typically these relate to renewable energy, emission reductions and so on. According to Moody's,[5] global green bond issuances are likely to surge by 60 per cent to a record $250 billion this year, with India and China leading the emerging markets in this space.

Catastrophe bonds

Catastrophe bonds (cat bonds, for short) are risk-linked securities that transfer a specified set of risks from a sponsor to investors. The aftermath of Hurricane Andrew and the Northridge earthquake led to their creation

[5] https://www.thehindubusinessline.com/markets/global-green-bonds-set-to-hit-record-levels-india-to-lead-emerging-markets-moodys/article22677873.ece

and they were first used in the mid-1990s. The use of catastrophe bonds helps ease the burden on poor and developing countries affected by increasingly devastating climate disasters. If specified disaster scenarios are met, these bonds are paid out towards recovery efforts. Investors get their money back along with interest if disasters are averted.

Global Environment Facility (GEF)

The GEF is an operating entity of UNFCCC's financial mechanism. An independently operating financial organisation, the GEF provides grants for projects related to biodiversity, climate change, international waters, land degradation, the ozone layer, and persistent organic pollutants.

Extreme Climate facility (XCF)

The Extreme Climate Facility is a new financial mechanism that will secure direct access to climate finance for African governments to respond to the impacts of increased climate volatility.

UN Land Degradation Neutrality Fund

The UN's Land Degradation Neutrality Fund draws on both private and public financing to rehabilitate and sustain 12 million hectares (29.64m acres) of land every year. This is for the land that has been mismanaged and degraded by human activity like unsustainable farming practices.

Climate Finance and COP21

A significant step towards creating a fund to address climate change as a global effort was achieved at the 17th Conference of Parties (COP) of the UNFCCC held in 2011 at Cancun (Mexico). This was done through the launch of the Green Climate Fund (GCF). One of the key objectives of the fund is to promote, and enable countries to make a paradigm shift towards low-emission, climate resilient and gender-sensitive development pathways. These objectives are met by providing suitable resources to meet the full and incremental costs of these pathways.

At the Paris COP21, the directors of GCF announced the approval of the organization's first eight projects. These investments will provide US$ 168 million for greenhouse gas emission reduction and climate resiliency efforts in African, Latin American, and the Asian and Pacific island nations. The projects range from investments in industrial-sector energy efficiency, to ecosystem restoration, water and wastewater infrastructure improvements, and development of climate change early warning systems.

TN 6: IMPACT INVESTING

Consider some facts. Access to safe water, health care, or financial services is not available to two billion people on this planet. Almost a billion people are deprived of access to electricity. Two hundred and fifty million children do not have access to education or childhood immunisation. The problems are immense and need quick solutions. With limited public funds, the need for private investment in public areas is acutely felt. The role of private enterprise is expanded by impact investing in addressing the world's most pressing social problems.

Impact investing is defined by The Global Impact Investing Network (GIIN)[6] as, 'Investments made into companies, organisations, and funds with the intention to generate measurable social and environmental impact alongside a financial return.' Impact investing also goes by several other names—socially responsible investing, social investing, mission-driven investing, responsible investing, among others.

Impact investing seeks to support organisations that will create social and environmental benefits, in addition to generating financial returns. Impact investors would like their money to make a difference for employees, clients, and other groups in society — at the same time creating financial value. Impact investors fund organisations that will positively impact society. They might invest in companies that develop affordable housing, install solar power plants, or improve women's lives, for example.

Impact investing should not be confused with 'negative' investing, for instance by refusing to invest in tobacco companies. It is not about protesting at a company's annual meeting or agitating for a change in policy. Neither is it about passive investment in companies that aim to be socially responsible.

Impact investing is gaining substantial traction. Industry research suggests that approximately 8,000 impact investments worth $22.1 billion were made in 2016. This amounts to almost a four-fold increase in investments from 2010. In India, the impetus is likely to come from the new Companies Act (2013) that mandates 2 per cent investment in CSR

[6] GIIN, Annual Impact Investor Survey. May 2017 https://thegiin.org/assets/GIIN_AnnualImpactInvestorSurvey_2017_Web_Final.pdf

activities (subject to certain criteria). According to Dr Maximilian Martin,[7] growth in impact investing is likely to come from four sources:

Massive pent-up demand at the bottom of the pyramid – People in the low-income segment are increasingly demanding products and services. The producers will need to tap this unfulfilled need.

Driving green growth – Investment in renewables is growing. A sharp rise in the renewables sector is also predicted.

Reconfiguration of the welfare state – Radical shifts in how we approach output of public goods will lead to opportunities for the private sector.

Emerging lifestyles of health and sustainability segment at the top of the pyramid – This is already a fast and growing segment.

Although traditional investors have been foundations, development financial institutions and high net worth individuals have contributed. However, the landscape is changing. Individual investors are increasingly interested and able to access dedicated mutual funds or community bonds.[8]

Impact investors also create new financial instruments such as social impact bonds and are a contract with the public sector in which a commitment is made to pay for improved social outcomes that results in public sector savings. For example, in 2016, the International Finance Corporation worked with mining company BHP Billiton, and the non-profit organisation, Conservation International, to issue a $152 million bond to protect forests and expand carbon-credit markets in developing countries.[9]

Impact investing has seen remarkable growth and visibility. However, significant challenges remain. It is often pointed out that the lack of track

[7] Maximilian Martin, Status of the Social Impact Investing Market: A Primer, Impact Economy and UK Cabinet Office, June 2013 https://assets.publishing.service.gov.uk/government/uploads/system/uploads/attachment_data/file/212511/Status_of_the_Social_Impact_Investing_Market_-_A_Primer.pdf

[8] Community bonds are interest-bearing bonds intended for small-scale, non-accredited investors and can only be issued by a non-profit organisation.

[9] https://nbs.net/p/why-impact-investing-matters-a-primer-ea88a0d5-14c3-4ecb-84eb-6ab01de4cf37

record of successful investments is a primary concern. Also, there are only a limited number of established players that are active in impact investing.

One of the critical challenges in impact investing is the measurement problem. Let us take the case where the impact of an investment is the creation of three jobs. Then the outcome would be increased wages to the workers, higher taxes to the state and reduced government subsidies. However, if one of the workers finds a job without the investment, then the effective benefit would be a net of two persons. The employment without the intervention of the programme is, often, not easy to find out. Hence it is difficult to track impact over time.

The much stricter fiduciary obligations of institutional investors is another challenge. Lack of a successful track record and the shortage of scalable and attractive investment opportunities create barriers to impact investing. A layering of financial instruments (e.g. grants and programme related investments) also makes it harder to define the impact of investing accurately.

Governance is an area of significant concern. Profiting from the poor can be a grey area. Significant attention needs to be paid towards creating frameworks that build an independent third-party monitoring mechanism.

Other roadblocks include investor scepticism about achieving both financial returns and creating social impact together, imperfect information regarding investment opportunity set, limited exit strategies due to insufficiently developed and illiquid markets.

According to a study by McKinsey,[10] in India, impact investing has grown steadily to a $5.2 billion value. The study shows that the average ticket size of a deal has grown from $7.6 million in 2010 to $17.6 million in 2016. The table below provides an indicator of the growth of impact investing in India. McKinsey's study estimates an average annual growth rate of 14 per cent and a weighted average internal rate of return (IRR) of 11 per cent and an average holding period of 4.9 years.

[10] Vivek Pandit and Toshan Tamhane, Impact investing finds its place in India, McKinsey Report, September 2017

Year	Value ($m)	No. of deals
2010	493	65
2011	772	63
2012	840	65
2013	438	81
2014	593	80
2015	1002	70
2016	1072	61

Source: McKinsey (https://www.mckinsey.com/industries/private-equity-and-principal-investors/our-insights/impact-investing-finds-its-place-in-india)

Despite several roadblocks, impact investing is expected to grow and become part of the mainstream finance.

TN 7: GUIDE TO THE CSR RULES

The **Companies Act, 2013** contains an important clause (Clause 135) that mandates CSR regulations for Indian companies. The final rules were notified on 27th February 2014, coming into force on 1st April 2014.

This piece provides a guide to the rules and how these rules affect your business.

Who are these rules applicable for?

The mandatory CSR clause is applicable to companies with net worth of Rs 500 crores or more, an annual turnover of Rs 1000 crores or more, or an annual net profit of Rs 5 crores or more.

How is net profit calculated?

1. Net profit before tax, not including profits arising from branches outside India.
2. The two per cent CSR spending needs to be computed as two per cent of the average net profits made by the company during every block of three years. For the purpose of the first CSR reporting, the net profit should be calculated as average of the annual net profit of the preceding three financial years ending on or before 31 March 2014.

2 per cent CSR Expenditure – What does it include?

1. CSR expenditure has to be in line with the amended Schedule VII of the Companies Act 2013. While the company can conduct CSR activities across a range of areas that it may deem suitable only investments in areas specified in Schedule VII will be considered as eligible CSR expenditure. Therefore, companies will have to draw up the policy and action plan to ensure that they spend the required 2 per cent amount on the activities included in Schedule VII.
2. CSR expenditure should exclude expenditure on activities undertaken in pursuance of the normal course of business of a company.
3. Foreign companies have to contribute to CSR based on the profits of their Indian business operations.
4. Companies belonging to the same group can set up a trust or not-for-profit company to undertake CSR. Companies can also join hands

with other companies to undertake CSR projects jointly. This would allow groups and companies operating in an area to come together and undertake projects of a larger scale.

Ten areas where the CSR Budget can be spent

i) **Eradicating hunger, poverty and malnutrition**, promoting preventative health care and sanitation and making available safe drinking water.

ii) **Promoting education** including special education and employment enhancing vocation skills especially among children, women, elderly, and the differently abled and livelihood enhancement projects.

iii) **Promoting gender equality**, empowering women, setting up homes and hostels for women and orphans; setting up old age homes, day-care centres and other such facilities for senior citizens and measures for reducing inequalities faced by socially and economically backward groups.

iv) **Ensuring environmental sustainability**, ecological balance, protection of flora and fauna, animal welfare, agroforestry, conservation of natural resources, and maintaining quality of soil, air and water.

v) **Protection of national heritage, art and culture** including restoration of buildings and sites of historical importance and works of art; setting up public libraries; promotion and development of traditional arts and handicrafts.

vi) **Measures for the benefit of armed forces veterans**, war widows and their dependents.

vii) **Training to promote rural sports**, regionally recognised sports, Paralympics sports.

viii) **Contribution to the Prime Minister's National Relief Fund** or any other fund set up by the Central Government for socio-economic development and relief and welfare of the Scheduled Castes, the Scheduled Tribes, other backward classes, minorities and women.

ix) **Contributions or funds provided by technology incubators** located within academic institutions which are approved by the Central Government.

x) **Rural development projects**

xi) **Slum area development**

Directives for Companies

1. Create a 'CSR Committee' made up of three or more Directors, one of whom must be an independent director.
2. Report details of all CSR initiatives undertaken by the company in the Directors' Report and on the company website at the end of each year.
3. Create a 'Corporate Social Responsibility Policy' that details which activities will be undertaken by the company, and what budget will be spent on them. This should be published on the company's website.

The rules have brought clarity to the apprehensions which the companies have had with regard to CSR expenditure. The range of themes is likely to promote national causes. It will now be up to companies to expand their range of activities.

TN 8: THE PARIS AGREEMENT (COP 21)

COP21, the 21st edition of the Conference of the Parties was a landmark event of 2015. After 21 years of intense debates and negotiations, governments world over have finally come to a legally binding agreement aiming to contain the increase in the global average temperature to 'well below 2°C above pre-industrial levels and to pursue efforts to limit the temperature increase to 1.5°C above pre-industrial levels.' This is a more ambitious goal than had been expected. This new climate deal will come into force in 2020.

The Paris Agreement aims to maintain and speed up that momentum. It offers clear directions setting out:

- long-term goals and signals,
- a commitment to meet periodically to strengthen climate action,
- a response to the impact of extreme climate events on the most at-risk,
- the transparency needed to ensure action takes place and
- finance, capacity building and technology to enable real change

The Agreement has five key principles:

Long-term mitigation goals

Governments have agreed to limit warming to 1.5°C above pre-industrial levels. Such a stiff goal would have appeared unthinkable just a few years ago. John Schellnhuber, a scientist who advises Germany and the Vatican, has taken a position that 1.5°C marks the point where there is a real danger of serious 'tipping points' in the world's climate. The goal of 1.5°C is a big leap below the 2°C that nearly 200 countries agreed as a limit six years ago in Copenhagen.

Five-Year Cycles of Action

To build on the momentum from countries' national climate plans put forward for Paris, countries have agreed to a process to ramp up action on emissions every five years. By 2020, countries aim to come back and either submit new or updated national climate plans (known as nationally determined contributions). Every five years after that, countries will submit new contributions. Countries have also agreed that their mitigation plans will represent a progression beyond their previous efforts.

Adaptation

A central issue for global climate action in the Paris Agreement is adaptation to climate change. It is on par with mitigation. It establishes a global goal of enhancing adaptive capacity, strengthening resilience and reducing vulnerability. It also includes an adequate adaptation response given the Agreement's temperature goal. A cycle of action for strengthening adaptation efforts regularly is created by the Paris Agreement, which is similar to the mitigation cycle. Countries will possess flexibility on the timing and methods for communicating information about their adaptation activities or efforts. Developing countries will be supported for planning, implementation and communication of adaptation activities.

Transparency

The Agreement establishes a common system for transparency for all countries. Through an enhanced transparency framework, companies will be expected to report on their emissions and track progress on achieving their nationally determined contributions on a regular basis. The information provided by all parties will be subject to a review by experts. This will facilitate multilateral consideration of progress. The framework provides flexibility and support that takes account of different countries' capacities. Developed countries will report on the money and support they provide. Developing countries will report on the finance and support needed and received.

Climate Finance

Finance will power the world towards a decarbonised, climate-resilient future. The purpose of the Agreement states that all financial flows—both public and private—need to be shifted from high to low-emissions activities and from risky to resilient investments. The Agreement makes clear that developed countries will continue to provide and mobilise finance to support developing countries. Developed countries have agreed to continue their 2020 commitment of mobilizing $100 billion a year until 2025. After that, governments will adopt a new, higher collective goal, though the extent to which finance will increase, and who will mobilise it, is a significant outstanding question. The Agreement provides an opportunity for developing countries to provide support to their peers, recognising that some developing countries are already supporting their peers.

Additionally, governments have agreed to balance public funding between adaptation and mitigation. They have also agreed to significantly increase support for adaptation before 2020. This is vitally important for the most vulnerable countries dealing with the impacts of rising temperatures. Countries also committed to improve reporting on finance, with everyone providing information about finance provided or received, as appropriate.

Timeline of COP meetings

Year	Event
1992	Governments craft UN Framework Convention on Climate Change in Rio to take steps, without specifying any, against climate change. Next five years, governments wrangle over role of developed countries over poorer nations
1995	COP1 - Berlin
1996	COP2 - Geneva
1997	COP3 - Kyoto: Talks of 5 per cent emission cuts compared with 1990 levels, by 2012. Each developed country allowed reduction targets. But, China, South Korea, Mexico and other rapidly emerging economies allowed to increase emissions at will.
1998	COP4 - Buenos Aires
1999	COP5 - Bonn
2000	COP6 - The Hague
2001	COP7 - Marrakesh
2002	COP 8 - New Delhi
2003	COP9 - Milan
2004	COP10 - Buenos Aires: Russia decides to pass treaty. Protocol came into force. But with the US remaining out of Kyoto, no agreement.
2005	COP11 - Montreal
2006	COP12 - Nairobi
2007	COP13 - Bali: New agreement on plan to replace Kyoto protocol.
2008	COP14 - Poznan

Year	Event
2009	COP15 - Copenhagen: Developed nations agree on greenhouse gas limits, but no treaty.
2010	COP16 - Cancun: rich nations agree to help poor countries.
2011	COP17 - Durban: Agree to start negotiations on a legally binding deal comprising all countries, to be adopted in 2015. Also progress regarding the creation of a Green Climate Fund (GCF)
2012	COP18 - Doha: produced a package of documents collectively titled The Doha Climate Gateway.
2013	COP19 - Warsaw
2014	COP20 - Lima
2015	COP21 - Paris: Legally binding agreement to limit global warming to well below 2°C compared to pre-industrial levels
2016	COP22 – Marrakesh
2017	COP23 - Bonn

Source: https://en.wikipedia.org/wiki/United_Nations_Climate_Change_conference

What do businesses need to do?

- Adopt science-based carbon reduction targets based on global emissions budgets.
- Put a price on carbon; both implement an internal price high enough to materially affect investment decisions and advocate publicly for policies that would require all businesses to do so.
- Procure 100 per cent of electricity from renewable sources.
- Engage with climate policy by internally auditing all activities related to climate, then communicate subsequent actions and outcomes.
- Help close information gaps by including climate change information in 'mainstream reports as a fiduciary duty', as outlined by the Climate Disclosure Standards Board.
- Commit to weeding commodity-driven deforestation out of supply chains by 2020.
- Contribute to faster results by eliminating short-term climate pollutants, like methane, black carbon and HFCs.

TN 9: SUSTAINABLE DEVELOPMENT GOALS (SDGs)

The United Nations has set out a collection of seventeen interrelated goals called the sustainable development goals (SDG). Each of the broad goals has targets. The total of all the targets is 169. A broad range of social development issues like hunger, poverty, education, health, climate change, gender equality, water, sanitation, energy, environment and social justice are covered under their ambit. These are also called 'Transforming the World: the 2030 Agenda for Sustainable Development'.

The SDGs were officially adopted at a UN summit in New York in September 2015 and became applicable from January 2016. The deadline for the SDGs is 2030.

The SDGs were set up to replace the Millennium Development goals (MDGs). Unlike the MDGs, the SDGs do not distinguish between the developing and the developed countries.

The seventeen SDGs are:

1. End poverty in all its forms everywhere
2. End hunger, achieve food security and improved nutrition, and promote sustainable agriculture
3. Ensure healthy lives and promote wellbeing for all at all ages
4. Ensure inclusive and equitable quality education and promote lifelong learning opportunities for all
5. Achieve gender equality and empower all women and girls
6. Ensure availability and sustainable management of water and sanitation for all
7. Ensure access to affordable, reliable, sustainable and modern energy for all
8. Promote sustained, inclusive and sustainable economic growth, full and productive employment, and decent work for all
9. Build resilient infrastructure, promote inclusive and sustainable industrialisation, and foster innovation
10. Reduce inequality within and among countries
11. Make cities and human settlements inclusive, safe, resilient and sustainable
12. Ensure sustainable consumption and production patterns
13. Take urgent action to combat climate change and its impacts (taking note of agreements made by the UNFCCC forum)

14. Conserve and sustainably use the oceans, seas and marine resources for sustainable development
15. Protect, restore and promote sustainable use of terrestrial ecosystems, sustainably manage forests, combat desertification and halt and reverse land degradation, and halt biodiversity loss
16. Promote peaceful and inclusive societies for sustainable development, provide access to justice for all and build effective, accountable and inclusive institutions at all levels
17. Strengthen the means of implementation and revitalise the global partnership for sustainable development

TN 10: INDIA'S WASTE MANAGEMENT LAWS

India's waste management is governed by a host of laws. Waste management is governed by the Ministry of Environment, Forests and Climate Change (MoEF&CC, earlier MoEF) and the state pollution control boards.

The Environmental Protection Act, 1986

This Act was enacted in 1986. It aims to establish a system for the protection of the environment and the regulation of waste. This Act confers powers to the Central Government to regulate all forms of waste. Some of the important provisions of this Act are given as under:

1. Section 7 of this Act places a prohibition on harming the environment by stating that no person carrying out any activity should emit or discharge environmental pollutants in excess of the prescribed standards.
2. Section 9 of the Act states that if any event takes place which harms the environment through any foreseen or unforeseen event, the person responsible for the harm is duty bound to prevent or alleviate the pollutant discharged as a result of such an event. The person is also obliged to inform the proper authorities about the event which may harm the environment.
3. The Act also contains provisions which remove the corporate veil. In case any environmental offense was committed by a company, with the connivance or consent of any director, manager, secretary or any other officer of the company, they will be held personally liable for committing offenses in the name of the company.
4. Environmental Protection Rules-Commonly known as the Environmental Protection Rules, 1986, these rules were formulated by the government under the power conferred to them by the Environmental Protection Act. Through these powers, the government has the authority to give specific directions, without changing the principle Act.

Bio-Medical Waste (Management and Handling) Rules, 1998

The aim of these Rules is to ensure that bio-medical wastes are safely disposed of. Bio-medical waste can be defined as any waste or by-product generated during the treatment, immunisation and treatment of human beings or animals or in research activities. Schedule I of the Rules, differentiates biological wastes into different categories like microbiological and biotechnological, human anatomical, animal anatomical, discarded medicines, chemical related waste, etc.

The Bio-Medical Waste Rules apply to various institutions like nursing homes, animal houses, veterinary homes, blood banks, dispensaries, pathological laboratories, etc. The BMW Rules prohibit mixing of biological wastes with any other type of wastes. The general rule provided is that bio-medical wastes can't be stored beyond the period of 48 hours without being treated.

The Batteries (Management and Handling) Rules, 2001

The Batteries Rules were notified to set up a mechanism in place which deals with the disposal of lead acid batteries. The Rules apply to every manufacturer, recycler, dealer, importer, assembler, bulk consumer (like organisations and department purchasing more than 100 batteries) and consumers. Rule 10 makes it compulsory for every consumer to deposit the used batteries back with the dealer, manufacturer, recycler or with labelled collection centres. Under Rule 6, if a recycler wants to import used batteries in India, for the purpose of recycling, (s)he must first obtain Custom clearance. Additionally, import of batteries will be allowed only upon producing valid registration with the Reserve Bank of India and MoEF and providing an undertaking in the prescribed format along with a copy of the latest half-yearly return.

The Hazardous Wastes (Management, Handling and Transboundary Movement) Rules, 2008

Management of hazardous waste is a very complex issue. Certain rules and regulations are required, which together form the legal regime. The Rules place an obligation on the occupier of hazardous waste to safe and sound handling of environmental waste. The occupier is that person under whose charge there is a plant or unit or factory which produces hazardous waste as a result of their operation. The occupier must sell or send the hazardous waste to a re-processor or recycler, who is authorized by the government to dispose of the waste in a safe manner. Any person who is engaged in storage, package, collection, destruction, conversion, processing, etc., also has to take authorisation from the State Pollution Board.

The recyclers, occupiers, re-users, re-processors can store the waste for up to 90 days.

Sale or transfer of hazardous waste can be done only after obtaining a valid registration from the Central Pollution Control Board (CPCB). Use of the waste as a source of energy also requires registration from the CPCB.

The cross-border shipment of hazardous waste is regulated by the Basel Convention, to which India is a signatory. Import of hazardous waste for disposal in India is prohibited by law, although import for the purpose of reuse, recovery as an energy source and recycling is allowed, subject to certain restrictions. India allows for the export of hazardous waste but only with the prior informed consent of the importing country.

The Plastic Waste (Management and Handling) Rules, 2011

The Plastic Waste Management (PWM) Rules is a regulatory framework set up to control the use, manufacture, and recycling of plastic waste. Plastic waste includes any plastic product which has been discarded after use or at the end of the product's life. The Rules have a uniform applicability towards all distributors, users, retailers and manufacturers of plastic products. Rule 9 makes it compulsory for every manufacturer of plastic products and recycler to obtain registration from the State Pollution Control Board and this has to be renewed every three years. Rule 10 states that no retailer can provide plastic bags free of cost. This is done to ensure that people use plastic bags judiciously. The PWM rules also specify the classification of plastic products such as compostable, recyclable or virgin plastic, thickness, and colour.

Recycling of plastic products is to be done according to a fixed procedure laid down by the Bureau of Indian Standard Specification.

The E- Waste (Management and Handling) Rules, 2011

The prime aim of the E-Waste Management (EWM) Rules is to put in place a system that manages e-waste in an environment-friendly way by regulating the issue of recycling and the disposal of e-waste. The large and growing information technology industry creates a lot of e-waste, disposal of which is necessary. A lot of e-waste also gets illegally imported into India, which worsens the problem.

E-waste defined under the Rule 3 (k) means any electronic or electrical equipment which has been rejected after use or has been discarded. The by-products which are discarded during the manufacturing process also fall under this category. The producer of electronic and electrical goods must obtain permission from the State Pollution Control Board under rule 4. E-waste Rules also delineate the responsibilities of collection centres, consumers, bulk consumers, dismantlers, and recyclers.

The Solid Waste Management Rules, 2016

Some of the key features of these rules are:

Segregation of waste: The new rules have mandated the source segregation of waste in order to channelise the waste by recovery, reuse and recycle. Waste generators would now have to segregate waste into three streams—Biodegradables, Dry (Plastic, Paper, metal, Wood, etc.) and Domestic Hazardous waste (diapers, napkins, mosquito repellents, cleaning agents, etc.], before handing it over to the collector.

Collection and disposal of sanitary waste: The manufacturers or brand owners of sanitary napkins are responsible for awareness about the proper disposal of such waste by the generator and shall provide a pouch or wrapper for the disposal of each napkin or diapers along with the packet of their sanitary products.

Collect back scheme for packaging waste: As per the rules, brand owners who sell or market their products in packaging materials which are non-biodegradable, should put in place a system to collect back the packaging waste generated due to their production.

Waste processing and treatment: As per the new rules, it has been advised that the bio-degradable waste should be processed, treated and disposed of through composting or bio-methanation, within the premises as far as possible, and the residual waste shall be given to the waste collectors or agency as directed by the local authority. The developers of special economic zones, industrial estates, industrial parks to earmark at least 5 per cent of the total area of the plot or minimum five plots or sheds for recovery and recycling facility.

Promoting use of compost: As per the rules, the Department of Fertilisers, Ministry of Chemicals and Fertilizers, should provide market development assistance for city compost and ensure promotion of co-marketing of compost with chemical fertilisers in the ratio of 3-4 bags is to 6-7 bags by the fertiliser companies to the extent compost is made available for marketing to the companies. Also, the Ministry of Agriculture should provide flexibility in Fertiliser Control Order for the manufacturing and sale of compost, propagating use of compost on farm land and set up laboratories to test the quality of compost produced by local authorities or their authorised agencies.

Promotion of waste to energy: The rules emphasise promotion of waste to energy plants. The rules mandate all industrial units using fuel and located within 100 kilometres from a solid waste-based Refuse-Derived Fuel (RDF) plant to make arrangements within six months from the date of notification of these rules to replace at least 5 per cent of their fuel requirement by RDF so produced.

Management of waste in hilly areas: As per the new rules, construction of landfills on hills shall be avoided. Land for construction of sanitary landfills in hilly areas will be identified in the plain areas, within 25 kilometres. However, transfer stations and processing facilities shall be operational in the hilly areas.

Constitution of a Central Monitoring Committee: The government has also constituted a Central Monitoring Committee under the chairmanship of the Secretary, MoEF&CC, to monitor the overall implementation of the rules. The Committee comprising of various stakeholders from the Central and state governments will meet once a year to monitor the implementation of these rules.

TN 11: NATURAL CAPITAL PROTOCOL

According to the Natural Capital Coalition, 'Natural capital is another term for the stock of renewable and non-renewable natural resources (e.g. plants, animals, air, water, soils and minerals) that combine to yield a flow of benefits to people.' Natural capital is one of the many recognised forms of capital. Other types of capital include financial, manufactured, social and relationship, human, and intellectual capital. Natural capital supports all of the other types of capital by providing essential resources such as air, water, soil and minerals, supporting a healthy planet that underpins thriving societies and prosperous economies.

The Natural Capital Protocol is a framework designed to help generate trusted, credible, and actionable information for business managers to inform decisions. Every business depends on natural capital. For example, the aluminium industry is dependent on and mining of bauxite. It also impacts natural capital through its decisions, like the degradation of forests cleared to make space for a factory. Each of these impacts and dependencies has either a positive impact (cleaner water) or a negative impact (air pollution).

The information provided through the protocol entails the following steps:

Get Started: Why should you conduct a natural capital assessment?

Defining the objective: What is the objective of the assessment?

Scope the assessment: What is the scope of your natural capital assessment?

Determine the impacts/dependencies: Which impacts and/or dependencies are material?

Measure impact drivers and/or dependencies: How can the impact drivers and/or dependencies be measured?

Measuring the changes in the state of natural capital: What are the changes in the state and trends of natural capital related to the business impacts and/or dependencies?

Value impacts and/or dependencies: What is the value of the natural capital impacts and/or dependencies?

Interpret and test the results: How can you interpret, validate and verify your assessment process and results?

12. 'The Viral Fever' founder Arunabh Kumar booked for alleged sexual harassment, Firstpost, https://www.firstpost.com/entertainment/the-viral-fever-founder-arunabh-kumar-booked-for-alleged-sexual-harassment-3359104.html
13. Eric Schmidt, Google and Privacy, MarketWatch, https://www.marketwatch.com/story/eric-schmidt-google-and-privacy-2009-12-11
14. Cyber Violence Against Women And Girls , UNESCO, http://www.unesco.org/new/fileadmin/MULTIMEDIA/HQ/CI/CI/images/wsis/GenderReport2015FINAL.pdf
15. Human Trafficking In Asia Going Online, East Asia Forum, http://www.eastasiaforum.org/2014/05/03/human-trafficking-in-asia-going-online/
16. Child-Snatchers Abducting as Many as 200,000 Boys and Girls And Openly Selling Them Online for Up To £10,000 in Kidnapping Epidemic Which is Destroying Families Across China, Daily Mail, http://www.dailymail.co.uk/news/article-2989404/Child-snatchers-abducting-200-000-boys-girls-openly-selling-online-10-000-kidnapping-epidemic-destroying-families-China.html
17. James Mayinka, et al, What the future of work will mean for jobs skills and wages, McKinsey Global Institute, December 2017 https://www.mckinsey.com/featured-insights/future-of-organizations-and-work/what-the-future-of-work-will-mean-for-jobs-skills-and-wages
18. Ibid.
19. The Global Risks Report 2017, World Economic Forum, https://www.weforum.org/reports/the-global-risks-report-2017
20. Transitions in the Indian Energy Sector - Macro Level Analysis of Demand and Supply Side Options, TERI, http://www.teriin.org/files/transition-report/mobile/index.html
21. India will be able to cater to 57 percent of its electricity capacity from renewable energy by 2027.
22. Report on India's Renewable Electricity Roadmap 2030, Niti Aayog, http://niti.gov.in/writereaddata/files/document_publication/RE_Roadmap_ExecutiveSummary.pdf
23. NITI Aayog Bats for Holistic Green Energy Policy to Bring Down Costs, *The Economic Times*, https://economictimes.indiatimes.com/news/economy/policy/niti-aayog-bats-for-holistic-green-energy-policy-to-bring-down-costs/articleshow/46306777.cms *and* Report on India's Renewable Electricity Roadmap 2030, Niti Aayog, http://niti.gov.in/writereaddata/files/document_publication/RE_Roadmap_ExecutiveSummary.pdf

24. Year End Review 2017 – Ministry of New and Renewable Energy, PIB, http://pib.nic.in/PressReleaseIframePage.aspx?PRID=1514215
25. India Could See 10GW Of Solar Installations In 2017, Says Report, livemint, https://www.livemint.com/Industry/xtRTwc5oLuqRsRpw5pQTRP/India-could-see-10GW-of-solar-installations-in-2017-says-re.html
26. Ibid.
27. Ibid.
28. Ibid.
29. India's NTPC Invites Bids for 24mwh Battery Storage to Pair With 17MW PV Farm, Energy Storage News, https://www.energy-storage.news/news/indias-ntpc-invites-bids-for-24mwh-battery-to-pair-with-17mw-pv-farm
30. Energy Storage Market to Touch 70 GW By 2022, India Energy Storage Alliance, https://indiaesa.info/news-menu/871-energy-storage-market-to-touch-70-gw-by-2022
31. Off-Grid Renewable Energy Storage Market To Be Worth Rs16,500 Crore By 2022: Report, Livemint, https://www.livemint.com/Industry/dMVXsavAUuGEsyIa04VERM/Offgrid-renewable-energy-storage-market-to-be-worth-Rs1650.html
32. Energy Storage Market for Off-Grid Renewable Energy in India to Touch Rs 16,500 Crore By 2022: CEEW, *The Economic Times*, https://energy.economictimes.indiatimes.com/news/renewable/energy-storage-market-for-off-grid-renewable-energy-in-india-to-touch-rs-16500-crore-by-2022-ceew/58697466
33. Global EV Outlook 2017, International Energy Agency, https://www.iea.org/publications/freepublications/publication/GlobalEVOutlook2017.pdf
34. India Leaps Ahead: Transformative Mobility Solutions for All, Niti Aayog, http://niti.gov.in/writereaddata/files/document_publication/RMI_India_Report_web.pdf
35. National Electric Mobility Mission Plan, Department of Heavy Industry, http://dhi.nic.in/UserView/index?mid=1347
36. India Considers 100% Electric Vehicles By 2030, Clean Technica, https://cleantechnica.com/2017/04/21/india-considers-100-electric-vehicles-2030/
37. Ibid.
38. Fame India Scheme, PIB, http://pib.nic.in/newsite/PrintRelease.aspx?relid=154119
39. Ola partners with Indian Oil Corporation Limited (IOCL) to establish

the first fast-charging electric vehicle station in a fuel station Ola Cabs website, https://www.olacabs.com/media/press/ola-partners-with-indian-oil-corporation-limited-iocl-to-establish-the-first-fast-charging-electric-vehicle-station-in-a-fuel-station

40. The mining sector in India (taking into account atomic, major and minor minerals and fuel) made up 2.4 percent of the GDP in 2014-2015.
41. Water Is the Next 'Gold', CISION PR Newswire, https://www.prnewswire.com/news-releases/water-is-the-next-gold-300536804.html
42. Larry Fink's Annual Letter to CEOs: A Sense of Purpose, Blackrock website, https://www.blackrock.com/corporate/investor-relations/larry-fink-ceo-letter
43. FinTech and Financial Inclusion, World Bank, http://pubdocs.worldbank.org/en/877721478111918039/breakout-DigiFinance-McConaghy-Fintech.pdf
44. Ibid.
45. Ibid.
46. The Equator Principles, Equator Principles website, http://equator-principles.com/about
47. Performance Standards, International Financial Corporation, https://www.ifc.org/wps/wcm/connect/Topics_Ext_Content/IFC_External_Corporate_Site/Sustainability-At-IFC/Policies-Standards/Performance-Standards
48. UNEP Finance Initiative website, http://www.unepfi.org
49. Principles for Responsible Investment website, https://www.unpri.org
50. CDP website, https://www.cdp.net/en
51. CERES website, https://www.ceres.org
52. Now called Public Eye.
53. Collevecchio Declaration: The role and responsibility of financial institutions, BANKTrack, https://www.banktrack.org/download/collevechio_declaration/030401_collevecchio_declaration_with_signatories.pdf
54. About Impact Investing," GIIN, http://www.thegiin.org/cgi-bin/iowa/resources/about/index.html
55. Social impact bonds, Social Finance, http://www.socialfinance.org.uk/sites/default/files/SIB_report_web.pdf Accessed October 3, 2013
56. Othmar M. Lehner (ed.) Routledge Handbook of Social and Sustainable Finance, page 679
57. The Utkrisht Impact Bond -- Improving Maternal And Newborn Health

Care In Rajasthan, India, USAID, https://www.usaid.gov/sites/default/files/documents/1864/Utkrish-Impact-Bond-Brochure-November-2017.pdf

58. Banking Responsibly at Yes Bank, *The Economic Times*, https://blogs.economictimes.indiatimes.com/ResponsibleFuture/banking-responsibly-at-yes-bank/

Chapter 7

1. Big Data and the Future of Privacy, epic,org, https://epic.org/privacy/big-data/
2. EU Court Backs 'Right to Be Forgotten' In Google Case, BBC News, https://www.bbc.com/news/world-europe-27388289
3. FTC Charges Deceptive Privacy Practices in Googles Rollout of Its Buzz Social Network, Federal Trade Commission, https://www.ftc.gov/news-events/press-releases/2011/03/ftc-charges-deceptive-privacy-practices-googles-rollout-its-buzz
4. Fitness App Strava Overhauls Map That Revealed Military Positions, Reuters, https://www.reuters.com/article/us-strava-privacy-exclusive/exclusive-fitness-app-strava-overhauls-map-that-revealed-military-positions-idUSKCN1GP1WE
5. KFC China Is Using Facial Recognition Tech to Serve Customers - But Are They Buying It?, *The Guardian*, https://www.theguardian.com/technology/2017/jan/11/china-beijing-first-smart-restaurant-kfc-facial-recognition
6. New Weapons and new Warnings Over Health Research, Applied Chemical Trials, http://www.appliedclinicaltrialsonline.com/new-weapons-and-new-warnings-over-health-research
7. Hacking Risk Leads to Recall Of 500,000 Pacemakers Due To Patient Death Fears, *The Guardian*, https://www.theguardian.com/technology/2017/aug/31/hacking-risk-recall-pacemakers-patient-death-fears-fda-firmware-update
8. The Equifax Hack Could Be Worse Than We Thought, CNN Money, http://money.cnn.com/2018/02/09/pf/equifax-hack-senate-disclosure/index.html298
9. Hackers Can Hijack Wi-Fi Hello Barbie to Spy on Your Children, *The Guardian*, https://www.theguardian.com/technology/2015/nov/26/hackers-can-hijack-wi-fi-hello-barbie-to-spy-on-your-children

10. This Advocacy Group is Saying 'Hell No' to 'Hello Barbie', Time, http://time.com/4093660/barbie-hell-no/
11. Spotlight on Srikrishna Committee, India's New Data-Privacy Law: 10 Points, *Bsuiness Standard*, https://www.business-standard.com/article/economy-policy/hands-off-my-fb-photos-india-s-new-data-privacy-law-takes-shape-10-points-118061800097_1.html
12. GDPR and accountability, ico., https://ico.org.uk/about-the-ico/news-and-events/news-and-blogs/2017/01/gdpr-and-accountability/
13. https://eur-lex.europa.eu/legal-content/EN/TXT/?uri=celex:32016R0679

Chapter 8

1. 5 Trends for The Future Of Manufacturing, World Economic Forum, https://www.weforum.org/agenda/2017/06/what-s-going-on-with-manufacturing-b013f435-1746-4bce-ac75-05c642652d42/
2. 25 Years Ago I Coined the Phrase "Triple Bottom Line." Here's Why It's Time to Rethink It., *Harvard Business Review*, https://hbr.org/2018/06/25-years-ago-i-coined-the-phrase-triple-bottom-line-heres-why-im-giving-up-on-it
3. Majmudar, Utkarsh, Namrata Rana and Neeti Sanan, Responsible Business Rankings 2018, Futurescape-IIM Udaipur Technical Report, 2018
4. Shell Scenarios, Shell Group website, https://www.shell.com/energy-and-innovation/the-energy-future/scenarios.html
5. Theory of Trusteeship, mkgandhi.org, http://www.mkgandhi.org/village_swaraj/09trusteeship.htm
6. Piketty, T. (2015). About capital in the twenty-first century. *American Economic Review*, 105(5), 48-53.
7. Facebook Knows More About You (Including Your Offline Activity) Than It Says, *The Scroll*, https://scroll.in/article/825345/facebook-knows-more-about-you-including-your-offline-activity-than-it-says
8. The EU Data Protection Reform 2012: Making Europe the Standard Setter for Modern Data Protection Rules in the Digital Age, European Commission, http://europa.eu/rapid/press-release_SPEECH-12-26_en.htm
9. We must ensure the Fourth Industrial Revolution is a force for good, World economic forum, https://www.weforum.org/agenda/2017/03/we-must-ensure-the-fourth-industrial-revolution-is-a-force-for-good/

Chapter 9

1. Delhi Participates in 'Chipko' Movement to Save 14,000 Trees From Felling, *Hindustan Times*, https://www.hindustantimes.com/delhi-news/delhi-participates-in-chipko-movement-to-save-14-000-trees-from-felling/story-4QfK3m3uleQXYv3Qe86WGO.html
2. To win war on plastic menace, Maharashtra needs to show resolve and not dole out concessions, Firstpost, https://www.firstpost.com/india/plastic-ban-to-win-war-on-plastic-menace-maharashtra-needs-to-show-resolve-and-not-dole-out-concessions-4598201.html
3. Indian Startups Still Don't Take Data Privacy Seriously, *The Economic Times*. https://tech.economictimes.indiatimes.com/news/startups/indian-startups-still-dont-take-data-privacy-seriously/64628154

Additional References

Adrian Henriques, and Julie Richardson, eds. The triple bottom line: Does it all add up, Routledge, 2013.

Here Are the Fortune 500's 10 Most Valuable Companies, fortune, http://fortune.com/2018/05/21/fortune-500-most-valuable-companies-2018/

Hindustan Unilever Limited, https://www.hul.co.in

Mahindra and Mahindra, Integrated Report: FY 2016-17, http://www.mahindra.com/resources/careers/pdf/mahindra-integrated-report-fy17.pdf

Namrata Rana and Utkarsh Majmudar, Nestlé India: Creating a New CSR Strategy, London, Canada: Ivey Publishing, April 2018 https://www.iveycases.com/ProductView.aspx?id=94986

Namrata Rana and Utkarsh Majmudar, Responsible future, ET Blogs, https://blogs.economictimes.indiatimes.com/ResponsibleFuture/

Nestle India, https://www.nestle.in

Utkarsh Majmudar and Namrata Rana, Hero MotoCorp: Championing a Cause, London, Canada: Ivey Publishing, June 2018 https://www.iveycases.com/ProductView.aspx?id=95967

Utkarsh Majmudar and Namrata Rana, Ambuja Cement: Measuring the Value of Water, London, Canada: Ivey Publishing, August 2017 https://www.iveycases.com/ProductView.aspx?id=87181

Utkarsh Majmudar and Namrata Rana, Dalmia Bharat: Social Return on Investment, London, Canada: Ivey Publishing, November 2017 https://www.iveycases.com/ProductView.aspx?id=89443

Utkarsh Majmudar and Namrata Rana, Finolex: Developing an Integrated Corporate Social Responsibility Strategy, London, Canada: Ivey Publishing, June 2017 https://www.iveycases.com/ProductView.aspx?id=86234

Why? The Need for Change, Integrated Reporting, http://integratedreporting.org/why-the-need-for-change/

Technical Notes References

Arya Tripathi, India: Waste Management In India: An Overview, May 2015 http://www.mondaq.com/india/x/396342/Waste+Management/Waste+Management+In+India+An+Overview

Blockchain is here. What's your next move?, PWC, https://www.pwc.com/gx/en/issues/blockchain/blockchain-in-business.html

Climate Policy Initiative, https://climatepolicyinitiative.org/

Corporate Social Responsibility (CSR) Policy, http://finance.bih.nic.in/documents/csr-policy.pdf

Ekta, Bahl, An overview of CSR Rules under Companies Act, 2013, Business Standard, March 10,2014

EY, Integrated Reporting: elevating value, 2014 https://www.ey.com/publication/vwluassets/ey-integrated-reporting/%24file/ey-integrated-reporting.pdf

GIIN, Annual Impact Investor Survey. May 2017 https://thegiin.org/assets/GIIN_AnnualImpactInvestorSurvey_2017_Web_Final.pdf

Integrated Reporting, IIRC, http://integratedreporting.org

Introduction to Climate Finance, https://unfccc.int/topics/climate-finance/the-big-picture/introduction-to-climate-finance

Lingane A, and S. Olsen, "Guidelines for Social Return on Investment", California Management Review. 2004 Apr 1;46(3):116-35.

Maximilian Martin, Status of the Social Impact Investing Market: A Primer, Impact Economy and UK Cabinet Office, June 2013 https://assets.publishing.service.gov.uk/government/uploads/system/uploads/attachment_data/file/212511/Status_of_the_Social_Impact_Investing_Market_-_A_Primer.pdf

Namrata Rana and Utkarsh Majmudar, Responsible future, ET Blogs, https://blogs.economictimes.indiatimes.com/ResponsibleFuture/

Natural Capital Protocol, WBCSD, https://www.wbcsd.org/Programs/

Redefining-Value/Business-Decision-Making/Measurement-Valuation/Natural-Capital-Protocol

Peter Debaere and Jay Shimshack, The Economics of Corporate Social Responsibility, Darden Business Publishing, Case UV7168.

SROI Network, "A Guide to Social Return on Investment", London: Cabinet Office, 2012. https://www.bond.org.uk/data/files/Cabinet_office_A_guide_to_Social_Return_on_Investment.pdf

Sustainable Development Goals, http://www.undp.org/content/undp/en/home/sustainable-development-goals.html

United Nations Climate Change Conference, Wikipedia, https://en.wikipedia.org/wiki/United_Nations_Climate_Change_conference

Vivek Pandit and Toshan Tamhane, A closer look at impact investing, McKinsey Quarterly, February, 2018

What Are Externalities?, International Monetary Fund, https://www.imf.org/external/pubs/ft/fandd/2010/12/basics.htm

What is Blockchain Technology? A Step-by-Step Guide For Beginners, https://blockgeeks.com/guides/what-is-blockchain-technology/

What is the Paris Agreement? https://unfccc.int/process-and-meetings/the-paris-agreement/what-is-the-paris-agreement

What You Need to Know about Impact Investing, https://thegiin.org/impact-investing/

World Economic Forum, The Green Investment Report The ways and means to unlock private finance for green growth. 2013 https://www3.weforum.org/docs/WEF_GreenInvestment_Report_2013.pdf

Acknowledgements

The past six years have been an exciting journey. We've met several people, members of senior management and their teams who were passionate about their commitment and shared their vision. We have visited places and beneficiary communities and learnt invaluable lessons on how large corporations build and retain their commitment to responsible business strategies.

We have no words to express our gratitude to thank Prof. Janat Shah, Director of IIM Udaipur, who has helped us begin this journey and has been a pillar of support throughout.

Many people have shaped our thinking on responsible business.

We are thankful to the industry leaders who shared their experiences and insights—Ajay Kapur, Akito Tachibana, Anant Goenka, Anil Kumar, Anna Swaithes, Anu Aga, Bhaskar Bhat, Hemant Kanoria, Ishteyaque Amjad, Jean-Francois Beaudoin, Jonathan Horrell, Jonathon Porritt, Mahendra Singhi, Mayank Ashar, Dr. Mukund Rajan, Onkar Kanwar, Piyush Pandey, Prakash Chhabria, Richard Howitt, Ritu Chhabria, Sanjeev Sharma, Sanjiv Puri, S. Sivakumar, Sudha Murty, and Suzzane Singh.

We are grateful to a host of professionals and friends for their perspectives and guidance—Adam Elman, Alok Mehrotra, Amit Chaudhery, Amit Malhotra, Anirban Ghosh, Anuradha Aggarwal, Anuradha Bhavnani, Anurag Rana, Apurv Nagpal, Ashish Kaura, Aswin Kumar David, Beenoxi Arora, Bibek Chattopadhyay, Bibhuti Ranjan Pradhan, Calvin Printer, Chandrakant Kumbhani, Deepak Ajwani, Dhenuka Srinivasan, Divya Rishi, Elmer Lenzen, Prof. Ganesh Prabhu, Gayatri Appaya, Jaison Banglavil, Jyotsna Bhatnagar, K.V. Rajendra

Hegde, Krishnan Chatterjee, Lovish Ahuja, Manoj Aggarwal, Manu Kapur, Meenakshi Ramesh, Mukul Rastogi, Namita Vikas, Nandini Basu, Naveen Soni, Navtej Johar, Neelima Khetan, Pearl Tiwari, Peter Vanderwal, Prasad Kumar, Prasad Pradhan, Prof. Prathivadi Anand, R. Rammohan, Rajib Saha, Ramadas Kamat, Randal Newton, Ranjit Singh, Rashika Kaul, Rashmi Bansal, Rinika Grover, Ritesh Sinha, Rohan Sukhatankar, Roma Balwani, S. Ravichandran, Sachin Nandgaonkar, Sanjay Khajuria, Sanjay Sindhwani, Sanjeev Minocha, Santosh Castelino, Satesh More, Prof. Satish Agnihotri, Saurabh Dhanorkar, Sumeet Chatterjee, Sharada Prasad, Sheetal Ahuja, Sheetal Gupta, Shefaly Yogendra, Shilpa Sanghai, Shubha Sekhar, Smriti Verma, Sohini Mookherjea, Sohini Roychowdhury, S.P. Mohapatra, Srinath Komarina, Sunil Mehra, Surya Velluri, Syamant Sandhir, Vijay Sethi, Vinod Mahanta, Vishal Bhardwaj, Vrushali Gaud, Yashmi Yadav, Zacharia James, and Zitin Munshi.

We would also like to thank Prof Neeti Sanan for her collaboration on our annual study. Prof. P.D. Jose and Prof. Rajesh Chakrabarti for their participation in the advisory board of the study. A special word of thanks for the lead researcher Neelam Agrawal for her support and insights.

A big thanks to Karthik Venkatesh, our editor from Westland, who helped us shape the book.

Namrata would like to thank her parents Jaishree Rana and Major Rana for their constant motivation; sister, brother and husband for their support; Syona, Avantika and Antara for bringing so much joy and above all the late Mr K.K. Sandhir without whom this book wouldn't have started.

Utkarsh thanks his best friend and wife, Kanan Mehta, for her constant support, his parents Mr Nitin Majmudar and the late Mrs Saroj Majmudar for inspiration. His sister Sonali and brother-in-law, Bharat Bisht for introducing him to the development sector. And his extended family, Mr Ramesh Mehta and Mrs Janakbala Mehta, and, Amit Mehta for their constant encouragement.

20 September 2018

